The Gentleman In Trollope

The Gentleman In Trollope

INDIVIDUALITY AND MORAL CONDUCT

Shirley Robin Letwin

A COMMON READER EDITION
THE AKADINE PRESS

The Gentleman in Trollope

A COMMON READER EDITION published 1997
by The Akadine Press, Inc., by arrangement with William Letwin.

A COMMON READER EDITION and fountain colophon are trademarks
of The Akadine Press, Inc.

ISBN 1-888173-22-X

10 9 8 7 6 5 4 3 2

To Joan Bennett
and in memory of H. S. Bennett

Contents

Preface

The idea that a human being is a compound of reason and passion and that the struggle between them constitutes the moral life has, since ancient times, been synonymous with morality. But in the more general sense, a morality is a conception of how it is decent to live. It is an answer to the question, How am I to understand myself and conduct my life? The morality that is the subject of this book denies that human beings are divided between reason and passion. And the consequence is a radically unfamiliar attitude to our mortal condition and in particular to the nature and significance of individuality. Individuality becomes the essence of humanity, but there is no suggestion here, as in so-called 'individualist' moralities, of any conflict between 'the individual' and 'society' or of any sanction for irrationality, egoism, or nihilism.

This unfamiliar attitude to a human condition is, I believe, what defines the gentleman. The many writers who, from medieval times onwards, have tried to discover his identity, have not taken this view. But they have succeeded only in reducing the gentleman to a heap of contradictions, despite their insistence that he is a coherent character. Nevertheless, there is a thread that connects the multifarious attributes that have been attached to the gentleman, and it can be found in the morality portrayed here. This morality can explain why it has seemed plausible to describe the gentleman as a man of ancestry, a useless idler, an exemplar of manners, as well as a leader of men and a paragon of unworldliness, and why all of these descriptions have also been rejected, not least by those who proposed them.

An abstract account of the gentleman's morality can, of course, tell us something important about it. But here, far more than in other moralities, it is impossible to understand what these abstractions mean as a moral practice without seeing what those who subscribe to this practice think, say, and do over many years. Such illustrations might have been taken from real life or from history, or they might have been invented. Instead I found them ready to hand in Trollope's novels, which first suggested to me that what gentlemen have in common is an unusual morality. Moreover, the novelist's art provides the kind of information about people's conduct that can be had only by knowing someone intimately for a long time and that is rarely available to historians or made available by them. I might have chosen some other English novelist, such as Jane Austen or Mrs Gaskell, but no other writer offers so wide a range of character and circumstance, studied in such full detail, as Trollope.

My attention to Trollope's novels should not, however, mislead readers into expecting a study of his literary devices, a 'structural analysis', or an account of his life and work. About a novelist, as about every other subject, many different questions may be asked. What students and admirers of Trollope can find here is an understanding of the distinctive atmosphere of Trollope's world, why he presented and judged his characters as he did, and why his novels have become the subject of controversy.

There is no need, however, to be familiar with the novels to which I refer. For readers who are strangers to Trollope, the characters discussed will be like the people whom they have come to know through anecdotes in conversation or reports in a newspaper. But instead of having merely a collection of incidents to go by, they will be able to see how the events are related in the context of a whole life and community.

Since the gentleman's morality flourished in England, what I say about it has implications for understanding English history. But this book is a philosophical study. What 'gentlemen' did through the ages, or how they regarded and were regarded by others and just what has been the role of a gentleman's morality in English life before, during, and since the time of Trollope remains for historians to establish. Although I have said something about its relation to other moralities, that, too, remains to be examined more closely by historians of ideas. In short, while I have, in passing, suggested certain possibilities, I have concentrated on explicating the morality that defines the gentleman. If I have succeeded in doing this, historians will find here an identification of a subject whose career they might study.

All this presupposes, of course, that how people conduct themselves depends on how they understand themselves and their world. Therefore anyone who believes that social 'forces', biological or psychological 'drives', 'class struggles' or universal 'structures' are what explain how people behave, will find nothing here to their purpose or taste.

I, myself, have come to think that the morality of a gentleman offers a more complete and coherent understanding of a human condition than any other known to me. Readers will no doubt discover reflections of that conclusion throughout the book, along with their own good reasons for condemning as well as admiring the morality of a gentleman. But to argue the case for accepting that morality as true or desirable is a separate and very different kind of task from the one that I have undertaken – to explain a neglected development in Western civilization and to clarify what connects and distinguishes moral ideas that have long been floating about haphazardly. If the reader finds that this book has made him acquainted with a new character, or enabled him to understand what before he could only recognize, it will have achieved its purpose.

*   *   *

Apart from Joan Bennett, to whom this book is dedicated, I owe to David Grene and to Michael Oakeshott a pervasive debt which goes far beyond what will be obvious to those who know their work. I am grateful to the Earhart Foundation not only for the grant that they gave me but also for the manner of giving it. But I might never have noticed the gentleman if my mother and father had not taught me to appreciate the unfamiliar by the steady example of their own remarkable courage and generosity.

Part I
The Oddity of a Gentleman

1 Englishmen in Search of a Character

The gentleman has become a figure of fun. He is supposed to be someone who has elegant manners and a fine appearance, owns an estate in the country but knows his way about London, covers his walls with ancestors, never seriously works, and looks with horror upon anyone engaged in trade – in short, a grand, inert and complacent idler. Echoes of this idea appear everywhere in popular usage – in the name of the famous cricket match, Gentlemen v. Players; in the opinion of Conrad's sailor that a gentleman must have a very thin backside because he sits so much; in letters to *The Times* arguing about whether a gentleman may wear a handkerchief in his pocket or own a Rolls Royce. And it is the idea of a gentleman firmly endorsed in the latest book on the subject, where we are assured that the species, defined in this fashion, still survives although it is not easily found by the uninitiated 'outside a few select private zoos called clubs'.[1]

But even those who take the gentleman more seriously, on whatever else they may differ, agree that a gentleman has the fixity of a work of art and the same lack of life. This immobility is usually attributed to his being a member of a privileged class, so long and so well fortified by land, rank, and wealth, that they are strangers to doubts as well as to aspirations and occupy themselves with rehearsing ancient and useless ceremonies. While it is acknowledged that others may learn to counterfeit these characteristics, the real gentleman is supposed to get them from his ancestors.

In saying this, those who now mock the gentleman seem to be echoing those who admired him in the past. The belief that he is 'a man of ancestry' appeared as early as Chaucer, and can be found also in Shakespeare. In discourses such as Defoe's *Compleat Gentleman*, we are told that 'our modern Acceptation of a

Gentleman is this, A Person Born (for there lies the essence of Quality) of some known or Ancient family; whose Ancestors have at least for some time been rais'd above the class of mechanicks'.[2] Distinguished historians like Hume, Macaulay, Stubbs, and Hallam have taken the gentleman to be a member of a social class called 'the gentry', who were landowners occupying a rank between that of barons and yeomen. It is the definition that has all along been preferred by the makers of dictionaries. Any derivation of the word other than that of a 'man of ancestry' was dismissed by Dr Johnson as 'whimsical', and of the five definitions that he gave, the first is 'a man of birth; a man of extraction though not noble'. In the seventeenth century dictionary of proverbs by Tilley, a gentleman without an estate is declared to be 'like a pudding without suet', which echoes Burghley, who instructed his son that a 'gentleman that selles an Acre of Land, looseth an ounce of credite, for Gentilitie is nothing but ancient Riches'.[3] Richardson's *New Dictionary of the English Language* of 1844 says that the gentleman is 'born of or descended from a good family'. This remains the first definition in the current *Oxford English Dictionary* – 'A man of gentle birth, or having the same heraldic status as those of gentle birth; properly one who is entitled to bear arms, though not ranking among the nobility. . . .'.

Nevertheless, the definition of a gentleman as a 'man of ancestry' was always rejected by some and never completely accepted by anyone. Nor can the dispute be resolved by consulting the derivation of the word because that is just as much at issue. The English 'gentleman' has been derived from the Norman-French *gentil-homme*, a man of birth and family; from the ancient Latin *gentiles*, someone belonging to the same class or family (*gens*), or, as Cicero maintained, a man of free-born ancestry;[4] from the medieval Latin, *gentiles*, used as a synonym for 'barbarian', to designate the Germanic conquerors of the Romans;[5] and also from the Greek *eugenia*.[6] But whatever its derivation, Sir George Sitwell established at the beginning of this century that the earliest use of 'gentleman' in England did not designate a member of a particular social class.[7] And this conclusion has been emphatically supported by the genealogical investigations of the former Garter King at Arms, Sir Anthony Wagner, as well as by other, recent work on the history of England.[8]

Sitwell pointed out that Chaucer speaks of knights, esquires, merchants, franklins and yeomen, but never of someone who has the status of a gentleman. In the *Lytel Jeste of Robyn Hode*, gentleman denotes a freeman. This meaning appears also in *Piers Plowman*, where it is said that the whole Jewish nation were originally 'gentle'men', but have since the death of Christ fallen to 'lowe cheorles'. In enumerations of classes in legal documents before the fifteenth century, whether in the poll tax, a certificate of non-villeinage, a subsidy of roll, or a petition, there is no mention of gentlemen. Only after the time of Henry VI was 'gentleman' used to designate a distinct social status, and this was because the statute of 1413 required every defendant to give his 'estate, degree, and mystery'. Younger sons of nobility, who had no title, land, military rank, or fixed occupation and therefore could not claim any established legal name, called themselves 'gentleman'. Anyone who insists that the word is in origin a label for a social status must conclude that the first 'gentlemen' were people charged with assault, murder, and house-breaking.

Sitwell produces equally strong evidence, which is supported by Wagner even though he was pursuing a different question, against the belief that a gentleman denotes a member of a class who have the right, by birth, to bear arms. Arms were first used merely as insignia to identify warriors and could be displayed on the shield of anyone who proved himself worthy of 'being known by arms'. Families with pedigrees that can be traced to Edward III, but never had any reason to bear arms, cannot claim any right to arms, whereas descendants of husbandmen can do so without question. If arms make a gentleman, then some of the oldest and grandest families are excluded by birth from the ranks of gentlemen, and some of the humblest are assured of the title. In later history, when the 'right to arms' became more widely spread it continued to be connected with service and birth. Arms could be claimed as a right by anyone who held public office, and a herald could not refuse a grant of arms to a mayor, provost, or bailiff of a corporate town. In the sixteenth century, when the heralds became powerful, they granted arms to masters in universities, doctors in the church, students of common law.[9] But it had always been permissible to adopt arms for oneself, provided that they belonged to no one else, from which it follows that, if arms make a gentleman, anyone who takes the trouble to invent an armorial seal for himself can be one.

In short, when 'gentleman' appears in medieval literature and legal records, the man so named might be of any rank going. He might as easily be a humble free tenant, a franklin, or a husbandman, as a baron, knight, or esquire. It is not at all unusual to find an identification such as 'husbandman, alias merchant, alias gentleman, alias woolman, alias yeoman'. There are references to the 'king's menial gentlemen', but also to the Earl of Salisbury as a gentleman. Lists of 'gentry' are a catalogue of knights, esquires, and men of influence and substance, who might at other times be designated as 'valetti'.[10]

That this floating quality in the social status of a gentleman remained unchanged in modern times is confirmed by a variety of witnesses. Discerning foreigners have regularly expressed their astonishment at finding that a man might come of a grand and ancient family and not be gentleman. Madame de Staël observed that being called a gentleman is 'the first condition for obtaining respect in England in any class' which not even the 'splendour of the highest rank' could induce knowing Englishmen to mistake, and that, however high his birth, if a man lack the moral quality, 'you will soon hear it said, even by persons of the lower class, "Though he be a lord, he is not a gentleman"'.[11] The remark that 'a king may make a nobleman but he cannot make a gentleman' is an ancient commonplace that has been attributed to Henry VIII.[12] Defoe reported a similar tale about Charles II: 'The king understood that a title no more makes a gentleman than the lyon's skyn would make the ass a lyon ...'.[13] Victorian children were told about how when his old nurse begged James I to make her son 'a gentleman', he answered, 'I'll mak' him a baronet gin ye like, luckie, but the de'l himsel'f couldn' mak' him a *gentleman.*'[14] And the reverse of this, that even a duke may also be a gentleman, just as tellingly establishes the title's independence from class.

The belief that the English regard for gentleman reflects a rigid social stratification is further undermined by the accumulating evidence that, from early medieval times, there has always been much movement in England from one status to another and a remarkable confusion of classes. England never conformed to the popular picture of a so-called feudal hierarchy which arranged everyone neatly under the headings of unfree villeins holding land in return for rural work, socagers holding by rent, knights and sergeants holding by military service, clergy holding by ecclesiastical obligations.[15] There was not one centralized hierarchy, but several parallel hierarchies, and a high place in one did not determine rank in another. A man who held the military rank of knight might have been lord of several manors, or of one, or of none.[16] And conversely, lords of manors and descendants of ancient families might, in the military hierarchy, rank as low as 'valet' or 'yeoman'. Within any single hierarchy, a man might hold a number of different ranks, each attached to a different sort of holding in land, and so have to meet several different kinds of obligation.

Even though there were references, in the twelfth and thirteenth centuries, to a distinction between free and servile (in the sense of villein or serf, not slave), recent research following Maitland, has emphasized that there was no hard line between free and unfree in medieval England, but rather many different combinations of obligations and privileges. With regard to one of his holdings, a man might owe work and be a villein; but on other holdings he might pay rent or owe different kinds of services, and for some purposes, the so-called unfree villein could sue his lord in the king's court just as if he were a free man. So confusing was the mixture, that the courts were regularly called upon to decide questions such as whether a man who rendered the services of a villein might not nevertheless claim the rights of free tenement, or conversely, whether a man who paid rent might not nevertheless be judged a villein.[17]

Nor was there any fixed relation between wealth and status – there were 'free' cotters who had hardly any land to their name, and villeins who not only bought their way out of labour services but collected enough savings to acquire the whole of the lord's demesne. Mixed marriages were one of the main sources of the confusion and their frequency indicates that there were no great barriers between one condition and another. The story of Cinderella could come true in England without the help of a fairy godmother – the son of a lord might marry the daughter of his father's villein. But it was also possible for the mighty to fall and there are knightly families who descended into servitude.

As a result, no man in England can safely boast of his ancestors. The founders of the great house of Howard, Dukes of Norfolk, are said to have been villeins, or perhaps Norfolk franklins of English origin. The Bishop of Winchester, who founded Winchester College and New College, Oxford, and became Chancellor of England, was probably a husbandman's son.

Geoffrey Boleyn of Salle, whose father was supposed to be villein, started as a hatter in London, married a baron's daughter and became Mayor of London; his great grandson, Thomas Boleyn, became Earl of Wiltshire and Ormond and the father of Queen Anne Boleyn, which makes Queen Elizabeth I the sixth in descent from a villein. In a later period, a typical example of the irregularities in English lineage is Jane Austen's family. Her great-grandfather was a scion of wealthy clothiers and had five sons. The eldest inherited the estate, and the others were apprenticed to an attorney, a haberdasher, a surgeon, and a stationer. The attorney, who grew rich, paid for the education of the surgeon's orphan son, who became the Rev. George Austen, married the great-niece of a duke, and was Jane's father. Of his sons, one became a clergyman, one a country gentleman, and two were admirals. Among their descendants, there are academics, members of the professions, a royal spouse, a grocer's assistant, and a bricklayer's apprentice.[18] And this pattern appears in her novels, unnoticed by those who keep insisting that all her characters belong to a highly restricted class. The very conventional Mrs Bennett, whose husband owns an estate of two thousand a year, is the daughter of an attorney, the sister-in-law of a solicitor, and the sister of a tradesman – and one of her daughters marries an aristocrat who seeks the company of the uncle who is a tradesman.

Many reasons have been suggested for the absence in England of sharp social divisions. It has been said that the Norman invasion shattered the old social system without replacing it so that there survived a multiplicity of orders and consequently much interlacing of classes. The strength of English kings is supposed to have prevented the formation of a closed order of nobility which meant that it was constantly receiving new blood, while on the other hand, the rule of primogeniture, that sent younger sons into the world of trade or adventure, led to a regular mixing of nobility with commoners in business enterprises and professions. But however the social set-up of England acquired its character, the pattern is clear. Though there were a great number and variety of social distinctions, they were never barriers to movement and did not isolate one order from another[19] with the result that it was impossible to identify anyone unequivocally or permanently with a given status. The English nobility was not distinguished by legal and fiscal privileges denied to outsiders;

poor freeholders possessed the same parliamentary franchise as their grander neighbours; and men of all conditions engaged in many common enterprises and regularly intermarried. That institutions like the public schools flourished testifies to a widespread belief that 'new men' could learn the ways of the old and join their ranks. And whatever else the controversy about the rise of the gentry may have failed to demonstrate, it established that what we now call 'social mobility' is an old English pastime.

The unusual freedom of movement in England and independence of individuals from fixed ties to any one group has impressed a distinguished line of foreign observers. It was emphasized by Montesquieu.[20] But Tocqueville felt that Montesquieu's remark, 'I am now in a country which has little resemblance to the rest of Europe', when he visited England in 1739, did not go nearly far enough. The most 'exclusive' and 'powerful' feature that made England 'so unlike the rest of Europe', Tocqueville insisted, was the complete destruction there of 'the system of caste': 'The nobility and the middle classes of England followed the same business, embraced the same professions, and what is far more significant, intermarried with each other.' Even though Tocqueville derived 'gentleman' from *gentilhomme,* neglected its medieval history, and mistook the character of medieval England, he linked the oddity of 'gentleman' to its not being confined to members of one rank.[21]

Mme de Staël gave a graphic account of the easy movement from class to class in England:

If the son of a common shopkeeper, or even of a mechanic displays superior talents at the bar, he may rise without obstacle to the rank of lord chancellor; enter the house of peers with an hereditary title ... One of his sisters may marry a descendant of the Howards or the Percies, and become related to all the great nobility celebrated in the history of England. Another, married at an earlier age, may be the wife of one of her own class, and remain in it. One of his brothers may have followed the profession of arms, and obtained a peerage by his bravery, as he has done by his learning and talents. Another, less fortunate may continue in the shop of his father, or in the office of an attorney: without this great difference between the members of the same family exciting astonishment in any one. I am not here making gratuitous suppositions: whoever has a little studied the domestic conditions of England, knows as well as I, that similar combinations have existed and may exist again.

But she emphasized as well another peculiarity of England, that the easy mingling of orders was combined with 'a decided propensity for distinctions of rank', indeed a remarkable interest in them. And yet, the people were free both from 'aristocratical prejudices' and 'jealousy of the higher classes'. Though intense and widespread, the English respect for rank never became servile, Mme de Staël found, because it was

> always united with a very just and even nice appreciation of the real merit of the persons on the one hand, and with a profound sentiment of their own rights as citizens of a free country on the other.

The people were 'too proud to claim anything but a free career'. And as a result England displayed a remarkable national unity.[22]

All of this makes it reasonable to conjecture that the title of gentleman flourished just because it had nothing to do with 'class', as defined by birth, occupation, wealth, or rank. In a society where distinctions of status and fortune were constantly changing, and were therefore confusing and unreliable, being known as a 'gentleman' may have indicated a more stable affinity among men of widely different origins and positions.

That is the moral of the Victorian story, *John Halifax, Gentleman.* When the hero, who started life as an abandoned orphan, had at last made his fortune, bought a house, and kept a carriage, his son said: 'We are gentle folks now', but John Halifax replied, 'We always were, my son.'[23] Much the same moral is taught in another Victorian novel, *Philistia*, which is a continuous conversation about class and culture. The well-bred person, who is the son of a shoemaker, explains to the Socialist, who insists on the importance of ancestry, that the 'gentleman may be the final outcome and efflorescence of many past generations of quiet unobtrusive, working-man culture', and that 'there are working-men's sons who go through the world as gentlemen mixing with gentlemen and never giving the matter of their birth one moment's serious consideration'.[24]

These Victorians echo what was said all along by their ancestors. In that widely quoted Elizabethan book, *The Gouverneur,* (1531) Sir Thomas Elyot, having derived 'gentleman' from the Greek *eugenia,* says that it signifies 'goode kinde or lignage, but in a more briefe maner it was after called nobilitie', which is 'only the prayse and surname of vertue' and not, as 'after the vulgarre opinion of men', dependent on ancient lineage or great possessions, and to suppose so is 'errour and folye'.[25] *The Institution of a Gentleman* (1568) declares that the first gentleman was he in whom 'vertuous and gentle deedes did first appear'.[26] A later Elizabethan book (1586) makes the same point: 'A Gentleman or a Nobleman is he (for I do wittingly confound these voices) which is knowne, and through the heroycall virtues of his life, talked of in euery man's mouth.'[27] In the seventeenth century classic, *Titles of Honour* (1614) Selden speaks of a threefold use of 'gentleman', theological or Christian, philosophical or from manners and virtue, and political or civil, and pays attention only to the last. [28] The moral is the same in *The Gentleman's Calling* of 1673: 'He that desired to ennoble his Family, would then begin at his Mind, cast out thence all base and degenerous Inclinations, and make himself a Gentleman without help of Heraldry.'[29] And it is what Steele wrote in the *Tatler* (1710), 'The appellation of a Gentleman is never to be affixed to a Man's Circumstances but to his Behaviour in them.'[30]

No doubt such remarks can be taken to indicate a concern with reassuring those who have risen in the world that they are the equals of longer established families. Certainly, the *parvenu's* friend, Samuel Smiles, said that, 'He is the true gentleman, whatever be his station in life – who possesses and displays the gentler graces.'[31] But if so, we must conclude that since medieval times, a considerable number of Englishmen have felt themselves and were recognized to be better than their antecedents would suggest.

Whatever the reasons for the gentleman's importance in England, how to identify a gentleman has continued to tease the English imagination. The large literature devoted to the subject shows that it has been something of a national hobby.[32] By the end of the sixteenth century there were a number of books entirely devoted to the subject: *The Institucion of a Gentleman, The Gentleman's Companion, The Gentleman's Calling, The Gentleman Instructed, The Compleat Gentleman.* The flow of discourses on the gentleman became a flood in the nineteenth century. *The Cornhill,* the *National Review,* and the *Contemporary Review* carried long essays. Sermons were preached on 'The True Gentleman' and 'What is a Gentleman?' And many books were written on *The Character of the Gentleman, The English Gentleman, A Fine Old English Gentleman, Quite a Gentleman.* This is to say nothing of incidental disquisitions in poetry, novels, and essays, in Locke's *Thoughts Concerning Education,* Lord Chesterfield's *Letters,* Newman's *Idea of a University,* Thackeray's *Book of Snobs* and *Pleasures of a Fogy,* John Mill's *Logic,* and Ruskin's *Modern Painters.*

The Victorian social reformers, who, like reformers to-day, insisted most stridently on identifying the gentleman by ancestry, nevertheless made wonderfully contorted efforts to deny, while affirming, the definition by birth. Ruskin started by declaring that the 'primal, literal, and perpetual' meaning of the word, gentleman, is "a man of pure race"; well bred, in the sense that a horse or a dog is well bred. The so-called higher classes, being generally of purer race than the lower, have retained the true idea and the convictions associated with it, but are afraid to speak out, and equivocate about it in public.' Then, by an ingenious twist, Ruskin attributed their equivocation to a desire of the upper classes to justify their living off the labour of others, 'with which the term has nothing whatever to do', and he went on to argue that, as the purity of moral habits transmitted by blood is what identifies the gentleman, someone of the lower classes may have noble blood 'since his family may have been ennobling it by pureness of moral habit for many generations and yet may not have got any title or other sign of nobleness attached to their names'.[33] John Stuart Mill managed to avoid committing himself more subtly by saying that 'the word, gentleman, originally meant simply a man born in a certain rank' but gradually came to 'connote all such qualities or adventitious circumstances as were usually found to belong to persons of that rank'. And this explained why, in 'one of its vulgar acceptations', it means 'any one who lives without labour' and in its 'more elevated significations', it signifies 'the conduct, character, habits, and outward appearance in whomsoever found which ... were expected to belong to persons born and educated in a high position'.[34]

The one thing clearly agreed on in this large literature is that a gentleman need not be 'a man of ancestry'. Even Dr Johnson included among his five definitions – 'a man raised above the vulgar by his character or post'. The current OED follows suit by adding that the word might also 'be applied to a person of distinction without precise definition of rank' and that the gentleman is one whose gentle birth is accompanied by appropriate qualities and behaviour; hence, in general, a man of chivalrous instincts and fine feelings'. Though Defoe gave what seems to be a clear verdict for defining the gentleman by blood, he went on to 'entreat' those who think of themselves as 'ancient gentry' to 'stoop so low as to admit that vertue, learning, a liberal education, a degree of natural acquir'd knowledge are necessary to finish the born gentleman . . .', and he ended with a plea for bringing 'the blood and the merit together' because only that can 'produce the best and most glorious piece of God's creation, a compleat gentleman'.[35] Others have had recourse to discovering a change of meaning over time in the manner of the *Quarterly Review,* which said that though 'the term, gentleman, signified nothing originally but "a man of family" it has come to be applied to all who share the position, manners, cultivation, etc. of men of family . . .'.[36]

The ambivalence about whether 'gentleman' designates a particular social status is far from a late development. It appears in Chaucer's 'though he be no gentil born he is gentil because he doeth as longeth to a gentleman'.[37] In the history of King Arthur, gentlemen are described as those who 'beare old armes, of right', but we are told also, 'For he that is of gentle blood will draw him until gentle tatches [dispositions] to follow the custome of noble gentlemen.'[38] There are many references in Shakespeare's plays to a gentleman's social standing, but also many lines which deny its importance.[39] Another Elizabethan, W. Harrison (1577), boldly faced both ways: 'Gentlemen be those whom their race and bloud, or at least their virtues, do make noble and known.'[40] Selden did the same by talking about gentlemen 'of blood' and 'by creation', although he concluded that 'morally the gentleman by creation be the better; for the other may be a debauched man . . .'.[41] Remarks about the social position of a gentleman often intrude into comments purporting to say that it is irrelevant, as in Lamb's remark that 'Joseph Paice of Bread Street Hill . . . though bred a Presbyterian and brought up a merchant was the finest gentleman of his time.'[42] Throughout, there are many firm and wholly unqualified assertions to the effect that any true definition of a gentleman must be wide enough to include *some* kings and *some* labourers. And there is no better summary of the difficulty felt by everyone who has tried his hand at defining the gentleman than the valiant Elizabethan effort to sort things out: 'Of gentlemen, some be called gentel gentel, others gentel ungentill, and a third sort, ungentell gentell.'[43]

That only the vulgar view of a gentleman makes him a person of fortune, rank, or fashion is a steady theme. It is the bluntly stated moral of *A Fool of Quality*, which from 1770 was steadily republished to the end of the nineteenth century.[44] The same idea appears indirectly in the condemnation throughout English literature of the 'snob' as the antipode of a gentleman, and Thackeray's definition of a snob is the standard one: 'You, who forget your own friends, meanly to follow those of a higher degree, are a Snob; you who are ashamed of your poverty and blush for your calling, are a Snob; as are you who boast of your pedigree, or are proud of your wealth.'[45] Nor would any of the snob's enemies soften the judgement that 'a gentleman in the vulgar, superficial way of understanding the word is the Devil's Christian'.[46] Even as late as 1961, the gentleman was described as a demanding model of moral conduct, which is peculiarly 'compatible with all forms of social and practical endeavour', and the author condemned the popular idea that a gentleman displays his lineage in the airs of an effete dandy as a gross misconception.[47]

But if the literature devoted to defining the gentleman bears out the historical conclusion that he is not a man of ancestry, wealth, power or fashion, the quality that truly defines a gentleman is hardly obvious. There are frequent references to something called 'the look of a gentleman'. Even so radical and unconventional a writer as William Hazlitt assures us that one can tell a gentleman 'infallibly at the first glance'.[48] Some say that the gentleman can be recognized by a special elegance and propriety in his appearance, that his carriage is 'neither apish nor sullen',[49] that he always dresses as cleanly as he speaks, and is as meticulous about the things that surround him as about his person and his clothing. But on the other hand, it is also said that a gentleman is indifferent to all such matters. Sterne said that 'Nature' had 'wrote Gentleman with so fair a hand in every line of his countenance' that even Uncle Toby's 'tarnished gold-laced hat and huge cockade of flimsy taffeta became him'.[50] There are many variations on the dictum that a gentleman's apparel 'is more comely than costly'[51] and that he never wears anything so fine that he is afraid of spoiling it. Both before and after the eighteenth century there are frequent denunciations of those who consider adornments like 'a bagwig, a tasselled waistcoat, a new fashioned snuff-box, a sword-knot'[52] essential for a gentleman, and there is complete support for the seventeenth century writer who declared that a gentleman is 'a man of himself, without addition of either taylor, milliner, seamster, or haberdasher'.[53] One might almost conclude that a gentleman is indistinguishable from a country bumpkin after reading Hazlitt's description of how far from elegant were the looks of a man whom he considers 'a gentleman of the first water', who 'sauntered down St. James's Street as if he were strolling along his own garden', wearing 'a large slouched hat and an old shabby drab-coloured coat buttoned across his breast without a cape', looking neither graceful nor dignified and yet every inch a gentleman. But what constitutes the look of a gentleman remains, as Hazlitt said, 'something more easily felt than described'.[54]

The gentleman's talent for being agreeable in a variety of circumstances with a variety of people is attributed by some to the fact that he manages what may now seem to be a miracle – to treat everyone as an equal without disregarding differences of rank. Coleridge said that a gentleman showed 'respect to others in such a way as at the same time implies in his own feelings an habitual and assured anticipation of reciprocal respect from them himself. In short, the gentlemanly character arises out of the feeling of equality acting as a habit, yet flexible to the varieties of rank, and modified without being disturbed or superseded by them...'[61] Hazlitt put the same observation somewhat differently: 'a gentleman is one who understands and shows every mark of deference to the claims of self love in others and exacts it in return from them ...'.[62] But others have fastened on the self-assurance of a gentleman which, they say, makes him good-humoured because it keeps him from taking offense. Still another explanation emphasizes that a gentleman is free from the vulgar disposition to put a high value on himself, which prevents a gentleman from supposing that he is or ought to be the centre of everyone's attention, and therefore renders him an agreeable companion. Cardinal Newman attributed a gentleman's pleasantness to what he refrains from doing, but added that a gentleman is anxious to remove 'obstacles which hinder the free and unembarrassed

action of those about him', is willing to fall in with whatever
others are doing, and generally 'carefully avoids whatever may
cause a jar, or jolt in the minds of those with whom he is cast, all
clashing of opinion, or collision of feeling, all restraint or
suspicion, or gloom, or resentment; his great concern being to
make every one at their ease and at home'.[63] The same stress on
mildness appears in A. and J. Hare's *Guesses at Truth.* The real
gentleman, they say, 'should be gentle in everything – in carriage,
temper, constructions, aims, desires. He ought therefore to be
mild, calm, quiet, even temperate – not hasty in judgment, not
exorbitant in ambition, not overbearing, not proud, not rapa-
cious, not oppressive; for these things are contrary to
gentleness.'[64]

About manners and the gentleman, there is at least as much
vagueness and confusion. Everyone agrees that manners count
and yet no one takes them to be of a gentleman's essence. The
notion that conformity to a 'code' of behaviour, to the 'convenan-
ces' of society, of etiquette, or the rules of fashion identifies a
gentleman is steadily denounced as a sign of vulgarity. The
stickler for the proprieties of the dinner table or the correctness of
his pronunciation is definitely held to be not a gentleman but a
genteel *parvenu.* Indeed those who merely pretend to be scrupulous about such matters offend less than those who genuinely
are. Lord Chesterfield[55] is regularly taken to task for failing to
recognize that naturalness is the mark of a gentleman. Some even
consider a degree of awkwardness essential, and many emphasize
that 'impudent ease' should not be mistaken for the bearing of a
gentleman. Hazlitt declared that a man may not only 'have the
manners of a gentleman without having the look', but also 'the
character . . . in the more abstracted point of view, without the
manners'.[56] The most systematic Victorian discussion of a gentleman flatly denies that manners belong to the 'actual nature and
substance' of a gentleman: 'We must, all of us, know a man whose
manners leave very much to desire, and yet to whom it would be
impossible to refuse the title. A *finished* gentleman such an one
may not be; but a gentleman he is notwithstanding.'[57]

Nevertheless, everyone agrees that, whether it is due to his
looks or his manners, he neither avoids nor courts notice, can be
as much at ease among gamblers as among lords, and that
generally there is a decorum about a gentleman that makes it
peculiarly pleasant to be in his company. Steele described him as,

'modest without bashfulness, obliging and complaisant without servility, cheerful and in good humour without noise'.[58] A similar description appears in the seventeenth century: 'His behaviour will be affable and civil, not insolent and imperious . . .',[59] and again in the Victorian book, *A Fine Old Gentleman*, where we are told not only that a gentleman displays none of the 'snobbishness of the upstart' or the 'arrogance' that 'sometimes makes established rank and position unsufferable', but also that his words are 'few and weighty' and spoken always in 'a calm voice'.[60] In short, it is regularly suggested that the modest, complaisant, cheerful, affable behaviour characteristic of a gentleman is somehow connected with certain inner qualities, but those named are far from coherent and often plainly contradictory.

But none of these writers explains how a gentleman can preserve such mildness while fulfilling the other obligations with which they saddle him – to defend the helpless against oppression, to fight valiantly for what he considers right, to stand ready to support a just cause against every opposition, to be capable of lasting indignation. In saying that 'the gentleman is just as well as firm . . . forgives or resents duly but is never revengeful . . . gentle, but not fearful', Samuel Smiles was repeating an old and steady refrain.[65] A gentleman is expected to be staunch also in maintaining his self-respect, to be able to go his own way and to disregard the opinions of others. Indeed throughout the literature on the gentleman, his readiness to stand fast and to fight is regularly contrasted to the disposition of the vulgar to falter and give way.

The many contradictions in the assorted virtues assigned to a gentleman are hardly surprising since there is no serious attempt to indicate what makes them hang together. Dazzling though they are, the lists of virtues are totally haphazard. To be told that a gentleman 'is in nature kind, in demeanour courteous, in allegiance loyal, and in religion zealous, in service faithful, and in reward bountiful . . .',[66] that 'if thou hast a good Soul, good Education, and art Virtuous, well qualified in thy conditions, Honest, Ingenuous, Learned, hating all baseness', thou art 'a true Gentleman, nay perfectly Noble, though born of Thersites',[67] that a warm heart, an affectionate nature, 'manly energy and uncompromising dignity of principle', prudence, tact and forbearance, an 'undaunted' spirit, indomitable 'bravery and masculine decision of character', 'tenderness and sweetness of disposition' make a 'fine old English gentleman'[68] hardly distinguishes a gentleman from a saint.

Nevertheless, the lists are not perfectly haphazard. Certain qualities are more regularly mentioned. There is always some reference to 'polish', 'calmness', and 'collectedness'. 'Polish' obviously refers not to manners but to a quality of character. Steele said that in all the 'great and solid perfections' that distinguish a gentleman, there is 'a beautiful gloss and varnish' which is like the genius of the poet that 'irraditates all the compass of his knowledge by the lustre and brightness of his imagination'.[69] This 'polish' appears to have some connexion with the 'collectedness of mind' and 'the liberal disposition' which are said to distinguish the gentleman from 'the clown, the gossip, the backbiter, the dullard, coward, braggart, fretter, swaggerer, ruffian, bully and blackguard'.[70] Defoe suggested that the gentleman's 'polish' and 'collectedness' spring from an ability to make distinctions that other men miss so that the gentleman can be 'frugal without avarice, managing without rigor, humble without meanness, and great without hautyness; . . . pleasant without levity, grave without affectacion, and posses learning without pedantry or pride . . .'.[71]

Another and more puzzling quality regularly described as essential is 'simplicity'. Archbishop Trench remarked that 'to say that a person is perfectly simple is, to my mind, the highest praise you can give'.[72] The *Saturday Review* celebrated the late Lord Hampden for being 'as fine an example as could be found of that union of simplicity with dignity . . . which we are apt to believe is the special characteristic of the genuine English country gentleman'.[73] The plainest statement of what is involved in simplicity is given by that seventeenth century master of definitions, Brathwaite, who said that the gentleman is 'a man of himself' because 'no object can withdraw him from himself' and 'he admires nothing more than a constant spirit, . . . embraceth nothing with more intimacie than a prepared resolution', and 'moderation of his affections hath begot in him an absolute command and conquest of himself . . .'.[74] But why 'simplicity' should be admired or considered a cardinal virtue for the gentleman remains unexplained.

Everyone agrees, too, that what distinguishes a gentleman is not unworldliness, but rather industry and practicality. And this is stressed as much in the seventeenth century as in the nineteenth. A gentleman, Brathwaite says, 'understands that neither health commeth from the clouds without seeking, nor wealth from the clods without digging', 'holds idlness to bee the very moth of man's time', and therefore, 'day by day', has his 'taske imposed'. Nevertheless, he is not so 'Stoicall' as to 'contemn' pleasure, but rather enjoys hospitality and other recreations, though he would never let 'a moment of content' deprive him of an 'eternity of comfort'.[75] Although the author of *A Gentleman's Calling* opens by deploring that 'a Gentleman is now supposed to be only a thinge of pleasure' which makes it seem 'a ridiculous solacism to define his Calling' since his 'very Essence is thought to consist in having none', he describes this idea as a project to rob the gentleman of his birthright and reduce him to 'that vulgar Mass, from which divine Providence and humane Laws have distinguished him'.[76]

The other virtues always attributed to a gentleman are courage, courtesy, and truthfulness, but there is a special stress on truthfulness: 'It is a common saying amongst us', Brathwaite writes, 'that a gentleman will doe like a gentleman; he scorns to doe unlike himself, for his word is his gage and his promise such a tie as his reputation will not suffer him to dispense with.'[77] Browne concludes his careful analysis with: 'This then is my definition: A gentlemen is one to whom discourtesy is a sin and falsehood a crime.'[78] All the writers take pains to point out that keeping promises and not telling lies are only symptoms of the deeper honesty that distinguishes a gentleman and reserve their most serious censure for the subtler manifestations of falsity such as affectation, inconsistency, hypocrisy. But we are not told just what constitutes the more profound honesty expected of a gentleman, or what connects the courtesy with the honesty, or for that matter, with the courage required of a gentleman. Certainly none of this enables us to see what made it so obvious to Robert Louis Stevenson that Scott, Gordon, Wellington, and Shelley were clearly gentlemen, and that Napoleon, Byron, Lockhart were 'as surely cads and the two first, cads of the first water'.[79]

Yet for all the elusiveness of the gentleman, everyone agrees that the word describes something so peculiarly English that it cannot be translated.[80] All candidates for a French equivalent – *gentilhomme, homme comme il faut, galant homme,* or *homme de mérite* – were firmly turned down by Mme de Staël.[81] In his *Notes on the English,* Taine explained that 'We have not the word because we have not the thing.'[82] The German, Huber, who wrote a classic history of the English universities, said the same about his country – 'we have nothing of the kind'.[83] And his opinion has been emphatically seconded in this century by another German, Dibelius, whose study of English character became a handbook for foreigners and instructed them that 'Among the things every Englishman is proud of is the fact that the idea of the gentleman is peculiar to England. It is a fact.'[84] It might seem that the Italians have a claim on the gentleman because of the popularity of Castiglione's *Il Cortegiano* in Tudor England. But though the book may have encouraged similar reflections on the gentleman, he had long before been established in England, and many of the arts that Castiglione required of the courtier, such as skill in dissimulation and flattery, have been utterly proscribed for gentleman. The Castilian *cavallero* perhaps comes closest to the English term, but it has never been adopted as a synonym.

Though Englishmen have occasionally awarded the title to men who were not English – Cicero, Charles X, Don Quixote have been called gentlemen – they have generally agreed that gentlemen are scarce abroad. Arnold is supposed to have reported a total absence in France.[85] Coleridge, who taught his countryman to appreciate Germany, declared the species to be unknown there, and even among the 'Anglo-Americans', he found rather 'the proper antipode of a gentleman'.[86] The only notable dissent has come from Sir Ernest Barker who declared the gentleman to be 'a phase and form of the development of European culture' from which the English 'perhaps drew far more than they gave'.[87] But he admitted that the idea had appeared in England with all its peculiar English complexity as early as Chaucer.

The agreement extends to seeing a connexion between the oddity of the word and certain distinctive qualities in English life, to the fact that, as the saying goes, *les Anglais ont des idées à eux, en amitié, en amour, en tout*. Taine held that 'those three syllables, so used across the Channel summarize the history of English social life'. Unlike the French *gentilhomme*, English gentlemen have not, he says, been 'ornamental parasites' but have become 'administrators, patrons, promoters of reforms, and good managers of the commonwealth ... well-informed and well-educated men who apply themselves to work and are capable, and who, as citizens, are the most useful of the whole nation'.[88] Huber was sure that England owed 'her power, her glory, and her importance' to the 'Old English Gentleman', who has 'ruled and represented England' and is 'one of the most striking and admirable forms of civilized national education in any period of time or in any nation'.[89]

Englishmen have not been too modest to agree. Harrington found that there is something in 'the making of a commonwealth, . . . in the governing of her', and 'in the leading of her armies, which . . . seems peculiar unto the genius of a gentleman'.[90] According to Burke, all that was best in English manners and civilization 'depended for ages upon two principles – the spirit of a gentleman and the spirit of a religion'.[91] Disraeli thought that gentlemen had provided 'proper leaders of the people'.[92] Dean Church admired Spenser for 'presenting before us, in the largest sense of the word, the English gentleman, who was that high type of cultivated English nature . . . common both to its monarchical and its democratic embodiments than which . . . our Western civilization has produced few things more admirable'.[93]

The history of the word makes it impossible to doubt that a gentleman is a character whose native habitat is England. But a coherent explanation of what identifies him is not be found among either the Englishmen or the foreigners who have written so much in praise of the gentleman.

2 Incompatible Qualities

To discover the identity of a gentleman from Trollope's novels may seem to be at least as difficult. The word is used in so many different ways that it might appear to be a label for a ragbag of characteristics from which everyone creates his own idea of a gentleman. Though Trollope assures us repeatedly that we will know what he means when he says that someone is, or is not, a gentleman, he always excuses himself from explaining. A gentleman remains 'that thing so impossible of definition and so capable of recognition', leaving readers with good reason to accuse Trollope of vagueness, if not coyness.

The difficulty of discovering Trollope's idea of a gentleman seems, moreover, to be connected with a larger uncertainty about the novels as a whole. Though they are universally acknowledged to be models of plain speaking, and though in his day and ours they have been favourites with the common reader, there has been a persistent disagreement about what Trollope was trying to do and what he achieved. And at the heart of these differences we regularly find something to do with gentlemen.

The disagreements are not, however, random. They follow a consistent pattern. And this pattern holds the clue to solving the mystery about the gentleman.

The character of the pattern is most obvious in the responses to Trollope's account of his own life because no one disputes the simple facts that Trollope gives in his *Autobiography*, while hardly anyone agrees with his own interpretation of them. Trollope was born in 1815, three years after Dickens, and his boyhood was full of the kind of suffering that Dickens's novels have made familiar to us. The father was a gifted and prosperous barrister, and a Fellow of New College, Oxford, but also an unpredictable, strict, and gloomy man. The spirit in which he discharged his parental duties is illustrated in his efforts to teach Anthony Greek and Latin while shaving: 'I was obliged', Trollope says, 'to hold my head inclined towards him, so that in the event of guilty fault,

he might be able to pull my hair without stopping his razor or
dropping his shaving-brush.'[1] Although the mother, Fanny Trollope, was energetic, cheerful and resourceful, she was hardly
more comforting as a parent. Until her middle years she was
highly erratic, and always regarded Anthony as the least prom-
ising of her children, which, despite her affectionate disposition,
she let him know.

At seven, he went as a day boy to Harrow, where his days were
filled with floggings and rebukes for being dirty, disreputable, and
generally a disgrace to the school. The least painful time was a few
years at a private school at Sunbury, though even there he was
regularly in trouble and severely punished for a crime, whose
nature he never learned and which the master later admitted to
knowing that Trollope had never committed. At twelve, he was
sent to Winchester, where his conscientious elder brother tutored
and thrashed him daily, and everyone else ignored him. He came
to think that this was the natural fate for someone so unprepos-
sesing as he felt himself to be – a 'big, and awkward, and ugly'
pariah, who 'skulked about in a most unattractive manner', and
was so lonely and downcast that his thoughts often dwelled on
climbing to 'the top of that college tower' in order to 'put an end to
everything'.[2] After three years at Winchester, the family's financial disasters forced him to leave, but not before it had been made
known to all the boys that Anthony Trollope's bills were unpaid.

What followed was still worse. He returned to Harrow, as a day
boy, and this time was obliged to walk twelve miles to school so
that he regularly arrived covered in mud and dust. And that was
only a small part of his miseries: 'I was never able to overcome –
or even attempt to overcome – the absolute isolation of my school
position. Of the cricket-ground or racket-court I was allowed to
know nothing. And yet I longed for these things with an exceed-
ing great longing. I coveted popularity with a coveting which was
almost mean. It seemed to me that there would be Elysium in the
intimacy of those very boys whom I was bound to hate because
they hated me.'[3]

The holidays from school hardly brought relief. His home was
a barely furnished farmhouse, ready to fall into the neighbouring
horsepond and appropriate only as a setting for the squalid life
led by the family: 'Our table was poorer, I think, than that of the
bailiff who still hung on to our shattered fortunes.'[4] His father was
ill and wholly absorbed in an ecclesiastical encyclopedia, one of

his many never to be realized dreams. His mother was in America, looking after the most disastrous of her husband's projects – a scheme for a great emporium in Cincinnati, Ohio, which became known as Trollope's Folly and absorbed all that remained of the family's funds. The boy could find nothing to do with himself and felt himself to be a burden to everyone. When bankruptcy could no longer be avoided, Fanny Trollope moved the family to Belgium and, at the age of fifty-one, while nursing her dying husband and three children through the last stages of consumption, began the writing that made her prosperous and famous. Even then Anthony continued to be 'an idle, desolate, hanger-on, that most hopeless of human begins, a hobbledehoy of nineteen, without any idea of a career, a profession, or a trade'.[5]

When at last he was packed off to a job in the Post Office, he contrived to make his start there highly precarious by being careless about hours and tasks and offending his superiors. As he had very little money and no knowledge of how to manage it, he was regularly followed into his office by a money-lender, and imprisoned for debt. In his free time, he gathered some fairly sordid experience as an innocent abroad in wicked London. And he disliked everything about his life – the office, the work, and most of all his own ineptitude. His first twenty-six years were summed up by Trollope as 'years of suffering, disgrace, and inward remorse ... I was wretched, – sometimes almost unto death, and have often cursed the hour in which I was born. There had clung to me a feeling that I had been looked upon always as an evil, an encumbrance, a useless thing, – as a creature of whom those connected with him had to be ashamed.'[6]

His appearance and manners never helped matters. To the end of his life, he remained very odd, without looking distinguished or interesting, what foreigners described as 'the bald-with-spectacles, underbred sort of Englishman'. No one took him for an easy or mild man. He was big and burly, with a bristly beard and piercing eyes. And the fierceness of his looks was matched by a disposition to interrupt and contradict everyone – it was not unusual for him to break in by declaring: 'I entirely disagree with you. What is it you said?' He often lost his temper, though he as often apologized, and even at his best he was abrupt and awkward, a bull in a china shop. He always made a great deal of noise – at the dinner table, his bellows of laughter were deafening, and he managed to make a racket even on the golf course. When he came on a visit, his presence was announced by violent knocking and loud calls, and when he entered, a tornado incarnate seemed to strike the house. He was the sort of man under whom chairs regularly collapse and where he might strike next was unpredictable, as he might also be found leaning against the sideboard, sound asleep. Nor was he any better in the country. Devoted as he was to hunting, he laboured at it under considerable handicaps – 'I am very heavy, very blind, have been – in reference to hunting – a poor man. ... Nor have I ever been in truth a good horseman.'[7] That the many mishaps on horses, so exactly described in his novels, were drawn from experience seems all too likely.

Nevertheless he became highly esteemed and successful both as a civil servant and as a novelist. It was Trollope who drew up the scheme that transformed the British postal service and gave it the shape that it still has, but with an unfamiliar efficiency. As a novelist, he ranked beside Thackeray and Dickens as one of the reigning triumvirate in the middle years of the nineteenth century.

His hours were organized by a rigid routine. While travelling about for the Post Office, he continued to write his novels by setting himself a daily quota from which he never excused himself. Even while crossing the sea, he remained shut up every morning in his cabin, producing his regular number of pages at the writing table which he had had built for him before sailing. The same meticulous persistence distinguished his work for the post. When planning the postal system, he himself rode through the most remote parts of England and Ireland in order to discover where the post might be wanted and what route would be the most efficient for a postman to follow.

Yet despite his formidable self-discipline, Trollope was, according to all accounts, anything but dour or ascetic. Prickly and clumsy though he could be, everyone considered him to be a man of profound good humour, who made the world seem a more cheerful place. He was welcomed and admired in the most discriminating social and literary circles of London, and he entered into the life of a literary celebrity with gusto. But hunting remained his chief pleasure, and his dedication to it was part of his intense feeling for the countryside. There is a romantic fervour in Trollope's descriptions of his best-loved haunts – 'sweet woodland nooks, shaws and bolts, and pleasant spinneys, through which clear water brooks run, and the birds sing sweetly . . .'[8]

The relish with which Trollope describes the variety of pleasures that he enjoyed would seem to support his conclusion that he had got through his life in a highly satisfactory fashion: 'To enjoy the excitement of pleasure, but to be free from its vices and ill effects, – to have the sweet and leave the bitter untasted, – that has been my study. The preachers tell us that this is impossible. It seems to me that hitherto I have succeeded fairly well. I will not say that I have never scorched a finger, – but I carry no ugly wounds.' He neither played down nor pretended to have forgotten the pain of his early life; he said bluntly that 'something of the disgrace of my schooldays has clung to me all through life'. Nor did he suggest that his early ill repute both among his family and friends had been wholly undeserved – 'Even my few friends who had found with me a certain capacity for enjoyment were half afraid of me.' And he was so far from taking the disappearance of past evils for granted that, when writing of how his life had since then improved, he said: 'remembering how great is the agony of adversity, how crushing the despondency of degradation, how susceptible I am myself to the misery coming from contempt, – remembering also how quickly good things may go and evil things come, – I am often again tempted to hope, almost to pray, that the end may be near . . .'.[9]

His own explanation of how the hopeless misfit had been turned into such a contented success was that he had learned the art of self-discipline. Whether or not he had discovered in his rigid routine an effective antidote to what may have been bouts of depression, it undoubtedly enabled him to accomplish a formidable amount of work. But he does not say how he came to adopt it. He is reticent, too, about his marriage, saying only that it was the foundation of his contentment, that he and his wife started on what others might consider too little money, and that otherwise it was 'like the marriage of other people, and of no special interest to any one except my wife and me'.[10]

The reticence is intrinsic to the spirit of the whole. Trollope condemned attempts to write confessions about one's inner life – 'No man ever did so truly, and no man ever will. Rousseau probably attempted it, but who doubts but that Rousseau has confessed in much the thought and convictions rather than the facts of his life?'[11] Certainly the spirit in which Trollope tells his story could hardly differ more from Rousseau's. There is no hint of self-pity or self-dramatization, indeed the tone of voice is so matter-of-fact that one might easily fail to notice, as many readers of the *Autobiography* have, how nasty are the trials endured by the hero. Trollope presents himself as a man who had known misery, struggle, and disappointment, and had nevertheless thoroughly enjoyed life, and bore no grudges.

This now makes his quiet *Autobiography* sensational. But even when first published, it provoked outrage because Trollope described himself as no better than a shoemaker, someone who happened to work at writing rather than cobbling. Worse yet, he made a great point of his delight in the money he earned, and gave the full details of his earnings from each novel. It has been said that this concern with money, along with Trollope's ridicule of the notion that novelists had to wait for inspiration and his boasting of his regular schedule of production, persuaded his readers that he had been merely a hack who was not worth serious attention. Whether or not that explains why Trollope's popularity declined so markedly after his death, readers have regularly bound in Trollope's *Autobiography* a man of incompatible qualities.

They cannot easily believe that anyone devoted to what are called the higher, spiritual concerns of a novelist could also care about mundane, material things; that it is possible to enjoy so much when one has suffered so much; that a man who changed so radically in fortune and character should nevertheless be all of a piece. And because they have found this combination unlikely, students of Trollope have occupied themselves with uncovering what Michael Sadleir described as 'the intriguing, wistful, lovable duality of Trollope's character'. Some have accepted Sadleir's view that 'the vehement shell which the world knew as Trollope, the successful novelist', hid 'a secret Trollope – diffident, defenceless, and forlorn'.[12] Others have said that Trollope contrived to make what was really a profound moral cynicism look like serenity. It has also been discovered that though the effects of Trollope's youth were for long suppressed, they came to the surface at the end of his life and led him to take an increasingly dark view of the world and to devote himself to exploring the more unpleasant aspects of human life.

Yet none of these surmises is supported by either the reminiscences of others about Trollope or his own letters. The attempts to turn his correspondence with the American girl, Kate Field,

into an episode of adultery display greater ingenuity than insight.
If Trollope dwelled more on the victory of vice over virtue in some
novels than in others, there is no consistent darkening of his
vision. The last novel that he completed, *An Old Man's Love*, is
a charming vignette of true love which could hardly be further
removed from the intrigues and disasters of *The Way We Live
Now*. If *He Knew He Was Right* is a searching account of madness, it was followed by novels in which there is nothing of the
kind: *Ralph the Heir, Phineas Redux, The Prime Minister,* and
The Duke's Children are full of triumphant sanity. The concern
with unpleasant behaviour which is supposed to constitute a new
departure in his later novels was discovered by reviewers even in
his very first novel, *The Macdermots,* as well as in pastoral novels
like *Doctor Thorne* and *Framley Parsonage.*

Although the efforts to explain away Trollope's contentment
have been strikingly unsuccessful, they have persisted. And this
persistence is revealing. For it indicates that what Trollope described as attributes of a single personality are seen by his readers
as qualities that could not exist together. And the same pattern
appears in the responses to the novels. The conclusions about
what Trollope did or was trying to do are wonderfully contradictory. But there is a regularity in the contradictions which
reveals a similar inability to account for incompatible qualities.

At the height of his reputation, when Trollope was a favourite
with the common reader, both the general public and many
literary men took him to be a great portraitist of character. *The
London Review* praised him for having 'lifted his characters out
of mere names, and endowed them with personalities'.[13] The
Athenaeum remarked on 'the hundred thousand readers' who
have 'gossiped and cried over Mark and Mrs Mark, as though they
had been living personal friends'.[14] Even the high and mighty
Saturday Review said that 'no London belle dared to pretend to
consider herself literary, who did not know the very latest intel-
ligence about the state of Lucy Robarts's heart and Griselda
Grantley's flounces'.[15] Adolphus Crosbie, the cad who jilted Lily
Dale, became as much a public figure as Lord Palmerston, and
two ships were named 'Lily Dale'.[16] George Eliot's friend, G. H.
Lewes, the most learned literary man of the day, considered
Trollope's *Orley Farm* to be an outstanding example of 'the
literature of character' as opposed to 'the literature of types'.[17]
And everything about the construction of the novels was found to

contribute to the effectiveness and subtlety of the characteriza-
tion. The fact that Trollope showed his character in so many
different social circumstances was said to be part of his insight
into the infinitely different shades of character and ways in which
people affect one another. There were complaints about the
many long passages of interior monologue in which he explained
not only what characters thought but how they had come to think
it, though more recently these monologues have been acclaimed
as one of the earliest attempts to treat what is supposed to be a
subject discovered in the twentieth century, 'the inner consciousness'. But both opinions support the picture of Trollope as a
portraitist of character.

This picture gets strong confirmation from Trollope's own
account of how he worked. He lived with his characters, he said,
'in the full reality of established intimacy'. He became so thoroughly involved in their lives that he responded to them as to his
family and neighbours, hating and loving them, quarrelling with
them, forgiving and submitting to them, crying at their grief,
laughing at their absurdities and enjoying their happiness. He
knew 'the tone of the voice, the colour of the hair, every flame of
the eye; the very clothes they wore and what they would or would
not say'.[18] Every word that was spoken by a character was connected in his mind to every other. When, in *The Prime Minister*,
Plantagenet Palliser refused to give Lady Glencora an office that
she wanted to hold, their conversation echoed a remark made by
Palliser in *Can You Forgive Her?*, published ten years before.
Though Trollope did not expect his readers to notice such references, it was by such details, he said, that he endeavoured to show
how his characters changed over the years and yet were the same.

All this evidence for Trollope's concern with character and his
success in bringing his creations to life has not, however, prevented others from discovering that he was incapable of drawing
character. He was said to have produced merely 'facsimiles' or
real people, so superficial and lacking in any distinct inner being
that they were little more than points on a chart of operations.
This was the verdict of Richard Holt Hutton, of the *Spectator*,
who complained that Trollope went about mechanically photo-
graphing a character from a great many different angles until
they added up to a complete figure and it was hardly surprising
that the result lacked the 'essence' and 'conscience' of human
beings. Much the same conclusion was reached in this century by

Rebecca West who declared that Trollope's characters have no
significance in themselves but derive their value solely from the
part that they play in social life, in a 'game of putting pegs into
holes, with far more pegs than holes'.[19] This opinion has been
supported by the most recent critics who have praised Trollope
for revealing the variety of 'social strategies' that people use to
beat down their rivals.[20]

The view of Trollope's novels as a vast, panoramic survey of
nothing more than the transient surface of life has led to his being
classified as a 'society novelist', who studied 'society as a whole'
rather than 'the working of other minds' and could not see past
the 'social costume' which disguises all the anomalies and discontents that lie in the 'passionate depths' of people. For those who
take this view of Trollope, *The Way We Live Now* is his greatest
novel, or at least the best embodiment of what is supposed to be
his dominant theme – how the lives of individuals are distorted by
their dependence on others and determined by social forces
beyond their control.

Distant though the society novelist may seem to be from the
portraitist of character, there is evidence for him, too, in Trollope's *Autobiography*. When he began a novel, Trollope tells us,
he always had an exact picture of the geography and all the inhabitants of the places that he described. He knew the roads and
the railroads, the towns and the parishes, the squires and their
parks, the rectors and their churches, the hunts and the fields over
which they rode. In supplying details about the 'surface' of social
life, Trollope displayed the zeal of a Mayhew. We are told not just
that a man is greatly in debt, but enabled to judge his difficulties
quite precisely by being given all the facts about his income, what
he paid for his hunters, what bills he signed and when they were
due, the prices not only of houses and horses, but also of bread
and mutton, as well as the dimensions of the house and garden
that had to be maintained and how the weather affected the cost
of doing so. If an interest in such matters defines a 'society
novelist', there is no denying the title to Trollope, however much
it is at odds with the fact that Trollope's characters have had a
remarkable reality for a great many readers.

Quite as striking a contradiction appears in the opinions about
what one might expect to be a less controversial matter –
Trollope's attitude to the society that he portrayed. One party
insists that Trollope's novels epitomise the complacency of the

mid-Victorians and their unquestioning belief in the church, the crown, progress, imperialism, and the ascendancy of the middle classes. They find Trollope teaching throughout that respectability is all in all and conclude that he is concerned only with a small part of the whole society – 'the steady, safe-going, port-wine, and country family society'.[21] There is a disagreement about whether that makes Trollope a good or a bad novelist. Whereas the earnest reformers of the *Westminster Review* found him trivial, just as today some consider him monstrously banal, the *Athenaeum* admired his ability to avoid scenes that were too painful or stirring, and others have commended his remarkable sense for the anatomy of practical pursuits. But all of these readers agree that Trollope was the 'supreme novelist of acquiescence'. Nevertheless, others have discovered in Trollope's novels a remarkable study of the changes, discontents, and antagonisms that afflicted Victorian England. Some have emphasized that Trollope wanted to show how 'the natural selves' of people were deformed by the 'social pressures' in a world that was rapidly changing. Others have concluded that Trollope was actively promoting the destruction of mid-Victorian society by exposing its nasty reality. At the present, Trollope is admired for doing so, but it was not so in his own day. His portrait in *Doctor Thorne* of the brandy-drinking stonemason, Roger Scatcherd, who became a disconsolate millionaire, was condemned for traducing 'the noble and energetic pioneers of the rising democracy of labour in our age of steam'.[22] He was attacked for trying to weaken the church by making an archdeacon 'a pillar of all clerical abuse', and he was accused of trying to disrupt the social order by approving of a marriage between an earl's daughter and a tailor.[23]

Certainly there is plenty of evidence to support the belief that Trollope was out to show, and even to commend, a world seething with social changes. Old and young often quarrel – about religion, politics, love-making, smoking, penny newspapers, hunting, and chignons. More than one marriage disregards distinctions of fortune and rank. The City is less suspect than it was; foreigners intrude everywhere; bustles are worn by ladies rather than tarts; clubs admit people who drop their aitches; Parliament is full of 'new men'; Conservatives try to disestablish the Church; old families can no longer afford to spend the season in London and dine with foreign swindlers. There is no denying that wherever we look in Trollope's novels, something is changing.

But, on the other hand, things seem to stay much the same. There is no suggestion that Parliament will be taken over by radicals. Though an American of humble descent becomes the highest of duchesses, she seems certain to maintain that position more stalwartly than her predecessor. Fathers and sons differ and sulk but they rarely part. The atmosphere is hardly stormy. No one expects the heavens to fall. The only uncertainty seems to be about whether the hero, who is an everyday sort of hero, will get his heart's desire. From his time to ours, many a reader has felt reassured that all is well when he sat down with a novel by Trollope.

The difficulty of denying either the peacefulness or the constant change in Trollope's world has led more enterprising commentators to conclude that there is the same hidden 'duality' in Trollope's novels as in his life. The seemly surface which, to the innocent, makes Trollope's world appear to be so decorous, calm, and comforting, they argue, hides awful depths which contain the nasty river of Victorian exploitation and depravity. That this conclusion turns plain-spoken, popular novels into an exercise in cryptography does not, of course, prove it to be false. But it does suggest that such critics are hard pressed to explain the coherence of Trollope's world.

Even more awkward difficulties appear in connexion with Trollope's attitude to the personal dilemmas that he describes. To many readers of his day, it seemed obvious that he was writing as a 'moralist', intending to teach his readers how to know and do what is right. The most respectable journals found his novels to be full of 'health', 'manliness', 'civilizing influence', 'sense', and 'principle'. And this accords perfectly with the many pages in Trollope's *Autobiography* devoted to explaining that he wrote as a moral teacher. 'I have ever thought of myself as a preacher of sermons', he says, 'and my pulpit as one which I could make both salutary and agreeable to my audience.' How people conduct themselves depends on what they learn to think of as good and bad, and as novels are read by everyone, they constitute a 'vast proportion of the teaching of the day'. Therefore a novelist should aim, just as a clergyman does, to 'make virtue alluring and vice ugly', and to show that 'things meanly done are ugly and odious, and things nobly done are beautiful and gracious'. If novelists teach their readers to admire and emulate heroes who try to get into Parliament by using 'trickery, falsehood, and flash cleverness', Trollope says sternly, they do more harm than ordinary criminals: 'There are Jack Shepherds other than those who break into houses and out of prisons – Macheaths, who deserve the gallows worse than Gay's hero.'[24]

Trollope felt sure that his own novels had never taught any youth 'that in falseness and flashness is to be found the road to manliness; but some may perhaps have learned from me that it is to be found in truth and a high but gentle spirit'. And this, he insisted, had been the object of all the great novelists, from Miss Edgeworth and Jane Austen to Thackeray, Dickens, and George Eliot. Of course, a novelist never says 'baldly and simply', as a preacher does in church, that 'because you Lydia Bennet forgot the lessons of your honest home', you shall therefore be 'scouraged with scourages either in this world or in the next'. The novelist shows, 'as he carries on his tale', that such a character will be 'dishonoured in the estimation of all readers by his or her vices', leaving the reader to feel – 'let me not be like that'.[25]

Since so much of what Trollope said in his *Autobiography* seems designed to offend conventional sensibilities and succeeded, and since he left it to be published posthumously, such remarks cannot be dismissed as a cynical offering to placate a priggish public. Nevertheless, both his contemporaries and ours have found Trollope's novels to be devoid of moral standards and judgements. A reviewer of *Is He Popenjoy?* declared that Trollope refused to admit into his novels even a breath of 'the sweet breezes of heaven'.[26] *He Knew He Was Right* was abused for exhibiting 'the morbid infatuation of modern novelists for plots and stories turning upon conjugal infidelity'.[27] *The Way We Live Now* was said to be polluted by an unrelieved 'atmosphere of sordid baseness'.[28] *The Eustace Diamonds* was condemned as a 'photographic delineation of human meanness'.[29] In *Orley Farm*, critics could not find any model of virtue who could neutralize the contamination by characters who were not 'what gentleman and Christians should be'.[30] Even *The Prime Minister* was taken to show that Trollope 'attributed to the majority of mankind an inherent vulgarity of thought'.[31]

The qualities that provoked Trollope's contemporaries to condemn him for immorality have since been found to be supremely praiseworthy. Nowadays he is admired for breaking through 'the smooth surface' to disclose 'the seething volcano underneath'. Whereas in his own time, Trollope was mocked for 'illustrating the immortal thesis that there are two sides to every question, and that there is so much to be said for each that it is really rather hard to tell them apart,'[32] to-day Trollope is venerated for his supposed unwillingness to distinguish between right and wrong. Michael Sadleir praised Trollope for being 'fundamentally detached' and having refused to insist, as his predecessors had, that everyone toe the line he drew. Whereas Thackeray and Jane Austen are always passing judgement based 'on a code of manners of which they, at least, claim to possess the secret', Sadleir says, Trollope never pretended to know 'the true paths of virtue or of social decency' any better than his characters.[33] More recently, this interpretation has been carried further to turn Trollope into a preacher of 'moral relativity' and 'situation ethics'. It has even been discovered that Trollope should be understood as a judicious Dostoyevsky, and a forerunner of Sartre, who was bent on exposing the absurdity and meaninglessness of human life.[34]

For this conclusion, too, readers with a short enough memory and sufficient determination can find confirmation in Trollope's own words. He did after all insist that the novelist ought to make his characters 'men and women with flesh and blood',[35] with the same mixture of good and bad as we know in ourselves. There are many explicit sermons commending charity and castigating those who presume to judge their fellows. He condemned the false moralizing of Dickens's novels, where the 'good poor people are so very good', and 'the hard rich people so very hard', where 'a pattern peasant or an immaculate manufacturing hero may talk as much twaddle as one of Mrs. Ratcliffe's heroines and still be listened to . . .'[36]

Nor can it be denied that Trollope's own characters are far from clear-cut or perfectly steady in either virtue or vice. Right and wrong, prudence and folly regularly get scrambled. Plantagenet Palliser, who, we are told, is a perfect gentleman, torments his daughter, unjustly accuses an old friend of treachery, and is rude to a guest. Phineas Finn, a poor man who thoughtlessly sets out to make a career in politics, makes a habit of falling in love with women able to assist him, and is hardly off with one love before he is on to the next, is nevertheless generally accepted as a gentleman. Mark Robarts neglects his duties as a parson and spends more money than he has by consorting with crooks and unbelievers, but gets off with no more than a reprimand from both that pillar of society, Lady Lufton, and

Trollope. The Vicar of Bulhampton befriends a declared atheist as well as a girl who enjoys sin and still Trollope seems to consider him a conscientious Christian and clergyman. Lady Mason commits a forgery and Cousin Henry hides a will, but Trollope judges each very differently. If one sets out to find ambiguity and inconsistency in Trollope, there is plenty of material at hand.

Should we therefore dismiss Trollope's novels as a patchwork of contradictory beliefs? Or, if we wish to be fashionable, celebrate him for his glorious inconsistency? Has he just beguiled simple-minded readers into believing that he has created a coherent world?

Even if there were no other reason for hesitating to accept this conclusion, there is the daunting fact that it would oblige us to abandon, along with Trollope at least two other giants of English literature – Henry Fielding and Jane Austen. Their novels are in many ways strikingly different. They dwell on different sorts of people and dilemmas. In Austen's highly compressed and taut novels, there is nothing like the variety in characters or social conditions that appears in those of the others, which are long and rambling. Nevertheless, about Fielding and Jane Austen, there are the same starkly contradictory conclusions as about Trollope.

Gibbon's remark that understanding Fielding is like understanding a Byzantine palace intrigue and involves nothing less than the problem of grasping the history of human nature has been proved true by the critics from his day to ours. Dr Johnson was sure that, magistrate though he was, Fielding wrote *Tom Jones* for the immoral purpose of denying the importance of good principles. More temperate critics have since found that Fielding attacked the harsh conventional morality of his time only in order to teach his readers a greater sympathy for their fellow sinners. And Fielding's antipathy to moral judgements has been explained by attributing to him an interest in promoting social mobility. But others have discovered in Fielding the very opposte – a typical product of the social stability of his age who emphasized the dependence of morality on a healthy social conscience. There is besides a Fielding who designed a new moral theory which does nothing less than refute both Hobbes and Dr Johnson, and is at once humanist, liberal, materialist and Calvinist. And in France, Fielding was discovered by André Gide to have shown that virtue could only be achieved spontaneously and effortlessly by love and is necessarily destroyed by a deliberate striving after goodness.[37]

Jane Austen's fate has hardly been more consistent. She has regularly been accused of dealing in nothing more than the trivialities and banalities of tea parties and regularly betraying her ignorance of the realities of life. She has been taken to task for having lived and written during the French Revolution without having once referred to it. Emerson went so far as to call her 'vulgar' and 'sterile'. And the truth of this opinion is supposed to be confirmed by her own famous description of her 'little bit (two inches wide) of Ivory, on which, I work with so fine a Brush as produces little effect after much labour'. But she has also been hailed as an anti-Jacobin novelist, who managed to insinuate the Napoleonic Wars into *Persuasion*. She has even been praised for having addressed herself to all the important 'social issues', such as the oppression of women by men, of the poor by the rich, and of everyone by Society. Her novels have been said to illustrate an 'Aristotelian' moral system by showing that fine and flexible discrimination are the essence of the moral life – as opposed to the 'Calvinist' disposition to draw hard lines between good and bad. But her novels have also been described as perfect illustrations for Dr Johnson's moral sternness and as a deliberate defence of Christian morality against the 'moral relativism' of Fielding and Shereidan. Some have agreed with D. H. Lawrence and Charlotte Brontë that Jane Austen was 'this old maid' who had no idea of the passions that move real men and women, while others have held that she disclosed more about the nature of passion than could be found in any of the Brontë manuals. She has been acclaimed both for revealing the 'terror which rules our moral situation', and for teaching us that the restrictions which reality imposes are not 'problematic', 'oppressive', or in the least 'mysterious'.[38]

Every one of these opinions about both Austen and Fielding points to something that is undeniably there in the novels. The difficulty is the same as in the case of Trollope and in the attempts to define a gentleman, that of explaining how attributes which are so incompatible can live together.

3 The Self-Divided Man

Something more than a whim inspires the belief in these incompatibilities. It springs from an understanding of the human condition that has dominated civilized thought since ancient times. Fulke Greville summed it up in verse:

> O wearisome condition of humanity
> Born to one law and to another bound
> Vainly begot and yet forbidden vanity
> Created sick, commanded to be sound
> What meaneth nature by these diverse laws
> Passion and Reason, self-division's cause.

Plato encapsulated it in an image when he described the soul as a charioteer and two winged horses, one noble and docile and the other an ugly, wanton brute who constantly thwarts the charioteer's efforts to drive to the realm of unchanging perfection. Aristotle wholly accepted this picture of man as a compound of reason and passion. It was central in Augustine's Manicheeism, but was not repudiated in his Christian theology. It provided the foundation for the Thomistic system, and neither Duns Scotus nor William of Ockham quarrelled with Aquinas on this point. It remains the basic postulate of modern philosophers – Kant, Rousseau, Hegel, Mill, Marx, Nietzsche, Dewey, Freud, and Sartre. Although it was seriously questioned by Montaigne, Hobbes, and Hume, still they used the moral vocabulary that had been shaped by the idea that they opposed. And the acceptance of this vocabulary throughout the civilized world has made morality synonymous in common parlance with recognizing that human life is a struggle between reason and passion. That is what we postulate when we say that reason should not be a slave to the passions, or that the spirit is willing but the flesh is weak, when we describe ourselves as rational animals or as minds attached to bodies.

These are all different expressions for the same idea – that a human being is an unstable compound of two elements struggling for supremacy, each connected to a different kind of being. One belongs to life on earth, where people need bread, feel want, taste grief, and all things alter, decay, and perish. The other links men to a realm beyond mortality where everything has a fixed place in an eternal unity. Each pulls in an opposite direction. Passion drives men into trying to satisfy their ever changing desires, to chasing ceaselessly after material things which change and decay, and a preoccupation with their mortal existence as separate individuals. But reason draws them to the immutable unity that it reveals.

In lives where passion dominates, there can be no stability or order, because the grounds for distinguishing between true and false, right and wrong, higher and lower, cannot be discovered in the mortal human world, where everything is constantly moving and altering and nothing is fixed. Only those who turn away from the human world and look to the changeless reality obscured by it can escape from the chaos of mortal life. But to do so requires a constant struggle. Therefore to be human is to be torn between reason and passion. And there can be no compromise because the qualities associated with the world of reason are wholly incompatible with those that belong to the world of passion.

This understanding of what men must suffer and strive for constitutes the morality which has shaped our civilization, the morality of the self-divided man. There have been many different, and more and less refined versions of this morality. But in all of them, the human world, whether it is described as a reflection, an impediment, a disguise, or a lower stage, appears as inferior to another better world. What makes the human world inferior is the changeable element in its composition. And this means that not only life on earth in general, but human individuality in particular, which gives rise to the transitory multiplicity and variety of the human world, is something to be deplored. The separate, bodily existence of men is what gives them individuality, and it follows that the cultivation of individuality is incompatible with finding the order and unity for which reason yearns. A human being can overcome his estrangement from the reality visible to reason only by transcending or losing his individual identity. Moral life therefore consists in striving to suppress the aspirations associated with mortal existence, and 'the consummation devoutly to be wished' is escape from life on earth, or what men ordinarily think of as death. When no man is anything, all can be one.

Most of those who have subscribed to this view of the human condition have refrained from pursuing such perfect consistency. But one cannot, without altogether giving up the idea of the self-divided man, refuse to measure everyone on the same scale. For if men are compounds of passion and reason, moral quality necessarily depends on the degree to which a man is free from concern with the mortal world which his body inhabits. Activities rank higher the further they are removed from a concern with material things; there is a hierarchy of activities. And those who are occupied with activities at different levels of this hierarchy cannot be of equal moral quality. Anyone who is content to do his work by day and sit under an olive tree at dusk must be but a poor thing. The cobbler, whose attention is fixed on the markings of a hide and the shape of a pair of feet, is necessarily inferior to the poet who soars on the wings of thought. Scientists who discover universal laws are superior to business men who occupy themselves with day-to-day affairs. Farmers who deal with soil and animals rank below lawyers and teachers who dabble in words. The leader who strives to impose a universal ideal on his fellows is as a god among swine compared to politicans who just try to let men live in peace.

In its more refined versions the morality of the self-divided man does not totally denigrate or neglect the concrete reality of human beings. Ancient philosophers and medieval theologians acknowledged that the eternal pattern of a good life may be realised in different ways, and insisted that changing circumstances and personal endowments should be taken into account when making moral judgements. In this way, they sanctioned a degree of variety in the way men live. But still they allowed no doubt about the moral inferiority of a farmer or a carpenter to a philosopher or a statesman. Nor could they do so because, as they equated moral quality with the triumph of spirit over matter, they had to rank men according to their degree of emancipation from the material world.

Some have tried to escape this difficulty by equating virtue with 'moderation' or 'temperance', that is to say, a pursuit of 'the mean', but they have only deluded themselves into forgetting that Aristotle's idea of the 'mean', upon which they are drawing, has moral substance only because its context is an Aristotelian pattern for the good life, which rests on the cosmic hierarchy of being. When Aristotle says that 'courage' is the mean between rashness and cowardice, he postulates knowledge of the universal pattern of a good life, which makes it possible to know when a readiness to face danger is neither more nor less than what is needed to fulfill human 'nature'. Without such knowledge, one man's extreme may be another man's moderation and there is no saying who is right. If, instead, 'moderation' or 'temperance' is used as a synonym for self-restraint' or 'self-control', then virtue is the capacity to submit passion to reason, which obviously postulates the morality of the self-divided man with its implicit denigration of individuality and diversity.

Cruder modern exponents have reduced the morality of the self-divided man to a set of orders, or what is called a 'code'. Morality is supposed to dictate the one right answer to every question about what to do here and now, just as a correct geometrical demonstration can have only one right conclusion, and the good man submits to these answers like a good soldier obeying his commanding officer. Since what is good is not only eternal and universal but also completely specified, any unusual behaviour, any personal oddity, any departure from the universal pattern necessarily signifies rebellion against morality. Deviations can be inspired only by irrational 'values', which are the effect of passion, those 'currents of life' which pull men back to the ever changing sensual delights of the human world.

But even in the older, subtler versions, the morality of the self-divided man equates reason and order with unity and fixity and this renders change and variety inseparable from irrationality and disorder. Men must choose either unity and fixity or change and variety. These are necessarily incompatible and the only alternatives, because each belongs to a separate realm of existence and human beings cannot avoid looking one way or the other.

The only escape from this choice is to renounce any interest in reason and order and to become what is called a 'relativist', who believes that it is impossible to discover any stable grounds for human judgements; or else to take the 'cynical' view that belief in the existence of such grounds is a pious fraud perpetrated by those who find it useful for getting what they want. Denying that there are stable grounds for human judgements implies that it is impossible to make objective distinctions between truth and falsehood, virtue and vice. The latest version of the 'cynical' view is the belief that all moral or theoretical arguments are really a justification for what someone wants to do to change the world, designed to persuade others to do his will. Although such formulations pretend to be rational, that is to say, founded on a perception of an unchanging reality, they are really masks for irrational desires and therefore rightly identified as rationalizations of practical decisions or what are described as 'ideologies'. It follows, of course, that what one man calls truth, another may denounce as ideology.

In short, all those who subscribe to the morality of the self-divided man are obliged to believe that reason, order, fixity, and unity are inseparable and the contrary of passion, disorder, change, and multiplicity. All questions about human beings are thus reduced to one question. It may be phrased as: Does he choose reason or passion? Or it may be put as a choice between order and disorder, spirituality and materialism, or science and irrational 'values'. But however the question is formulated, it defines the human predicament as a choice between two incompatible sets of qualities, one of which is inseparable from change and diversity, and the other identical with fixity and unity.

In the twentieth century, the fundamental choice demanded by the morality of the self-divided man has been translated into a conflict between morality and individuality. Individuality is supposed to belong to the realm of change and variety, and moral standards to the realm of eternal order, and therefore they cannot be reconciled. This conflict between individuality and morality is supposed to produce a tension between the 'private' and the 'public' self. The private self appears in the resistance of the wild, ebullient, irrational forces of passion to the stultifying constraints imposed on them by the guardians of public order. Once the passions are suppressed, the public self dominates and therefore such people can have a coherent and steady attitude to life, but for the same reason they must also be joyless, pinched, narrow, dessicated. Anyone in whom the private self still flickers must be seething with unrest, unpredictable and aggressive because they act as their impulses dictate, and are committed to nothing. These are the signs of life because they reflect the resistance of free passion to the constraints of reason. Or, to put it in another way, human beings are divided into conformists and deviants. In the former, the public self is securely victorious and they are consequently calm and dead: the latter are ill at ease and unruly because their private self continues to assert itself. A man who lives quietly, is constant in love and accepts adversity with equanimity, must be a prig, a stick of a man, a stranger to feeling. But anyone who offends against propriety or disappoints conventional expectations must be a private self rebelling against the tyranny of the public self. And all those who display such symptoms are heroic rebels whose individuality enlivens the dead world of public selves.

In its most extreme modern version, the morality of the self-divided man offers no ground for distinguishing among different sorts of oddity in personal responses or for understanding how a man might depart from conventional behaviour without being rebellious. That some rebels ruthlessly pursue power, while others retire to a remote village to write poetry, is of no moral significance. As every one must either abjectly accept or else challenge and disrupt the established order, every individual response necessarily becomes an instance of either submission or rebellion. The possibility that people may behave in unusual and diverse ways for a variety of reasons, which have nothing to do with submission or rebellion, is excluded.

It follows that an orderly community must always take the same form. There must a fixed structure in which each man, woman and child has a given place and function. This explains the disposition to describe people in terms of their 'functions' or 'roles' in 'society', and the belief that if a ruler does not impose a unifying plan directing the activities of the ruled to the service of an overriding purpose he is a useless figurehead. As dominating and submitting are the only alternatives, social life is in essence a struggle for power between those who try to impose unity on diversity and those who resist, and order cannot be reconciled with a regard for individuality.

Nor can order be reconciled with any alteration or uncertainty in social arrangements because any departure from fixity signifies disorder. A change whose outcome is unknown, which may or may not take place, indeed any unpredictable event or concurrence of events, can only be explained as an outbreak of the irrational forces that always threaten to break through the fixities imposed by reason. That changes should occur imperceptibly, through mutual adjustments between one man and another without anyone's having deliberately arranged the whole, that innovations should be introduced and disagreements settled without making a revolution, that a government should preserve order without imposing a goal or a plan, that a society should be constantly changing and yet stable, none of this is conceivable in a world divided between unity and chaos. A community can be orderly only if its members are passive and docile, ready to aquiesce in whatever those above them command. Though a relatively mild repression might do to secure an adequate uniformity, there is no escape from the choice between submitting to a set pattern and rebelling against order. The self-moving man, who makes his own life must, by definition, be rebelling against the established order. Self-reliance, enterprise, originality, and courage can be expressed in only one way – in disdain of all that is respectable.

In the morality of the self-divided man, individuals can have no meaning in themselves. They are essentially parts of a whole, fragments of a cosmic unity as in the ancient picture, or players of roles or performers of functions as in the modern picture. Either way every individual response is merely a symptom of the relation between part and whole. Asking about someone's ancestry, occupation, wealth or status signifies a question about how he fits into his assigned slot and therefore constitutes what is called 'a preoccupation with class'. If a man is careful about decorum, it means that he willingly submits to his assigned role, and if many people do so, it means that the whole is functioning well. But a proliferation of oddities, regardless of whether they are due to eccentricity or wickedness, show that the social order is crumbling, for it is inconceivable that a society should be full of change and diversity and also stable, or that a man should be both respectable and independent.

The only way to explain anyone who appears to combine such qualities is to discover a conflict between the surface and the nature of a man. Since the true, inner, natural self, which is the product of unruly passions, is bound to be rough, awkward, unrestrained, any conduct that is gentle and courteous must belong to the outer, conformist self, to the shell imposed by 'social constraints'. There is only one way to get on in the world without losing one's individuality and that is to hide, but not truly repress, the natural self by wearing a 'mask of gentility'. Such a hidden individualist appears to be respectable because he assumes a slick appearance to conceal the crude reality of his 'natural' self. It follows that if people of marked individuality wish to live together in peace, they must hide their true selves. They must recognize that the cement of society is hypocrisy. For hypocrisy is the only alternative to the chaos produced by an uninhibited lurching from one 'self-expression' to another or what is called 'spontaneity'. A person can no more be both decorous and honest than be in two places at once.

Nor can one, in a world divided between shadow and substance, combine wordliness with profundity. How people go about getting and spending, speak to their friends, decide whom to marry, bring up their children – all that belongs to the material world of constantly changing appearances, the land of shadows. The serious concern of human beings lies beneath that surface, in the struggle to transcend material life, to resist the temptation to enjoy morality, to find eternity. This is what preoccupies those in whom an 'inner self' speaks with a higher voice. They are people of profundity because they feel obliged to struggle against passion which reduces each man to an isolated pool of egotism and alienates him from the eternal spiritual whole.

This higher voice is commonly described as 'conscience' and the struggles to which it calls are what in the morality of the self-divided man constitutes the 'inner, personal' life of human beings. But 'conscience' is personal only insofar as it is private rather than public. In essence, conscience is universal because it is the voice of the eternal spiritual reality speaking through a particular man. In other words, conscience has nothing to do with individuality. And since heeding one's 'conscience' constitutes the moral life, the particular words and actions of a man as he moves through the everyday world have nothing to do with his 'inner moral being'. The twists and turns of a man's conduct are but manifestations of his individuality and reveal nothing about his moral quality.

Many variations have been rung on the morality of the self-divided man. No doubt there are others to come. But it is logically impossible to develop a truly individualistic morality on this basis because it offers no way of making the individuality of human beings one with their rationality. If human beings are divided between reason and passion, and if reason is the power to impose unity and fixity on disorder, individuality can only be explained by accidental differences, either in the circumstances in which people find themselves, or in their genes. Reason can, of course, take account of these differences, but they are of no worth in themselves, because the differences among men are all due to the mortal element in their nature which causes their deviations from the one true, universal, eternal standard which reason recognizes and tries to achieve. In the universe of the self-divided man, all diversity is necessarily a deviation from the rational ideal, which is necessarily a universal uniformity. And there would be no deviations if all men were virtuous.

From the standpoint of the self-divided man, Trollope talks only about the unimportant. He is wholly absorbed in relating how men and women manage to get through their time on earth and the diversity in what they think and do. When he shows how a modulation or an omission or an emphasis distinguishes one person from another, he discloses nothing about a struggle to transcend mortality. Anyone who sees such a cosmic struggle as the true 'inner, personal, moral life 'of human beings can only conclude that Trollope does not reveal 'the depths of a character'. His preoccupation with how differently men respond to the constant change and uncertainty in this world makes him a 'society novelist', who merely skims the surface of life. For what does the price of bread have to do with eternity?

Among the many charges of superficiality brought against Trollope, the harshest has come from Henry James. In a review of *Miss Mackenzie* in 1865, James declared the novel to be 'monstrous', and 'totally lacking in the supreme virtue of possessing a character', indeed with nothing in its favour but the 'virtues of detail' such as one finds in a photograph.[1] In the following year, he called *The Belton Estate* a 'stupid book ... essentially and organically stupid ... without a single idea'.[2] But that was not James's last word.

His final appraisal, written after Trollope's death, could hardly have been more approving. He praised Trollope for a 'happy instinctive perception of human varieties', for his ability to put before us a person who has – 'in spite of opportunities not to have it – a certain particular nature'. Moreover, James had come to see his earlier opinion of Trollope as part of a common disposition to misread all the English novelists who were often dismissed as 'the society school'. They could not, James declared, be fitted into the categories which were popular in controversies among literary men. James rejected the 'droll, bemuddled opposition between novels of character and novels of plot' as an 'idle controversy' which would never have been taken seriously by a writer of Trol-

lope's 'great good sense'. He rejected also the other popular
dichotomy between 'drawing character' and 'social photography'.
These were not exclusive of one another, but complementary,
James insisted, because we care about what happens to people
'only in proportion as we know what people are,' and we can
know what people are only by observing how they conduct themselves and respond to others. Trollope was such a good delineator
of character just because of his 'great apprehension of the real',
which was displayed both in the 'spacious geographical quality' of
his novels, and in the 'homely arts' by which Trollope built up the
details of social life that brought his characters alive. Because of
his remarkable 'knowledge of the stuff we are made of', James
concluded, Trollope could rightly be called 'a man of genius'.[3]

The qualities that led some critics to describe Trollope as a
social photographer and as the voice of mid-Victorian complacency, and others to condemn him for being indifferent or
hostile to morality, propriety, and decorum, were given a radically different interpretation by James. He found in Trollope's
novels the human world portrayed with perfect truth, without
any descent into 'morbid analysis' or 'a grain of the mawkish or
the prudish'. This unusual ability to tell the truth both straight-
forwardly and decently was attributed by James to 'the natural
decorum of the English spirit'. It enabled Trollope, he said, to
judge and talk 'plainly and frankly about many things like a man'
and even with 'a certain saving grace of coarseness', while holding
fast 'to old-fashioned reverences and preferences'. Nor did James
accept the opinion, fashionable now among admirers of Trollope,
that he never revealed his own opinion about what should be approved or condemned. James found and admired the opposite.
He praised Trollope for his sparse use 'of the quality of irony', for
never being 'paradoxical or mystifying' or 'juggling with the sympathies of his reader'.[4]

These virtues, according to James, were not confined to Trollope but were an 'English talent', what the French described as
'something peculiarly *honnête* about the English mind'. And
James connected the 'natural decorum' of English novelists with a
special interest in the 'moral world', as opposed to the 'so-called
scientific view' which had 'lately found ingenious advocates
among the countrymen and successors of Balzac'. Though the
French were superior in audacity, neatness, acuteness, and intellectual vivacity as well as in 'characterizing visible things', the

English had a genius for making fine discriminations, an instinctive knowledge of the fine distinctions in words and actions that constitute the moral life. Their 'great taste for the moral question' not only gave them a 'more just and liberal' perception of character than the French. It also made them more attentive to how people go about the ordinary business of life. Though to outsiders this seemed to be an odd combination of interests, it signified, James insisted, that the natural home of the English novelists was the moral world. 'They know their way about the conscience.'[5]

The most surprising thing about the final verdict of Henry James is not that it runs contrary to much of the critical opinion about Trollope but that it is entirely in keeping with the popular view of him in his own day. The many readers who made Trollope's fortune seem not to have been troubled by the mysteries that have occupied sophisticated critics. In the middle decades of the nineteenth century, when Trollope was at the height of his popularity, the common reader seems to have found him as straightforward and coherent as Henry James finally did. And this curious discrepancy between the popular and the critical response to Trollope points to the solution of the mystery about the novels and the gentleman. For it coincides with a profound change in opinion[6] whose effects can be traced in the reception of Trollope.

The years during which Trollope became a popular novelist saw the spread in England of a new way of thinking. By the 'seventies and 'eighties, the last decade of Trollope's life, it had became common in intellectual circles to denigrate English achievements. Her philosophers were found to have produced nothing but partial and superficial schemes which did not even aspire to give a coherent view of the universe and revealed nothing, as Carlyle charged, 'about our mysterious relations to Time and Space, to God and the Universe'. The qualities that Henry James praised as the distinctive virtue of English writers were condemned for making English literature nothing but a domestic convenience, a trivial and boring collection of moral truisms flavoured with 'a few immoral refinements and paradoxes'. What James saw as the 'dauntless decency' of the English was interpreted by these critics as the mark of an unimaginative, philistine nation of shopkeepers, too engrossed in shillings and pence to have an 'inspiring vision' of a 'higher purpose' in life.

Among such denigrators of England, the names to conjure with were all German – Niebuhr, Richter, Goethe, Kant, Fichte, Schiller, Tieck, Novalis. That these writers were in many respects profoundly different from one another went unnoticed because their English hierophants were so dazzled by the simple contrast between the 'profundity' common to all the Germans and the 'superficiality' of the English. The first leaders of the German vogue were Coleridge and Carlyle, and it became established in Cambridge early in the century under the influence of distinguished dons like the scientist and philosopher, William Whewell. The German library of the classicist, Julius Hare, initiated brilliant undergraduates into the new learning. The group, called the Apostles, dedicated to spreading what was described as a 'Platonic-Wordsworthian-Coleridgean' gospel, helped to make 'trancendentalism' the rage among undergraduates and became the dominant influence on the essays that appeared in the *Athenaeum*. One of the Apostles, John Sterling, became the close friend of John Mill and helped to convert him to the new enthusiasm. By the 'thirties and 'forties, everyone with intellectual curiosity was interested in Germany and found there something that they believed to be lacking in England. John Austin, the jurist, came back, after a year in Germany, a confirmed admirer. His wife, Sarah Austin, compiled an anthology of German literature. Learning German and reading German works became popular. John Stuart Mill studied with Sarah Austin; George Eliot translated Strauss's life of Jesus; Bishop Thirlwall translated Schleiermacher; Carlyle's essays made German writers familiar outside academic circles.

The Germans, it was felt, opened a window to eternity. Their peculiar virtue was described as 'earnestness', which, though it was first used to indicate that they were not overwhelmingly witty, came to mean that they were capable of seeing beyond the joys and sorrow of human life to a higher reality. They showed that man was more than a dazed mortal, that there is something 'godlike within us' because the human soul is a fragment of the eternal spirit.

Once profundity came to mean a disdain for mortality, the ill repute of English writers was bound to follow. For none of them had any use for the idea that man is a fragment of a cosmic spirit. The most influential English philosophers – Hobbes, Locke, Hume – attacked just those aspirations that preoccupied the admirers of the Germans – the search for ultimate truth, for a complete view of the universe that would restore men to oneness with the whole and rescue them from the separateness of their mortality. The denigrators of English thought, even those who, like F. D. Maurice, retained a suspicion of grand systems, rightly felt that the German writers provided what they were seeking and could not find at home – assurance that they were part of an eternal reality.

Though not all who joined the German vogue were Christians, some were. For others it was an alternative to the Christian faith that they had lost. F. D. Maurice was inspired by the new creed to join the Anglican Church; John Sterling, on the same grounds, rejected Christianity; and Julius Hare tried to reconcile orthodox Christianity with the Apostolic pantheism. The German message was reinforced by other imports, such as Comtist positivism, as well as by native inventions like Social Darwinism. Though each sect used a different vocabulary and emphasized a different aspect, they all taught a version of the morality of the self-divided man and fed the same aspiration – to see the 'vast and glorious unity' of the cosmos.

At the heart of many apparently distinct Victorian controversies, whether about teaching science in the schools, the truth of Darwin's theory, the comparative merits of Byron and Wordsworth, ecclesiastical practices or theological doctrine, there was a more profound issue – whether men should strive to overcome mortality. In popular discussions during the middle decades of the century, the argument was focused on whether the account in Genesis could be reconciled with Darwin's theory of evolution, and the issue appeared to be about the relationship between science and religion. In fact there were Anglicans who saw no difficulty and Darwin himself never suggested that he wished to cast doubt on religion. Nevertheless there was a good reason for the heat in the controversy. 'Darwinianism', as taught by T. H. Huxley, was not a scientific theory – it was a rival religion to Anglican Christianity, a pantheist religion. Though it seemed to concern itself with rocks and bones, it introduced England to a new conception of the human condition which was the same as that taught by the admirers of Germany and the disciples of August Comte.[8] And that affinity was recognized at the time by a number of leading philosophers, scientists, clergymen, and literary men, who came together in the Metaphysical Society to explore and spread the new truth. Although their declared purpose was to reconcile religion with the new scientific discoveries, the essence of their teaching was that man is one with God and nature. That some of the converts placed the source of unity in heaven, while others found it in the bowels of the earth, was unimportant beside the belief common to all of them – that men could discover and join the unchanging unity that lies behind the transitory variety of the human world.

The new creed appeared in diverse sorts of doctrine – scientific, religious, philosophical, and political, but the moral was always the same. To give meaning to their lives, individuals had to become integrated into a higher unity. Some identified the desired unity with God or Spirit; others preferred to describe it as Nature, the Evolutionary Process, Humanity, the Human Species, or the State. But these differences did not prevent the new believers from being at one in their horror of any resignation to mortality. What they despised as English philistinism was the refusal to think of life on earth as a procession of phantoms concealing an eternal unity, which is man's essence.

A typical example of the literary men who came under the influence of such foreign ideas was the editor of the *Spectator* and the most assiduous reviewer of Trollope, Richard Holt Hutton, who was also one of the leading spirits of the Metaphysical Society. Like many others with his convictions, he came from a non-Conformist background, was educated at University College, London, which was a stronghold of non-Conformity, and studied for the Unitarian ministry at Manchester New College. He became acquainted with German ideas directly when he studied at Heidelberg. Because he often wrote about theological subjects, Virginia Woolf described his writing as 'the voice of a man stumbling drowsily among loose words, clutching aimlessly at loose ideas'. But in fact his theology was of the same pantheist variety that attracted atheists along with the non-Conformists and Evangelicals who dominated the late Victorian intellectual scene. Hutton talked of God as a spiritual principle making the world a unity. Man, nature, reason, the human soul were for him just different aspects of the cosmic whole shaped by a single ruling spirit. Throughout his essays, whatever the subject, there is an unmistakable echo of the pantheist dictum, 'all is one'.

It is hardly surprising that Hutton found Trollope devoid of any insight into the essence of man. For if what matters is, as

Hutton put it, 'the humanity that is our bond with fellow men', and 'humanity' means 'the universal self', the eternal spiritual reality which makes men one underneath the 'merely flying surface of life', then Trollope's characters are bound to look, as Hutton said, like superficial photographs of numberless accidental incarnations of humanity. When Hutton criticized Trollope for being indifferent to the 'conscience' and its struggles, he meant that Trollope did not write about 'that voice within every man which is his participation in the eternal spirit'.[7]

The same defect undoubtedly afflicts all the so-called society novelists with whom Hutton identified Trollope. A reader who is seeking the one, unifying Truth is not likely to care, or even to notice, that when Jane Austen says 'a' Harriet Smith, she is alerting us to Emma's attitude to her friend; nor are they likely to see the difference between the garrulity of Mrs Elton and of Miss Bates, or be persuaded that they should. Such details can only seem supremely unimportant to readers who have become drunk on the joys of pantheism. What seems trivial and banal in Jane Austen is certain to become monstrously so in the more elaborately detailed novels of Trollope. While he is painstakingly exploring all the intricacies of mortal thought and conduct, the reader who is waiting for eternity to break through is bound to wilt with boredom.

As long as the infatuation with eternity and unity remained confined to literary and academic circles, Trollope continued to be popular with the common reader. He was for long treated charitably even by some disciples of the new outlook among the critics because they retained enough interest in the words and actions of individuals and the subtleties of human relationships to appreciate Trollope for what he did. And that a journal like the *Academy*, which prided itself on promoting a new kind of literature, regularly dismissed him as a hopeless philistine did not much matter. But as the message that men of letters had been spreading began to extend beyond the universities and journals and to shape popular thought, as it did increasingly in the later decades of the century, the attitude to Trollope changed. Along with other old English verities, his novels came to be regarded as trivial and tiresome.[9]

Their subscription to the morality of the self-divided man explains why the more learned critics in Trollope's day and nearly everyone later found Trollope, along with other English novelists, full of incompatible qualities. But even those who were self-consciously protesting against English philistinism did not realise how their belief in the self-divided man affected their thinking. They did not see that it rendered them incapable of understanding a vital idea which, to the common reader, who had made Trollope's fortune, was so familiar that he just took it for granted. And it is no wonder that those who lacked this vital idea should have reached irreconcilable conclusions about Trollope as about other English writers. They are like people locked in a dispute about whether a red ball is round or red because they think that redness and roundness cannot exist together.

Part II
The Definition of a
Gentleman

4 Virtue without Struggle

The missing idea is nothing less than a hitherto unidentified morality – an understanding of what men are and should be (which until the other day had never been formulated) where virtue does not require a struggle against mortality. Intimations of this unidentified morality can be found all through European civilization, in the philosophies of Plato, Aristotle, and Cicero; among the late Scholastics; in Rabelais' Abbaye de Thélème, the essays of Montaigne and the aphorisms of Vauvenargues. The most substantial suggestions for it have come from Christianity. But that it flourished in England, as nowhere else, has been unwittingly suggested by everyone who has remarked on what, until recently, distinguished England – an ability to tolerate without strain a combination of qualities that were elsewhere considered incompatible. On the one hand, the English have been unusually intent on guarding their personal independence and have made their country a haven for the original, the bold, the adventurous, for hermits as well as eccentrics. But on the other hand, the English have shown unusual fidelity to traditional ways of doing things, to rules, formalities and conventions, and they have been suspicious of innovation. Though to outsiders these appeared to be conflicting dispositions which should have torn it apart, England was generally acknowledged to possess a genius for order and stability. In a world accustomed to thinking that men must either submit or rebel, England has stood out as a country where people did neither.

This genius of England has been regularly connected with her other peculiarity – the gentleman. The reasons suggested for the connexion have been as various and conflicting as the definitions of a gentleman. But if the connexion is historically true, a likely reason for it is that the gentleman subscribes to a morality in which the dichotomies that plague the self-divided man disappear.

One might expect to find the morality of a gentleman explained in the writings of English philosophers, especially as since late medieval times they have been as odd as everything else about England. They have been unusually preoccupied with individuality and, unlike their colleagues elsewhere, they have been given to insisting that there is no escape from mortality and no need to lament the fact, all of which suggests that they were pursuing an alternative to the morality of the self-divided man. Nevertheless, these philosophers never succeeded in finishing a new picture of the human condition. Indeed the incompleteness of their accounts may have helped to drive those Englishmen who were interested in abstract reflection to look abroad.

What English philosophers failed to do, however, was inadvertently achieved, in a somewhat different fashion, by the so-called English 'society novelists', of whom Fielding, Jane Austen, and Trollope are the most eminent. There is so much talk in their novels about 'gentlemen' not because, as it is fashionable to believe, they were concerned with class distinctions but because they were exploring the moral world of the gentleman. That is why they were so attentive to 'character' and why they endlessly record details of word, gesture, and circumstance which readers, who are attuned to the morality of the self-divided man, find so tedious.

The common reader, who was the contemporary of those writers, unselfconsciously accepted the same morality and therefore felt completely at home with them. There still are such readers. But the others who, because they can understand the words believe that they understand what is being said, read the novels of Trollope or Austen as if they were written from the standpoint of the self-divided man, and accordingly find them full of incompatible qualities.

What has made the relation of the gentleman's morality to these novels, as to the character of a gentleman, so elusive is that in both cases the bearers of the morality have been unaware of it. This raises the question: How can one attribute a morality to people who did not recognize its existence? The answer is: in the same way as one can discover the grammar of a language which has long been spoken by people who do not themselves recognize its grammar, who even lack the concept of grammar. No one expects an Englishman to ask himself, before uttering a sentence, what constitutes correct English syntax, any more than one expects distinguished writers to be adept at explaining why they write so well. Nevertheless a grammar can help to explain, after the fact, why a speaker of a language chooses to arrange his words as he does. Though a foreigner cannot discover from a grammar how to do justice to the peculiar flavour and texture of a language, he can learn something about what distinguishes that language from others and be guided towards understanding its usages. In other words, the grammar of a language is an abridgement of the practice of that language; its rules are a shorthand for indicating the character of the practice. They can neither replace a knowledge of that practice nor tell us what anyone will or should say in that language. But neither are the rules of grammar irrelevant for understanding the language being spoken, even though those who speak it may break or, on occasion, dispute or deny the grammarian's dictates.

In short, to understand what a gentleman is we must make explicit the grammar of a language which has been spoken without being identified. To construct this grammar, we need examples not only of a pure and consistent usage, but also of the variety of usage allowed by the language. And there is no better source for such examples than Trollope's novels because Trollope explores in fine detail so broad a range of character and circumstance.

That may be why Trollope was more severely depreciated when Englishmen were turning against their traditional beliefs. But it may also explain why, now that there is a revival of interest in all the 'society' novelists, the vogue for Trollope is especially strong. Considerable ingenuity has been spent on demonstrating that he can satisfy our current obsession with the crude and brutal; others have dismissed the vogue as an attempt to escape from the unpleasant reality of our own world to a more agreeable one. But the true reason for Trollope's return to popularity is more likely to be that the descendants of those late Victorians who disparaged Trollope for shallowness, having had enough of heady pantheist profundities, are now trying to recover that moral understanding which, though it suffered the curious fate of having nearly disappeared without having been recognized to exist, once made a gentleman, like the country that bred him, such an admired oddity.

But even when its distinctiveness is recognized, the morality of a gentleman remains difficult to understand because it offers no ideal to realize, no goal to achieve, no pattern to fulfill, no absolute targets, indisputable commands, inevitabilities, or final solutions. Nor is anything given in the form of drives or structures from within, or forces from without, pushing men to do this or that. In this picture, the only thing given to a human being is the power to choose what to see, feel, think, and do, which constitutes his rationality and his humanity. In other words, rationality has a totally different character. It is not a link to something outside the human world, neither to Nature nor Spirit; nor is it a power of discovering any other non-human source of eternal truth such as natural 'processes' or 'structures'. Though called reason, it must not be confused with a cosmic principle of 'Reason'. It is a purely human property which enables men to make of themselves what they will.

This way of understanding rationality implies that there are no 'real desires', what are called 'needs', as opposed to 'apparent desires' or 'wants'. For if human rationality does not provide a link to an eternal, non-human reality, it becomes impossible for men to discern or 'intuit' any indisputable, universal, and eternal pattern to which human life ought to conform or any 'nature' which it ought to realize, and which constitutes an indisputable ground for judging the claims that men make. All talk about 'nature' and 'needs', 'natural rights', and 'natural laws' must then be human talk that pretends to carry a cosmic sanction. Or else it is merely metaphorical. A man's 'needs' and 'rights' can only be what someone believes that he ought to have.

Of course, a human being has to eat in order to survive and generally has to deal with biological processes within his body and physical processes outside. But that cannot determine how he behaves. Even a brute physical fact, like the emptiness of a man's stomach, in itself determines nothing since he can choose to think of his sensations in many different ways – as gratifying evidence of abstention, as a biological fact beneath his notice, as good preparation for a feast, or as unbearable hunger. While a person is in full possession of his faculties, it is he who determines how to interpret his experience and how to respond to it. He decides how far to exert himself in order to survive, how to get his food, and whether just to fill his gut or to make an art of eating; he can even decide to choose death. Human behaviour is never a mechanical reaction to a cause, like the motion of a billiard ball to the cue that strikes it, but a chosen response.

Therefore experience is not what happens to a man; it is what a man does with what happens to him. It is the dealing with events, not the events themselves. There is, in short, no non-rational experience for a human being. This does not mean that experience consists only of self-conscious thought in the shape of geometrical demonstrations. Nor does it exclude recognizing that experience is accompanied by changes in the body. But it does exclude supposing that electrical charges or chemical reactions can explain the meaning of what is felt, supposed, concluded, said, or done, or that the conditions needed for physical survival dictate behaviour. Human experience is composed of desires, feelings, hopes, habits, dispositions, skills, at different levels of consciousness, as well as of trains of thought, associations of ideas, propositions, and arguments. But though it takes different forms, all of human experience is rational because it is made by the subject of the experience who connects his experience with his awareness of selfhood. The accurate name for human behaviour is 'conduct' because a human being leads himself to do everything that he does.

In no circumstances is a human being, in full possession of his faculties, potter's clay being 'conditioned' by something other than himself. He is himself both potter and clay. Phrases such as 'irrational action', 'overcome by passion', or 'driven to do something' cannot easily be avoided because all civilized vocabulary has been shaped by the morality of the self-divided man. But when such phrases are used by gentlemen, they become metaphors indicating that someone has acted injudiciously, without enough reflection, knowledge, sense of proportion, or clarity, or perhaps that he has violated certain canons of decency and effectiveness. In the same way, talk about 'human nature', 'needs', and 'rights', becomes a short-hand for describing similarities of disposition or belief among men, some of whom are perhaps long dead, who, because they share certain practices, agree on giving priority to certain wants.

If all of human experience is rational, a man is not a self-divided being, with 'higher' and 'lower' parts; he is not a 'rational animal' born to one law and bound to another. He is all one, an intelligent being. His consciousness consists neither of urges emanating from a lower, passionate, animal element, nor of a 'voice' speaking from beyond the human world through his 'higher' or 'true' self, but of all the feelings, imaginings, memories, and reasonings that sit in conclave to determine the meaning of his experience.

This consciousness constitutes a man's personality. And therefore, human individuality is not due to passions escaping from the control of reason; nor is it the product of 'alienation' or of adopting an independent standpoint; it is simply the inescapable quality of a rational being. One may choose to play down or to emphasize one's distinctiveness from other human beings, to give up what one wants for the sake of others, to regard individuality as an evil, to seek the uniformity of a commune. But short of destroying his rational faculties, a man cannot lose his individuality because he cannot cease to be the maker of his own experience.

Individuality has no more to do with either fixity or disorder than with passion or alienation. A human being constantly changes because he is always understanding and responding. But as understanding and responding consist in making connexions among ideas, the consciousness of anyone in full possession of his faculties is a network of connexions. And this gives his conduct a certain regularity. Therefore human individuality has neither the amorphous quality of a 'bundle of perceptions' nor the fixity of a 'core of personality'. It is a personal identity which is more or less stable and becomes fixed only at death. This changing but steady distinctness is most accurately described as a 'character'. Seeing human beings as 'characters' means recognizing that they make their individuality for themselves by how they choose to understand and respond to what they encounter, and that this individuality is the essence of their humanity.

If the capacity to shape a character defines a human being, the only way to understand the human world is by understanding characters. One may, of course, be more concerned with the uniformities than the differences in conduct. But any general or universal conclusions about the human world are necessarily abstractions from a reality that consists of distinctive individuals, of 'characters', each of whom has to be known in himself and may always do something unexpected. Such abstractions may explain that reality by disengaging some aspect of it, but they are not an advance to a 'higher truth' any more than a dressmaker's pattern is superior to the finished garment.

This is another way of saying that the human world acquires a new importance. Its ceaseless change and diversity are not the shadow of a substance that lies elsewhere or the fleeting appearance of an eternal fixity which reason seeks to discover. Change and diversity are the reality of a world inhabited by characters. The untidy human world is the real world.

But men have to pay a high price for acknowledging their own reality. If individuality is of the essence of human beings, the men and women who walk and talk on earth are not just ephemeral manifestations of something else that constitutes their 'real being'. They are not 'really' parts of a whole. Each is in himself a whole. This means that the human world is not merely an aspect of an all-embracing Nature. There is no cosmic unity such as pantheism postulates. All is not one. In short, belief in a cosmic unity must be renounced. And if the universe is not a pantheistic cosmos, there is no hope of escaping from mortality and uncertainty. For only if reason links men to a 'higher' reality, as it does in all pantheistic views, is there any way of climbing out of the human world to a non-human vantage point. Without such an independent ground for judging human ideas, there can be no indisputable knowledge. Any such knowledge, whether proposed in the form of science or philosophy or religion, whether it offers to disclose the destiny or the structure of human life, postulates a pantheist cosmos and is therefore incompatible with taking individuality seriously. Otherwise, uncertainty is incurable and human life is surrounded by a mystery which men can probe but never dispel.

The human predicament acquires a new character. It does not, in this picture, consist in the difficulty of imposing a given order on a given disorder or in the resistance of passion to reason. The human predicament consists rather in the absence of anything given or fixed and is produced by the unlimited creativity of reason. Just as the capacity to make sounds must be shaped before words can be uttered, just as a man who sets off in all directions will not go anywhere, so the activity of reason must be constrained in order to give definition and meaning to the buzz of experience. Limits must be set to the human power of annihilating limits.

The way out of the human predicament is to acquire what only a life among other men can provide, that is to say, the constraints of civilization. But these are not to be confused with the repression or suppression of 'irrational forces'. If men are understood as 'intelligent beings', and not as 'rational animals', the constraints imposed by civilization are the shape and definition that human reason gives to itself. In the arts, disciplines, skills, manners, habits, institutions, conventions, traditions, and rules that constitute civilization, men find the limits that can shape their experience. They learn to make distinctions and connexions in what is presented to them and so to make their world meaningful.

A man is then what he learns to be. And learning requires submitting to a teacher. But that does not turn learning into 'an imposition on a given self'; it is rather the making of selfhood. Learning carries no threat to individuality and it makes no sense to talk about 'a conflict between the individual and society'. The pupil has the character of an apprentice, not a disciple, and he is only temporarily so until he acquires the skills, not the style, of the master. For learning the arts of civilization does not consist in copying patterns but in mastering a language of one sort or another, and knowing a language does not dictate what should be said. Of course, a pupil must start by accepting someone's word not only for what he has to learn but also for whom he should listen to. Nevertheless, he can in time choose what to learn and from whom because he can refuse to listen to those among whom he is thrown, make efforts to counteract their influence, or seek out others. He is obliged only to recognize that submission to some teacher is a condition for cultivating his individuality.

Another condition is acknowledging the authority of rulers. Again, the commonplaces belonging to the morality of the self-divided man must be rejected. Ruling and being ruled acquire a new meaning. That men need to be ruled does not mean that they have to be saved from themselves or reduced to unity. The rationality, not the bestiality, of human beings creates work for rulers. Because reason can invent infinitely various responses, men living together can always arrive at irreconcilable interpretations of their shared practices. Even if everyone were ready to yield, some way would be needed to decide when the yielding had to stop. If men can always disagree, yet wish to live and work together in peace, they need some way of coming to an agreement. Rulers are wanted not to destroy diversity but to 'arrange' a peaceful communal life, to maintain a civil association. They exercise authority to make rules and procedures for settling disputes and to enforce them, when necessary, by physical coercion. But such repression is an adjunct, not the essence of ruling. The ruled, in obliging themselves to recognize the authority of their rulers, 'subscribe' to rules governing their relations with others. Their subscription constrains them as they go about their business and it may entail obeying commands. But such obedience is not what defines subscription to the rules of a civil association. It sets conditions to be observed in the pursuit of their business; it does not dictate what that business shall be. And therefore subscription to rules is a form of constraint compatible with diversity. Nor need subscription to rules, even when they remain unaltered, prevent change. On the contrary, it makes accommodation to change easier by providing a steady way of attaching the new to the old. Subscription to rules reconciles change with order by preserving continuity. For all these reasons, in the morality of a gentleman, order is not identified with either repression or fixity. Order consists in stability secured by arranging and subscribing. Those subject to such order may be prevented from doing just what they would like. But no one need rebel to go his own way.

Here then we have a picture of human life in which individuality emerges from the society of other men and can only be expressed in the context of that society. There is a clear distinction between the social and the private but no incompatibility because social life is the context within which the private flourishes. And the human world, instead of being an arena of conflict, is a web of responses. The hum of many voices is not an ominous sign of alienation from order, but a welcome evidence of human rationality.

None of this promises escape from the tribulations of mortality. But they lose the sensational quality of a natural evil or deviations from a natural perfection, and acquire the banal character of the stuff out of which mortals have to make their lives. That this stuff should in some respects be poor or good is simply part of the mystery that surrounds human existence. But the mystery has its compensations. As nothing is eternal in human life, nor anything just what it seems to be, and the consequences of our actions are never just what we intended, then to-day's evils, like to-day's blessings, may not seem quite so bad or good tomorrow. They certainly cannot last forever. Hopefulness is not only reasonable, but obligatory, because despair betrays an arrogant pretension to foresee the future with certainty, to know what mortal beings may not hope to know.

Instead of being a struggle to repress given evils or to achieve given goals, human existence becomes an exploration in which the destination is always being discovered in the course of arriving. It is full of uncertainty but in many different degrees. About some things, men may think that they know the right answer 'with certainty'. In other cases, the ineradicable contingency of human knowledge is more obvious. And this makes it sensible to distinguish between 'knowledge' and 'opinion'. But it is merely a distinction between convictions held with greater and less confidence. In order to decide what degree of confidence is appropriate to any opinion, men can only refer to their civilized inheritance.

By comparison with the certainty available in the pantheist cosmos, inhabited by the self-divided man, the gentleman's mortal knowledge may seem a poor thing. But gentlemen do not mock it because they are content to have at their disposal the whole of human civilization, to the degree of course that they are educated and aware of it, which enables them to act and think always on something that is truly given. Only it is given by the past, not by God or Nature. Since it has been made by human beings over time, it is subject to unceasing emendation; and there is nothing in it that can be known to be indisputably valid. Nevertheless it provides solid enough ground for distinguishing steadily between true and false, beautiful and ugly, just and unjust, right and wrong.

But as there are no universal patterns, there is no one 'good life', and the shape of moral excellence cannot be generic. It must be personal. And yet the personal is inseparable from the social. Although a man's moral excellence is bound up with the community in which he moves and he is obliged to heed what others prescribe, virtue does not consist in conformity to such prescriptions.

The result is an unusually complicated morality. But the complexity allows for a possibility that is excluded in moralities of the self-divided man – cultivating individuality without embracing either nihilism or narcissism. For a gentleman, individuality has nothing to do with rejecting all constraints or pursuing 'self-realization'. Both are ruled out because a gentleman's selfhood is made by him out of materials provided by his communal life. The richer the materials, the more subtle and various can be the product.

In a way, the moral problem for a gentleman is analogous to the traditional one. A gentleman, too, is trying to discover some fixity in an existence where everything is ephemeral. But the fixity sought by the gentleman is of a very different sort. It is a conquest of mutability not by renouncing or trying to overcome or stifle it, but by developing a steady way of dealing with it. This manner of conducting himself constitutes the moral excellence that defines a gentleman and is called 'integrity'.

The quality of integrity may or may not be present in a character because the connexions constituting a character may be more or less jumbled. Just as a picture may be nothing more than the shapes and colours contained within a finite frame, or may be a self-contained unity without the frame, so may the connexions that constitute a man's character be unified only by being attached to the same person or by such a profound coherence that everything about him seems to be a necessary part of a whole. Such coherence constitutes the integrity of a gentleman.

It might be said to make a gentleman self-possessed, self-determined, self-contained, well regulated, or collected. But each of these words carries distracting connotations. It is perhaps less misleading to see a gentleman as the opposite of someone whose steadiness depends on conformity to something outside himself and, where such a support is missing, contradicts himself and fragments his life. When a man contradicts himself, he becomes an adversary of himself, and when he divides his life into separate compartments, he hides himself from himself and is only partly alive, like someone who walks in his sleep. Because a gentleman is aware of himself as engaged in shaping a coherent self, he would not do either.

The self-awareness of a gentleman must not be confused with self-preoccupation or self-absorption, or with a disposition to take an hourly census of one's virtues and vices, pleasures and pains, successes and failures. It is a profoundly different kind of sensitivity to the context of all the moments that make up one's life. It appears in a gentleman's care to consider whether the meaning of what he does today is consistent with what he did yesterday or is likely to do tomorrow, and in his readiness to question whether he has accurately observed what should have been taken into account. A gentleman's self-awareness is, in other words, a delicate sense of responsibility for the coherence of all his thoughts, words, and actions.

Self-awareness need not be self-conscious. Indeed, the more deeply rooted and complete is a man's sense of responsibility, the more it will resemble an 'instinctive' quality because the more difficult it will be for him to behave otherwise and the more surely and easily he will behave in this manner. Deliberate, self-consciousness in conduct, far from being essential to a thorough and profound sense of responsibility, may distort judgement. Or it may indicate an affectation of the genuine quality. But on the other hand, the more serious the anomalies that a gentleman encounters in his life, the more self-conscious he may need to be.

To conduct himself responsibly, a gentleman must take accurate note of the world that he inhabits. In that world, he recognizes himself to be one among others who have the same distinctiveness and in whom this quality has been nurtured by the communal life that they share. Therefore the notion that 'others' are an intrusion on him, that they are by nature antagonists or competitors, or that they in any other way necessarily threaten his individuality, is foreign to a gentleman. He does not see himself and others as bundles of interests scrambling to produce and acquire satisfactions which are in short supply. To his way of thinking, that is only one of many possible relationships among human beings, just as producing and acquiring goods is but one of many human activities and can play different roles in the different lives that men lead. What constitutes a human relationship in the gentleman's world is neither the presence nor absence of hostility but speaking the same language. As a common language does not dictate what is said, it cannot threaten the individuality of the speakers.

How a gentleman is obliged to treat others is derived from how he understands himself. Though that understanding is learned from his life among other men, it is the ground for both how he thinks of himself and how he relates himself to others. In his understanding of himself, the idea of integrity is central. And he cares about his integrity because the more coherent a character, the greater its integrity, the more perfect the humanity. But this raises the question: Why is it worth fostering the quality of humanity?

There is no answer to this question in the morality of a gentleman. Only if human reason were linked to a source of non-human eternal truth, if it were the ordering principle of a rational cosmos, could reason demonstrate that man heads the hierarchy of being and is superior to all other kinds of being. But that would be the Reason of the self-divided man and not a merely human property, as it must be in a gentleman's morality.

A gentleman might, however, regard his humanity as a trust given to him by God, and justify that belief by reference to Scripture. But that justification need not impress anyone who does not believe in the same God and his revealed word. In short, the gentleman's fundamental postulate, that men are not for eating, is an article of faith. He cannot demonstrate that his way of understanding what men are is indisputably true, and that any alternative, such as the morality of the self-divided man, is false. The morality of a gentleman denies that it can be proved to be the only true one. It is in this sense a sceptical morality.

The obligation to recognize that his morality is founded on an article of faith raises a serious difficulty for a gentleman. It means that others may not accept his morality and that he cannot claim a demonstrable right to impose it on them. But it does not follow that he has to refrain from doing anything to preserve the kind of life that he values. He may even be obliged to fight, subjugate, or destroy others. Whether he is justified in doing so is a practical judgement that can only be decided in each case in terms of the particular circumstances. Therefore a gentleman accepts the existence of other moralities alongside his own, and also the necessity sometimes to defend himself against them. His readiness to acknowledge that his belief in the superiority of his own morality is an article of faith rather than a demonstrable truth, and his willingness nevertheless to fight for it without being certain when it is right to do so, is part of his ability to accept the limitations of his mortal condition.

Certain obligations do, however, follow necessarily from the fundamental postulate of a gentleman's morality. The equation of virtue with integrity follows from a gentleman's understanding of what it means to be human. And since an antipathy to self-contradiction is at the heart of integrity, and a gentleman understands himself as one among others like himself, his respect for his own integrity entails respecting the integrity of others. He will think of others in the same way as he thinks of himself. He will recognize them as personalities, as characters, whose distinctiveness he is obliged to respect, and whom he must treat as he wishes himself to be treated. He is not thereby bound to regard all men as equally good, any more than he is obliged to deny his own failings; the ability to respect others, like the ability to respect oneself, requires taking accurate note of the different qualities of different characters. What it rules out is manipulating, taking advantage of, managing others as if they were instruments for achieving the purposes of others.

This implies that men may not be defined as beings whose essence is to be found in the species to which they belong or in their fulfilling their proper function in a social organism. For such definitions imply that individuals are means to a higher end such as the survival of the species or the supremacy of the nation. It also follows that there can be no such thing as a 'gentleman burglar'. That Raffles robs only from guests and never from his host, has excellent manners, and patriotically captures a spy makes him an eccentric burglar but not a gentleman because he makes use of others. The Golden Rule, 'Treat others as you would have them treat you', is not a bad summary of the idea that governs a gentleman's relations with others. But it presupposes, what is neglected in popular references to the Golden Rule, a gentleman's self-awareness and respect for his own integrity.

A gentleman's integrity gives him a kind of fixity. And this makes him resemble a work of art. But nevertheless, he is full of the movement of life. For his steadiness does not arise from conformity to a code or pattern or from pursuing a given goal or ideal. It consists rather in a certain way of understanding himself. Therefore, the virtues that produce integrity differ from the traditional ones.

The traditional virtue of wisdom is replaced by discrimination. This is because a gentleman is obliged not to discover 'the real unity' underlying the 'apparent diversity' but to take accurate notice of the human world. In order to do so, he must distinguish nicely between similarities and differences. And therefore he needs discrimination.

Discrimination is displayed by recognizing that the same sort of action may have been inspired by different motives, by an ability to acknowledge ideas and purposes alien to oneself, by care to distinguish between malice and error, disagreement and depravity. It does not prevent a gentleman from making moral judgements. On the contrary, it keeps him from evading an obligation to judge through confusing prudence with weakness. Discrimination enables a gentleman to recognize that though charity is admirable, charity to a murderer may imply indifference to the fate of his victims; that if he rejects a friend's criticism of someone else, he is criticizing his friend; that whereas even unjustified censure may have been preceded by a serious effort to understand

and excuse, tolerance may be inspired by nothing more generous than a servile desire to please; that though being suspicious is ugly, unseemly conjecture should be distinguished from reasonable doubt and that squeamishness about suspecting a conspiracy may hand over his country to enemies. Instead of renouncing rules, a gentleman will recognize that rules mean different things in different circumstances, and that, if in some contexts firmness about rules is more important than achieving perfect justice, in other contexts, since rules are abridgements of a practice, they should be ignored. When faced with transgressors, he will consider whether he is dealing with an eccentric, a ruffian, or a villain.

Far from giving him an aversion to decisiveness,, his discrimination enables a gentleman to take into account a rich variety of considerations and to master a rich vocabulary of responses, so that he is not at a loss even in strange circumstances. That is why resolution is said to be the mark of a gentleman. To those who do not understand what considerations govern his conduct, his discrimination may give him an appearance of inconsistency, but it is only because they fail to see the intricate connexions that are all important to him.

The second, and perhaps the most surprising, of the gentleman's virtues, is his diffidence. Unlike the traditional virtue of humility, it carries no connotation of unworthiness or inferiority. Diffidence is rather a pervasive awareness of the limitations of all human reason. It follows from believing that no human being can know the ultimate origin, ground, or purpose of his existence. And it gives a gentleman a profound repugnance to all pretensions of transcending mortality by predicting the future or discovering inevitablities.

Diffidence does not prevent a gentleman from taking action, but it does keep him from supposing that everything is or ought to be subject to his control. Nothing could be more alien to him than the dream of constructing 'a sure plan' which would substitute certainty for 'petty and probable conjectures'. Proposals for reconstructing the world to match some vision of perfection are, to a gentleman's way of thinking, absurd and dangerous. Nor will he accept the sordid belief that everyone's words and actions are instruments for changing the world so as better to satisfy his interests. To be constantly active on behalf of the future is not, for a gentleman, a virtue, but a vice.

The oddity of a gentleman's diffidence is perhaps most obvious in his attitude to altruism, to putting others before himself. If it means pursuing self-sacrifice, altruism is a sin rather than a virtue for a gentleman because he feels obliged to respect his selfhood. If it means seeking to do good to others, altruism strikes him as perilous. His awareness of the ultimate mystery of personality and his concern to respect the integrity of others makes him wary of doing harm instead of good by mistaking the characters and circumstances of others. In any case, he never considers himself indispensable in the scheme of things. Therefore, in his view, equating altruism with morality is a sign of arrogance and a vice. But because he bears it in mind that his own estimate of what is true and right may be wrong and because he is not disposed to exaggerate his own importance, a gentleman will relent and forgive where others might insist, resent or fight. And therefore magnanimity is the other side of a gentleman's aversion to altruism.

But though a gentleman may hold back where others rush in, his diffidence should not be mistaken for the aloofness of someone who lacks zest for life and sympathy for others, or for the meekness of someone who dare not act. His awareness both of his own unimportance and of his fallibility not only keeps him from intervening arrogantly. It also prevents him expecting things to go his way. This both saves him from disappointment when men and things resist his will and allows him to hope that something worthwhile may be salvaged. And consequently, when others give in, he may go on fighting.

To sustain his diffidence and discrimination, a gentleman needs courage, which is the third of the cardinal virtues. Without it he could not endure the special awareness that distinguishes his frame of mind. For he recognizes that while it is impossible to live without constantly making judgements, nothing can guarantee the correctness of a judgement or render it immune to criticism, and yet a man swayed by every hostile voice will soon reduce his life to absurdity. A gentleman's courage consists in honestly hearing objections that may prove him wrong, while steadfastly enduring criticism once he has taken his decision. What distinguishes his courage from obstinacy or arrogance is that he keeps to his judgement because he has rigorously questioned it and has become persuaded that it is the right one, and not because it was the first one to hand or because he finds it the most comfortable to hold. This makes a gentleman's courage peculiarly strenuous because it requires much more than ability to face what he would rather avoid; it is the capacity to take a firm stand while recognizing that the rightness of doing so is questionable.

The last of a gentleman's cardinal virtues is honesty. Though it has a peculiar importance for him that is connected with his regard for individuality, it bears no resemblance to what is now called 'authenticity' and is understood as the resistance of a given, fixed self to the distortions imposed upon it by others. For a gentleman, honesty is a necessary condition of his respect for himself and others and it consists in taking account of – not, it should be noticed, conforming to – three different kinds of objectivities.

One consists of all the impersonal ways of understanding and judging made available by the arts and sciences. What makes a man honest in this respect is not how much he knows, but his clarity about what he does and does not know and about what kind of knowledge is appropriate to answering the questions in hand. Though he recognizes that all of these objectivities were made by men and not given by nature, he respects them as if they were eternal verities.

Secondly, and more profoundly, a gentleman's honesty rests on recognizing his own integrity as an objectivity. To do so, he must know what belongs to himself, and instinctively connect every utterance and action with that selfhood. What matters is that his words should be consistent with a steady understanding. A man who lacks integrity cannot speak honestly because what he thinks now has only a fortuitous connexion with what he thought yesterday and may think tomorrow. Though the utterances and actions of such a man may be true self-expression, they cannot have any intrinsic, steady, personal content, and they are therefore merely affectations of the moment. A man of integrity, on the other hand, though he may and probably will change, either deliberately or unselfconsciously, will always feel obliged to recognize that he has done so by connecting what is new with what has gone before, even if only by acknowledging a change. And therefore everything that he says has a reliable connexion with the coherent consciousness that constitutes his personality.

The third kind of objectivity that a gentleman takes into account is the character of other people. He exerts himself to notice carefully what they say and do and to understand how they connect their words and deeds. Deceit is repugnant to him because it is a means for manipulating others and treating them as objects for his use, and because he would be betraying himself by pretending to be other than he is in order to produce the response he wanted. Merely refraining from lying is not enough. A gentleman feels obliged to recognize that a literal truth can deceive even more effectively than a bold falsehood, and to notice with precision whom he is addressing, for what purpose, in what time and place. He does not excuse a disregard for the contingent human world by pleading a saint's or a philosopher's absorption in a 'higher' reality or in universal abstractions. To discern and to take into account the personal identities and particular circumstances that constitute the reality of human life is for him always a duty. His honesty leads him to speak differently to friends and to strangers, in private and in public. He will lie to a murderer in order to save his friend, though his honesty will keep him from pretending, to himself or others, that he has not lied. But at the same time, he is careful to distinguish a respect for the concrete context of utterances from a wilful denial of objectivity. As honesty depends on taking accurate account of the weight and limits of words, anyone who uses words promiscuously cannot be a gentleman.

All of this means that the virtue of a gentleman does not depend on his doing or thinking this or that. His motives are more important than his intentions or actions. The crucial thing is how his thoughts, feelings and actions fit together and are related to the world in which he moves. Such a moral quality cannot be conveyed by an abstract discussion or even by a collection of examples. We can come to understand what constitutes being a gentleman only by following what a gentleman notices, what questions he asks, what considerations he entertains, how he responds on different occasions, in short, by knowing people who are gentlemen intimately over long stretches, either in life or through reading a novelist like Trollope.

Getting to know people in this sense means noticing not just their words and actions as they go about their daily life, but also their tone of voice, inflexions, and gestures and the particular circumstances in which they appear, as well as their relation to other sayings and doings, both of the actor and of those to whom he is responding or whom he is affecting. From the standpoint of the self-divided man, such nuances and connexions are merely matter for gossip or food or a childish interest in story-telling, and hardly pertinent to a theoretical discussion of moral conduct. But they are the very essence of the moral life in the gentleman's morality because there the moral quality of people depends on how they understand themselves and their world and each is taken to be an individual consciousness with his own way of achieving coherence. The important question is always *why* someone behaves as he does and there is no short-cut to the answer. Therefore an interest in the moral life is necessarily an interest in the details of how individual human beings conduct themselves.

5 The Meaning of Integrity

The most perfect gentleman in Trollope's novels is Madame Max Goesler. She was the daughter of a humble German Jewish attorney, and her only endowments by birth were beauty and intelligence. But she inherited a fortune from her husband and with these assets Marie Goesler moved from Vienna to London, hoping to make her way into the top social circles. She succeeded so well that the highest duke of all offered her his coronet.

According to the morality of the self-divided man, Madame Goesler has no claim to being a model of virtue and there is a good case for dismissing her as a crass social climber. She did not struggle or yearn for spiritual perfection. Far from despising worldly things, she pursued a wholly material kind of success. The fact that despite her great wealth, she chose a small house in Park Lane, entertained only a few guests at time, and refused at first to admit the Duke of Omnium whom other hostesses were delighted just to have cross their threshold, suggests that she proceeded with low guile.

But this interpretation of her conduct makes it impossible to explain the rest of what Trollope tells us about her. Why, when at last the Duke of Omnium asked her to become his duchess, did Madame Goesler refuse him? She felt certain of her ability to play the part brilliantly and believed that 'a woman ought to wish to be the Duchess of Omnium'.[1] The life of a duchess would have been much more congenial to her than living alone. It was, besides, her professed belief that love was not essential to marriage; the only man whom she could love was pursuing other heiresses; and she not only felt a genuine affection for the duke, but was convinced that she could 'add something of brightness to his life'.[2] Nor was she in the least frightened by the opposition of his family. When Lady Glencora told her that such a marriage would disgrace the duke, Madame Goesler demanded an apology and declared that nothing stood 'in the way of her being as good a duchess as any other woman'. Nevertheless, after playing with the coronet in her lap for a day or two, she rejected the duke and without regret – 'the gem was not worth the cost . . .'.[3]

The difficulty of reconciling Madame Goesler's ambition with her refusal of the duke is not the only anomaly in her history if interpreted from the standpoint of the self-divided man. As she takes great care to observe the established conventions, she appears to be guilty of slavish conformity; but as she goes her own way with unwavering determination, she must be a rebel. The suspicion and hostility aroused by her being a foreigner, a Jewess, a woman, and clever make her 'a victim of society'; but on the other hand, she displays throughout the easy assurance of those in a position to do the victimizing. Her perfect propriety suggests a complete capitulation of the 'private' to the 'public' self; but her uninvited offer of her hand and fortune to a man of no importance is the behaviour of an unrepressed, passionate, 'private' self. In fact, Madame Goesler is none of these things, neither a self-sacrificing martyr nor a ruthless go-getter.

What distinguishes her character is suggested by small details about her house and person. We are told not just that her house was pretty and charming, but that although the rooms were adorned by many 'precious toys', nothing 'annoyed by its rarity or was distasteful by its richness'; that while the seats were graceful and 'as costly as money could buy', they were 'meant for sitting and were comfortable as seats'; that there were not only books, but means for reading them at hand and the books were in fact read.[4] The same 'studious absence of parade', Trollope says, marked the appearance of the woman herself. She did not play down her foreignness; she wore dark ringlets as no one else did, and gowns made of unusual, rich fabrics cut in a strange fashion. And yet she was never obtrusive. Even her stationery was neither ordinary nor ostentatious – its small monogram was 'fantastic without being grotesque'.[5] Though everything about her was odd, nothing jarred or demanded attention. It all might have grown upon her. These details reveal something more than a highly cultivated aesthetic sensibility. The quiet charm of Madame Goesler's house as of her appearance was due to its being the natural expression of someone who knew herself, took careful notice of her circumstances, and was all of a piece. This clarity about herself and others shaped her conduct and led her to refuse the duke's offer.

With her beauty, wit, and wealth, she easily might have dazzled the gatekeepers of London society into overlooking her lack of pedigree. Or she could have bought her way in as there were plenty of willing sellers among the highest in the land. But she took care to do neither. She took a small house and entertained modestly because she wanted to make herself known only gradually. She refused at first to receive the Duke of Omnium in order to make it clear to him that displaying his presence as a trophy was not her object, and that she would no more accept condescension from him than from anyone else. In their meetings, she took pains to be agreeable but without flattery – when the duke referred sadly to his advanced age, she did not tell him how young he looked but remarked on 'the difference between oak-trees and currant-bushes'.[6] And this was generally her style. She spoke her mind without pandering to the opinions of others, yet she never offended because she had a graceful way of expressing her true opinions. In short, she was out not just to win, but to win by playing well and fairly. She wished genuinely to persuade those by whom she hoped to become accepted that, despite her strangeness, she was someone whom they could genuinely respect and like. And she succeeded because a superior imagination enabled her to avoid ruffling sensibilities without betraying her convictions.

Madame Goesler is no more 'a victim of social pressures' or a 'rebel' than she is a crass social climber. When she took careful account of the prejudices and conventions of the people among whom she had come to live, she did not think of herself as 'battling against society'. What moved her was the conviction that in a well ordered and closely-knit community, a strange woman with a foreign name, foreign sources of income, and a foreign history was bound to seem a questionable creature. Even later, when she had made her place fairly secure, she still kept 'a conviction in regard to herself, that hard words and hard judgements were to the expected from the world – were to be accepted by her without any strong feeling of injustice . . .',[7] and in thinking so, Madame Goesler was not depreciating either herself or the decency of others. She was merely acknowledging that the present could not be divorced from the past; that as the knowledge that we have of someone else's motives and intentions is necessarily incomplete, misunderstandings cannot be ruled out; and that therefore, as she had chosen to live among strangers, she had to accept the conditions attached to doing so. Her attitude was like a good craftsman's sense for the texture of the materials on which he works and his determination to do his job well. 'If a man is a servant,' she said, 'he should be clever enough to be a good one.'[8]

The same sort of consideration made Madame Goesler fastidiously careful not to take advantage of her intimacy with the great, without affecting either her opinion of herself or the whole-heartedness of her friendship. It appears only in her care to distinguish between friendship and familiarity, and to draw the line differently according to the circumstances. She felt free to scold the duchess with the familiarity of an elder sister because the duchess was a grown woman, notoriously capable of holding her own. But when, after the duchess died, Madame Goesler took charge of the daughter, she continued to address the girl as Lady Mary because, though she knew that her friendship was perfectly disinterested, she knew also that she had to guard herself against any appearance of manipulating the girl. For it would not have been unreasonable for strangers to suppose that a young girl, soon after her mother's sudden death, would be extremely susceptible to the influence of her mother's friend and might be used to strengthen the position of that friend, if she were an outside like Madame Goesler.

This manner of understanding herself and others led Madame Goesler to decline the coronet. She refused it because she felt that she – not the duke – would have been degraded by her acceptance. But her reasoning started from a delicate understanding of what respect for him required.

She saw that the duke's only accomplishment was his regard for his role in the social hierarchy – he stood above all other aristocrats and went near royalty only as a 'disagreeable duty, incident to his position'.[9] And he played his part to perfection. His presence was unquestionably that of the greatest of dukes and effortlessly won him the deference due to his station. That in this way he helped to reinforce the sentiments essential for preserving the aristocracy made his life meaningful to him. This sense of himself would have made it inconceivable earlier that he should have thought of marrying a Marie Goesler.

But he had gone through life missing he knew not what. He had the wistfulness of a departing guest who wondered why he had not enjoyed the party more and hoped that in the few moments left to him the evening might still be redeemed. In that state of mind, an unusually beautiful and witty woman, altoge-

ther unlike anyone he had ever known, could easily distract the
duke into forgetting himself. Madame Goesler did not doubt that
he had a real affection for her. But she also recognized that if
they had met at the beginning of the party, his response would
have been very different. Though he understood what he was
deciding and was aware of the opposition to his project, he was
not in complete possession of himself. Like a child surfeited with
all his presents, he was grasping at the top brick in the chimney.
If at this time, Madame Goesler had accepted his proposal she
would have been no better than her maid who could see nothing
but the glow of the coronet. She would have been taking something that, though it was given voluntarily, was not in truth being
given freely. As untitled and foreign Marie Goesler, she felt equal
to the Duke of Omnium, but to have become his duchess, because
she had failed to understand or to consider that she was taking
advantage of an old man's weakness, would have demeaned her.
In thinking of what was due to the old duke and giving up the
coronet, she was not sacrificing herself but doing the opposite –
preserving her self-respect. 'As Madame Goesler, I can live, even
among my superiors, at my ease,' she wrote to the Duke. 'As your
Grace's wife I should be easy no longer.'[10]

In other contexts, the same kind of considerations led Madame
Goesler to conduct herself very differetly. When she quarrelled
with the younger duke, she pressed her own claims as forcefully as
she could. She had become the wife of the duke's close colleague,
Phineas Finn, had for long been on intimate terms with the
entire family. and when, upon the sudden death of his duchess,
the duke asked her to act as companion and guide for his
daughter, Mrs Finn found herself the custodian as well of an
awkward secret. Lady Mary had become engaged to a commoner, and had been encourged to do so by the duchess who,
though she knew how distasteful such an alliance would be to the
duke, expected that she could persuade him to accept it. But she
died too suddenly to tell him anything. As it seemed natural to
confide in her mother's dearest friend, Lady Mary did not see
what was painfully obvious to her confidante, that her doing so
required Mrs Finn to betray the duke by condoning what she
knew he opposed and should have been told long ago. To avoid,
as well as she could, violating the confidence of either the father
or the daughter, Mrs Finn urged Lady Mary to reveal the truth
and immediately left the duke's house. But when the duke was

told, he at once concluded that Mrs Finn had plotted against him and wrote her a curt note accusing her, banishing her, and declaring an end to their long friendship.

Her response was neither servile nor rebellious, but firm, consistent, and charitable. Even at the height of her anger, she recognized that, had the accusation been justified, the duke could not have done less. He would have shown a despicable lack of self-respect to have continued to admit into his life someone mean enough to exploit his friendship in order to impose upon him. But the same consideration, that would have justified the duke in banishing a devious friend, moved Mrs Finn to be equally forceful about obtaining an apology from him.

She understood that the duke was being so wildly unjust to her because he could not accept the truth that he easily guessed. Not only had his beloved duchess conspired against him. She had favoured the engagement because it seemed to realize a dream that she herself had once entertained and lost, and of which he was aware. To be reminded of this just when he was both overwhelmed with grief for his wife and faced with evidence of her having wronged him was peculiarly painful. He could not accuse the memory of his wife, and to turn against his daughter, the one consolation left to him, was out of the question. Therefore he seized upon a more bearable explanation – that Mrs Finn, who had recently been intimate with his daughter and had left his house with a mysterious suddenness, had arranged it all.

Mrs Finn insisted on getting an apology just because she held the duke in such high regard and saw his injustice as an aberration. Had she not tried to persuade him of his error, she would have frivolously let one action of his transform an estimate of his character that she had formed over many years, and in doing so she would have violated both consistency and charity. Ha she dismissed the offence, she would also have been lacking in self-respect. Other misunderstandings had been disregarded by her as mere annoyances. But this one came from someone whom she loved and respected and who had known her intimately for a long time. It was, moreover, an accusation that struck at the very heart of her sense of herself: 'The thing of which I am accused is so repugnant to me, that I am obliged to do something and to say something, even though the subject itself be one on which I would so willingly be silent.'[11] The opinion of the world she easily ignored, but not that of an old friend and on such a vital matter.

In her letter to the duke Mrs Finn minced no words: 'Had I
been . . . a participator in that secret I could not have honestly
remained in the position you assigned to me. Had I done so, I
should have deserved your ill opinion. As it is I have not deserved
it, and your condemnation of me has been altogether unjust.
Should I not now receive from you a full withdrawal of all
charges against me, I shall be driven to think that after all the
insight which circumstances have given me into your character, I
have nevertheless been mistaken in the reading of it.' She pointed
out that he had violated an obligation to be especially careful
about bringing such charges against a stranger of inferior station
who was peculiarly vulnerable to accusations of deviousness. And
finally, she told him that she knew him to be an obstinate man
reluctant to change his mind, but that if he was as honourable as
she believed him to be, he would strive to overcome his obstinacy:
'You are not one who from your nature can be brought easily to
do this; but you are one who will certainly do it if you can be
made to feel that by not doing so you would be unjust. I am myself so clear as to my own rectitude of purpose and conduct, and
am so well aware of your perspicuity that I venture to believe that
if you will read this letter I shall convince you . . .'[12]

Her tone of voice was in keeping with her conception of what
was at issue. She argued her case as directly and as effectively as
she could, without either whining or surliness, and so managed to
voice her grievance without imposing her feeling of grievance. It
would have defeated her purpose to bully or distress the duke into
apologizing because only if he were truly persuaded of his mistake
could his apology he meaningful to her. She had no desire to
revenge herself on the duke, or to renew the friendship, and there
was no advantage that she could gain from the duke's apology.
She was moved only by her respect for herself and for him, which
demanded that she should not let a wrong of this kind pass
without making some effort to correct it.

Madame Goesler's integrity is so impressive partly because her
circumstances provided her with many tempting invitations to
confusion. Her wealth removed the most ordinary constraints; as
an outsider, she had no inherited pattern to follow; she had to
make her way against suspicion and to be more than ordinarily
responsive to the opinions of others. Yet she managed to be at
once decorous, honest, consistent, and independent. But her
ability to combine qualities which, in the morality of the self-

divided man, are taken to be conflicting is only part of what makes her an unusual model of virtue. Judged by the consequences of her conduct, there is nothing grand or even especially admirable about her. Her moral quality depends entirely on her motives – that her conduct was governed by an unfailingly meticulous respect for the personality of herself and others, and on her remarkable ability to distinguish fine shades in the interpretations and responses available to her, which enabled her never to betray that respect.

*   *   *

Plantagenet Palliser, Duke of Omnium (*Can You Forgive Her? Phineas Finn, Phineas Redux, The Prime Minister, The Duke's Children*), Trollope says in his *Autobiography*, 'is a perfect gentleman. If he be not then am I unable to describe a gentleman.'[13] But it would be difficult to imagine a character more unlike Madame Goesler. He conforms to the stereotype of a gentleman as thoroughly as she departs from it. His rank was the highest; his property and wealth, immense; his occupation, governing; and his manner, reserved. And he has a full measure of the faults from which she is so remarkably free.

The story of how he came to marry Lady Glencora suggests that he was incapable of love. Respected advisers presented Lady Glencora to him and as he believed that he would find it agreeable to contemplate her across the table, he was prepared to love her – he understood love to be the regard that a man ought to have for his wife and for no other woman. Though he was told that she had once succumbed to an imprudent attachment, he assumed that it resembled his meaningless hour of infatuation with Lady Dumbello. After his marriage, a number of people told Palliser that his wife continued to regret what might have been and was thinking of leaving him for her former lover, Burgo Fitzgerald; it was true, but Palliser noticed nothing and refused to hear what he was told.

The history of his married life confirms the picture of Palliser as a man who cold and stiff. When in an effort to distract herself with public activities Lady Glencora asked him to make her Mistress of the Robes, he refused. When she tried to help him gain the following that he was unable to achieve by himself, her efforts were not appreciated. He made her life more difficult, the duchess said, than Lady Macbeth's: 'Her lord appeared and misbehaved himself; my lord won't show himself at all.'[14] When he did appear in his drawing room, he either hid behind a screen, or retired to a corner with one person; or else he went walking with a dreary old spinster who talked about cork-soled shoes. He was capable even of being extremely rude – he turned his back on a guest who had made a displeasing remark. The feeling of many of his colleagues was expressed by the duchess when she remarked that he seemed to expect a majority to drop into his mouth. But a closer look at how Trollope tells the story shows why, despite all his faults, Palliser is as good a model of integrity as Madame Goesler.

An apparently trivial disagreement between the duke and his duchess over the garden at Gatherum Castle is telling. In preparing for the great receptions that she proposed to give to promote his government, the duchess had completely reconstructed the grounds. She had moved earth, laid down grass, scattered exotic plants, constructed gravel paths, produced a great ha-ha. The duke did not mind the expense and had no objection to setting the flag waving over the Castle – the practice belonged to his rank and station and he would not take it upon himself to imperil 'the benefits accruing to his country from established marks of reverence'.[15] But ruthlessly transforming the grounds to impress their guests was another matter. The garden had been the work of many generations and had a quality that could be acquired only in that way. Lady Glencora's changes had brutally substituted something that had a look of raw newness and an 'assumed and preposterous grandeur'. The falsity was all the worse because it was done only to impress a horde of strangers – 'Why, on earth, should a man's grounds be knocked about because he becomes Prime Minister?' and so the duke ended by telling Lady Glencora that her projects were 'vulgar'. She acknowledged that they were and saw no reason to regret it: 'But why shouldn't she be vulgar, if she could most surely get what she wanted by vulgarity?' Everything that she had done was designed to promote his popularity – 'When a man wants to be Prime Minister he has to submit to vulgarity, and must give up his ambition if the task be too disagreeable to him ... that had been understood, at any rate ever since the days of Coriolanus.'[16]

The duke had a very different conception of his obligations as Prime Minister, and it was not because, like Coriolanus, he was so sure of his superiority or so determined to have it acknowledged. Just as Madame Goesler wanted her social acceptance to depend wholly on her true qualities, so he wanted only followers who were convinced that his policies were desirable. He would spare no effort to persuade them by argument; he considered it a fine thing to entertain one's friends and went so far as to grant that in a public position a man acquired more 'so-called friends'. But Lady Glencora's idea of entertainment substituted bribery for persuasion – 'the idea of conquering people, as you call it,' he told the duchess, 'by feeding them, is to me abominable'. The same sensitivity to the difference between fake and genuine things that made the duke dislike the new gardens, led him to escape from a party full of strangers to go walking with the spinster who talked about cork-soled shoes. She never bored him because 'she was natural, and she wanted nothing from him. When she talked about cork soles she meant cork soles.'[17]

His unusually profound courtesy explains the duke's notorious rudeness to Major Pountney. The major accosted his host in the garden, was not at all discouraged because his compliment on Gatherum Castle – 'A splendid pile' – was answered by, 'It is a big house', and moved on to announcing that he wanted to be made the candidate for the duke's borough: 'You would find that you would have a supporter than whom none would be more staunch ...'. The duke's reply was short: 'I think, sir, that your proposition is the most unbecoming and the most impertinent that ever was addressed to me', and the major was left standing open-mouthed as the duke walked away; later the major received a note saying. 'The Duke of Omnium trusts that Major Pountney will not find it inconvenient to leave Gatherum Castle shortly.'[18]

The significance of the incident is underscored by the very different response of the duchess to a similar request. She knew that the duke was scrupulously careful not to behave as a 'borough-mongering lord', but when another of the strange guests, who seemed amiable, mentioned his hope to stand for the duke's borough, she responded in her usual ebullient fashion without thinking of what that implied about the duke. When the rumours that he was supporting one of the candidates reached the duke, he categorically denied them. But when the man argued that he had acted on expectations aroused by the duchess which were then disappointed, the duke insisted on compensating him, regardless of the scandal that was promised and realized.

Trollope has been widely criticized for the implausibility of the duke's treatment of Major Pountney because a gentleman, it is said, would never be rude to a guest in his own house; the real prime minister would have uttered some dry or humourous excuse and then avoided his guest. But the scene is not a mistake. It shows that the duke required of himself something more than pleasantness that would lead people to think well of him. The duke recognized that to such a man at such a party, in order to guard against false expectations, he had to make it brutally plain that he was not selling seats. He held himself responsible for what he had suggested, even indirectly, by the manner in which he entertained. And therefore the duke's dismissal of the major was more truly courteous, in the sense of being respectful of others, than the friendliness of the duchess. The duke was rude because he was a perfect gentleman. It is true that on other occasions he might have managed to be more amiable without running much danger of displaying irresponsible warmth. But as he lacked the deftness to get such things right, he erred on the side of coldness. That kept him from being an amusing companion, which he saw and regretted, but it was less likely to impose on others than the opposite excess illustrated in the behaviour of Lady Glencora.

In a similar fashion, Palliser's unawareness of his wife's unhappiness indicates something very different from insensitivity. It arose from his general attitude to those with whom he was connected. Those whom he identified as gentlemen, he regarded as his moral equals and never suspected of behaving improperly because to do otherwise would imply that they were inferior: 'I never gave the lie to a gentleman and hope that I may never be driven to do so.'[19] The contrary of this understanding of people appears in Mr Bott's certainty that Lady Glencora was planning to run off long before she was. Bott saw other people as bundles of movements and words from which it was his duty to extract proof of whatever he wanted to believe about them. When he found Lady Glencora doing something that might indicate disloyalty to her husband, he at once concluded that she was disloyal without stopping to consider how the incident accorded with her character.

Whereas the concept of a character was unknown to Bott, for Palliser it was always in the foreground of his thinking. It led him to assume that his wife took their marriage vows as seriously as he did and kept him from suspecting her of unfaithfulness. And when she confessed that she had considered leaving him, it led him to think first of the unhappiness that had moved her to entertain such an idea. He accepted her description of how useless and unhappy she had felt as his wife and yet reluctant to break her vows as a true account of an unfortunate predicament. His lack of the kind of imagination that distinguished Madame Goesler had kept him from seeing his wife's troubles for himself, but he could understand how someone who was not given to falseness might nevertheless be unfaithful, and he did not suppose – as did Bott – that all unfaithful wives are alike.

Palliser made the discovery that his wife could not love him at the same time as he discovered that he loved her. But he responded by acknowledging all the uncomfortable implications of what had happened without feeling debased, or looking for a scapegoat, or succumbing to despair. That she did not love him, he told her, was 'a misfortune' for both of them.[20] Neither he nor she could have just what each wanted, but something else, not to be despised, remained possible. And in offering to take her abroad, even though he was giving up an opportunity to be Chancellor of the Exchequer, he was not asserting his rights as a husband, treating her as an inferior who needed to be saved from herself, or sacrificing himself for her, but giving her the help for which she had asked him.

Lady Glencora's 'wild impulses' continued to create difficulties for Palliser. But he loved what made her distinctive to the point of cherishing the accompanying faults, and that was why he was shocked by her desire to become Mistress of the Robes. His own occupation, he told her, had required him to accept the constraints of public life: 'I have put myself into a groove, and ground myself into a mould, and clipped and pared and pinched myself all round – very ineffectually as I fear – to fit myself for this thing.' But she had lived 'free as air': 'You are what you have made yourself, and I have always rejoiced that you are as you are, fresh, untrammelled, without many prejudices which afflict other ladies, and free from bonds by which they are cramped and confined.' Though he had occasionally grumbled, he had been proud of her disdain for 'the swaddling bandages of court life'.[21] In short, Palliser had more respect for his wife's individuality than she herself did.

Though he never turned into the romantic hero for whom Lady Glencora yearned, and she never ceased to find him slightly ridiculous. She came to think that it was best that she had been 'kept in order, and made to run in a groove' and that she did almost love her husband.[22] Nevertheless, he went through life with a painful awareness of her unsatisfied dream, yet without resentment. And he could manage to do both because he felt obliged, and was able, to see things as they are and to be content with imperfection.

But if Palliser displays remarkable steadiness in his relations with his wife, in other matters, he radically changed his convictions and conduct. He not only first wronged and then apologised to Mrs Finn: 'I did you a wrong, and therefore write to ask your pardon.'[23] By the end of his life, he had deliberately abandoned some of his strongest beliefs. Can a man alter so much and yet preserve his integrity? The answer appears in the story of the duke's battle with his children.

The duke believed that a nobleman was no freer to marry than a king. His own marriage had been faultlessly correct and he expected his children to marry in the same fashion. Otherwise 'all restraint would be lost and there would be an end to those rules as to birth and position by which he thought his world was kept straight'.[24] But in another part of his thought, the duke had sealed off a different set of convictions. As a Liberal, he believed that if a man could 'raise himself by his own intellect to become Prime Minister,' no gentleman would think of his father or grandfather. The peerage had been, and should be, continually refreshed from 'the ranks of the people'. In keeping with his beliefs, the duke was as content to work with Mr Monk, 'whose father had risen from a mechanic to be a merchant, as with any nobleman who could count ancestors against himself,' and the peer he sat next to in the House of Lords, 'whose grandmother had been a washerwoman and whose father an innkeeper, was to him every with as good a peer as himself. He also took pains to teach his children that not birth but character determined the quality of a man. How much rank or money a man possessed might make his life more or less easy, he told his son, but what mattered was whether he had learned 'those lessons without which no man can live as a gentleman'.[25]

The duke held both these views without noticing the inconsistency until his daughter proposed to marry a gentleman with no rank or wealth. As Frank Tregear was clearly an ambitious man, it seemed plausible that he was an adventurer impudent enough to select his victim from the highest family of all. His great physical beauty made his resemblance to the man whom his wife had loved, complete in the duke's mind – Burgo had been poor and irresponsible and anxious to get lady Glencora's money, and Tregear was, the duke told himself, the same story again. His wife's history made it clear that young people should not be given what they wanted just 'because they have declared themselves to be in love'.[26]

But even at the outset of the troubles, the duke suffered from uncomfortable doubts. For something more was involved in his antipathy to letting Lady Mary accept Tregear. To admit now that inclination need not be sacrificed to propriety would imply that his own marriage had been a mistake. At first, he did not let himself see how the unhappiness in his own life had influenced his judgement. But before long, he began to consider whether after all things might not have been better if his duchess had been allowed to have her way – 'might she not have been alive now, and perhaps happier than she had ever been with him?' He had after all been no more than a 'respectable husband'. As he reviewed the manner in which his own marriage was arranged, he found that 'the idea when picked to pieces is not a nice idea'. He ordered that his daughter should be exposed to eligible young men in the conventional manner, but the procedure was repulsive to him.[27]

When Tregear addressed to him all those sentiments about the equality of gentlemen and the irrelevance of rank and money that he himself had often professed, the duke was outraged, though he acknowledged 'that he had to deal with a man'. When his daughter declared that Tregear was a gentleman, the duke replied that every clerk in all public offices considered himself a gentleman. But all the time he kept asking himself whether he was being cruel and dishonest, until he discovered that the resemblance to Lady Glencora's situation was superficial. Lady Glencora had been flighty and weak and Burgo had been unreliable and greedy, but Lady Mary knew what she was about and Tregear, though poor, had a strong and good character. This was not a case of a princess and an adventurer but of true love. And so the duke came to acknowledge his mistake – 'now I will accept as courage what I before regarded as arrogance'.[28]

His son's proposal to marry an American, the grand-daughter of a poor dockworker, instead of the daughter of Lord Grex, was even more trying since the blood of all the future Dukes of Omnium would flow from that marriage. Yet the duke came to admit that an aristocracy, consisting of peers like Lord Grex, not only would 'go to the wall'[29] but had better do so, whereas Isabel Boncassen, descended though she was from an American labourer, had all the necessary qualities. With his usual candour the duke said so, though he made no pretence of having always liked the marriage, or thinking that Silverbridge might not have found a suitable bridge in more orthodox fashion.

Close as he came to obsession in his obstinacy as a father, Palliser's integrity is especially impressive in that context. Whereas Madame Goesler had to make her way against the prejudices of others, he had late in life to make his way against his own prejudices. He had to question what he had never before doubted. But it was only a more marked version of how he behaved generally, even as a politician. At the lowest moment in his career, when he was clinging to power and trying to bring himself to give it up, he told Phineas Finn that a man should not go into politics as he had, as a 'ready-made' Liberal, who discovered only near the end what his Liberalism had meant and why he had held to it.[30]

His ability to change is an essential ingredient of the duke's remarkable integrity. Though his obstinacy is a serious flaw, there is a connexion between the two qualities. His obstinacy was an exaggeration of his care not to take up a stand thoughtlessly and his courage to endure opposition. And that same care and courage appear in his determination to open questions that he had considered closed and to acknowledge unpleasant truths. It is important that he did not lurch from one whim to another or grab frenetically at new ideas or rewrite the past, but changed to correct what he came to see as an incoherence in his thought. His perfection consists in his conscientiousness and persistence in asking himself hard, searching questions and in scrutinizing the answers that he gave to himself. However certain his tone of voice, he was never free of doubt. But though he doubted he did not flinch from being firm. And when he made his most radical changes, he was being most careful to see himself as a coherent whole.

Palliser's history makes it plain that being a perfect gentleman has nothing to do with perfection, changelessness, conforming to a certain pattern, doing this or that. The excellence of a gentleman depends on the 'manner' in which he conducts himself. And his 'manner' consists in the kinds of considerations that he takes into account when deliberating and how he connects what he thinks and does here and now with what he has thought and done in the past. Just as a ballet dancer may perform a great many different movements in different moods and roles and still be recognized as a ballet dancer because of the manner in which she moves, so may there be great diversity in how gentleman behave and live. Of course shallow, unimaginative people may identify being a gentleman with always being pleasant to one's guests, just as the vulgar may expect a ballet dancer always to wear white net and pirouette on her toes. But those who know better will not be astonished even by rudeness in a gentleman.

Because the quality of a gentleman is compatible with great diversity in concrete behaviour, gentlemen can disagree and yet live together in harmony. And this is illustrated in another aspect of the duke's relationship with his children. The battle over the marriages was not the first time that the duke had differed with his children. How unlike the sons were from their father is made plain in Trollope's account of a 'family breakfast'. Whereas the duke considered it wicked to have more than toasted bacon before lunch his sons liked an elaborate feast. When the salmon and kidneys, that they had ordered, were brought in, the duke commented on the change in the breakfast arrangements and the sons explained sheepishly that they were 'awfully hungry of a morning'. That provoked the duke into a little sermon to the effect that 'eating is an occupation from which . . . a man takes the more pleasure the less he considers it' and that 'a rural labourer who sits on the ditch-side with his bread and cheese and an onion has more enjoyment out of it than any Lucullus', which culminated in an ardent speech about the kind of happiness brought by the 'grind' of parliamentary life. Lord Gerald tried to break the flow with a mention of 'books', while stuffing himself with kidneys; Silverbridge defended the comfort of having 'a second horse out hunting'; and after they finished eating they quickly retired to some distant part of the house where they could smoke without being noticed by the duke.[31]

The differences between the duke and Silverbridge went beyond the breakfast table. Not only had Silverbridge been sent down from Oxford. He spent many hours at the disreputable

Beargarden Club; worse still, he devoted himself to racing of which the duke strongly disapproved; when finally he did enter politics, he stood as a Conservative rather than as a Liberal, which the duke considered to be the natural party of his family. The duke made his dissent on all these subjects perfectly clear; Silverbridge disliked causing him pain, but was also determined to go his own way; and the duke, though he disapproved, did not try to prevent him.

Despite these differences, no one who understood the duke and his family had any doubt about their regard for one another. When the younger son broke the rules of his college in Oxford to attend a race with Silverbridge, and was sent down, the elder brother went to plead for him with the Master of the college. What concerned Silverbridge was the pain that the affair would cause their father: 'If you knew how this would, – would, – would break his heart,' he said, and the tears in his eyes brought tears to the Master too – 'That a young man should pray for himself would be nothing to him ... A father asking for his son might be resisted. But the brother asking pardon for the brother on behalf of the father was almost irresistible.' Only a vulgar scoundrel like Major Tifto supposed that because the duke differed with his son, they must be on bad terms. When the conflict over the marraiges was at its height, and Major Tifto announced that 'There have been no end of quarrels', Tregear answered firmly: 'there has been no quarrel at all ... nothing on earth would make Silverbridge quarrel with his father, and I think it would break the Duke's heart to quarrel with his son'.[32]

Father and son are not two opposed forces fated to collide because each is a choir of many voices, comprehending a multitude of hopes, dreams, fears, disappointments, loves, convictions, prejudices, information, habits, inclinations and judgements, which keep shifting and have no fixed anchor. It is not the case that the old hold fast while the young try to break away and move forward along the road that lies ahead. There is no one road and no given goal – only a multitude of paths, some already well-worn, others yet to be made. Therefore when a difference arises, it is not a simple clash. A variety of ideas and sentiments enters into the stand taken by each, and the adjustment can come about in any number of ways and take many different forms.

What remains constant is the manner in which gentlemen conduct themselves – their agreement that what matters most is maintaining integrity. And this agreement is expressed in a readiness to observe certain formalities in their intercourse with one another. Formalities consist in outward forms of behaviour, whether of speech or of gesture, which are established by convention and by law. A gentleman's respect for formalities has given plausibility to the common misconception of a gentleman as someone who is governed mechanically by 'a code'. But the real reason why a gentleman respects formalities is that it enables him to distinguish between agreeing with others on fundamentals, on a certain manner of conducting oneself, and a substantive agreement on what to do here and now. This distinction makes it possible for gentlemen to live together amicably without committing themselves to approving of all that the others do and think. Gentlemen need not therefore dissimulate when they disagree. They can differ and remain friends without hypocrisy because their concord is not founded on either a real or a feigned uniformity.

Formalities are not, however, sacrosanct. This further complicates the meaning of integrity, and explains why, though some gentlemen may be as correct as Plantagenet Palliser, others may be eccentric.

*　　*　　*

The story of Mr Scarborough (*Mr Scarborough's Family*) shows how a gentleman may disregard formalities. Mr Scarborough lied about his marriage not once but repeatedly: he deceived both his sons, as well as his devoted legal adviser; in the eyes of the world he was a reprobate because he lived with his wife 'on and off, as people say'; he devoted himself to 'arranging tricks for the defeat' of the law that put him beyond its reach, and when reproached for doing so, declared that 'he did not care a straw what the world says'. Nevertheless the impeccably correct lawyer, Grey, insisted that Scarborough was not a rascal and confessed that, though he could not account for it, he felt for Scarborough 'a spark of love', and would not have been outraged by Scarborough's saying, 'I doubt whether Grey is so absolutely honest as I am.'[33]

The clue to the reasons for Grey's tolerance of Scarborough appears in the contrast between Mr Scarborough's two sons and his attitude towards them. By conventional standards, Augustus was virtuous, and Mountjoy was a rascal. Whereas Augustus never told a lie or broke a rule that gentlemen are expected to observe, Mountjoy gambled away his fortune and was barred from all the clubs for being unable to pay his debts. Every conscientious mother regarded Augustus as the perfect husband for her frail daughter, and treated Mountjoy as a sure disaster. Those were the appearances.

The reality is suggested by the meeting between Mountjoy and Captain Vignolles. Though the captain had never cheated or failed to pay his debts, he had something else which 'stood him well in lieu of cheating'. When his opponent was drunk, he took care to remain sober; when others became impetuous, he remained cool; and he regularly sought out people whom he could rely on to become drunk and impetuous and to be anyway much inferior in skill. He lured Mountjoy into playing with him when he knew that Mountjoy had regularly lost to him and had good reason not to play, and of course the captain won. Though he had never slipped a card Trollope says, the captain in effect sat with his fingers in his neighbour's pocket and his eye on his purse, knowing that his studied calculations would get the best of his victim. The moral of the story is that 'there is much that is in truth dishonest even in honest play'.[34] While by conventional standards, Captain Vignolles remained respectable and Mountjoy did not, Mountjoy had none of the captain's dishonesty.

Mr Scarborough accepted the opinion of 'the world' insofar as he recognized that there was a great deal to be altered in Mountjoy before he could go to heaven. That he had gambled when he could not pay, promised to pay when he had no money, and was indifferent to whether his breeches belonged to him or to his tailor was 'bad'. Mountjoy had been 'very bad', Scarborough thought, in thinking himself to be a fine fellow just because he had dined with lords and dukes, and he was 'very bad', too, for having been so 'passionately fond of women'. But not only had his sins brought trouble upon himself rather than on others. He possessed a great redeeming quality – a capacity for loving others. He was genuinely devoted to his mother, his father, and the girl whom he wished to marry. What worried him most, when his father declared him a bastard was the insult to his mother. Nor did he turn against his father. Disinherited and disgraced as he believed himself to have been, Mountjoy genuinely mourned for Mr Scarborough.

Augustus cared for no one. He did not even hate the brother whom he tried to destroy. About his mother, he took it for granted, as he did about everyone else, that the worst was probably true. About his father, he felt only that he had violated the canons of respectability and was therefore an inconvenience that he wanted to kick away, like a stone that sat in his path. He had no friends and wanted none, desiring only 'someone who would do his bidding as though he were such a friend ... who would listen to his words, and act as though they were the truth'. And like everything else that Augustus did, his telling of the truth was merely an instrument for getting what he wanted. He used the truth to destroy the reputation of a man whom he pretended to befriend and knew to be blameless. He welcomed the truth when it gave him an estate, without giving a thought to its effect on his mother's reputation or his brother's fate. And because he always behaved correctly and was devoid of right motives, he was 'odious all around'.[35]

That Augustus, who never lied or broke a promise and yet ruthlessly exploited everyone and loved no one, was considered superior to Mountjoy, who though he misbehaved was capable of real love and never took advantage of anyone, moved Scarborough to redress the balance. What Scarborough admired was the kind of honesty that made a man incapable of 'mean or dirty conduct', by which Scarborough meant using others. The law was 'mean and dirty' because it allowed a man to exploit others and pass for honest. By making it appear that honesty consists in observing formalities, the law promoted dishonesty. What Scarborough found dishonest, he hated and, as he could hate 'to distraction' and with 'a terrible persistency', he was unrelenting in his hostility to the law.[36] That the law should bestow his estate on the son born earliest regardless of his character was just the sort of iniquity that outraged Scarborough. And so he tried to arrange his affairs in a way that would allow him to outwit the law.

Here as elsewhere, what matters for how moral quality is judged is the motive, and the deepest motive of Scarborough's campaign against the law was love. Indeed 'in every phase of his life'. Trollope tells us, 'he had been actuated by love'. He had never served himself at anyone else's expense and had steadily thought of what was due to others. He had all his life been a generous man. To his tenants, he had given liberal allowances and offered to keep a school, though, characteristically, his insistence that dissenters should be allowed to attend established him, in the eyes of the respectable, as an unregenerate atheist and a menace to social order. He had given his sons the best education. Though he had his own ideas about marriage 'and that kind of thing', he had esteemed his wife, declared her to have been the best wife in the world and, we are allowed to think, had made her reasonably happy. In all other respects, his tastes were, as he said, 'simple and not especially vicious'. It is important, too, that in trying to arrange his affairs so as to reward the worthier son, even though he had long disliked Augustus, he did not reach his conclusions hastily but carefully gave both sons an opportunity to display their true character. In the end, we were persuaded that Mr Scarborough was right when he said, 'Most men have got some little pet tyranny in their hearts. I had none.'[37]

Though his various ploys distressed Mr Grey, Scarborough never imposed anything worse than inconvenience on others. Even if he believed that Augustus had behaved 'damnably', was determined to punish him and greatly enjoyed his success in doing so, still he saw to it that Augustus was provided for and not deprived of anything that he had a right to expect. All this establishes that Scarborough was not haphazardly indulging whims but had arrived at a genuinely impersonal notion of justice, however unconventional. That was why Grey, though a lawyer who revered the law, could love and praise Scarborough and why, when the three persons who had known him intimately, assembled at his deathbed, they 'did respect him, and had been made to love him by what he had done'.

The conventional misunderstanding of Scarborough is summed up by the doctor's remark to Mountjoy. His father had 'a capacity for love, and an unselfishness,' the doctor said, which 'almost atones for his dishonesty. And there is about him a strange dislike to conventionality and to law which is so interesting as to make up the balance. I have always regarded your father as a most excellent man; but thoroughly dishonest. He would rob anyone, – but always to eke out his own gifts to other people. He has therefore to my eyes been most romantic.'[38] But Mr Scarborough was not, as the doctor implies, a kind of Robin Hood, setting up his own ideas of justice against the established ones. He was not robbing the rich to give to the poor. He was out to preserve the distinction between a merely conventional honesty, which consists in observing established rules, and a more profound honesty, which scrupulously rejects undetectable injustices that do not violate the rules of law and convention.

The story of Scarborough's antics establishes that a gentleman at his best can see beyond conventional good behaviour to judge correctly the moral quality of those with whom he has to deal and, if necessary, defy conventional opinion. But the qualities required for being eccentric without falling into wilfulness are fairly rare.

One of these qualities is indicated in the counterpoint to the shifting fates of Scarborough's sons, the story of Mr Prosper's attempt to disinherit his nephew. He disowned Harry Annesley suddenly upon hearing that he had beaten up a man in London. The report was untrue and, in any case, implausible because Annesley had never been known to misbehave in such a fashion. But Mr Prosper did not stop to enquire before disinheriting the nephew whom he had invited to depend upon being his heir.

The real reason for Mr Prosper's readiness to believe the worst was his annoyance with Annesley for his persistent refusal to hear his uncle reading sermons. But Mr Prosper had no idea that his indignation over the sermons had anything to do with his outrage over Harry's escapade in London. Mr Prosper meant well and he generally conducted himself well. But unfortunately he was 'a fool', and unable to stray from the well trodden ways without getting lost. He had not the wit required to follow an eccentric course sure-footedly.

The other quality essential to keep an eccentric from going wrong is revealed in the story of the stonemason, Sir Roger Scatcherd, (*Doctor Thorne*). He appears to be similar to Mr Scarborough insofar as he was also bent on defying the world, and was perhaps even more independent, having raised himself from a simple workingman into a titled man of enormous wealth, through extraordinary stamina and a remarkable power for succeeding in jobs where others failed. In addition, Scatcherd took the law into his own hands more definitively than Scarborough ever did. When his sister was wronged, Scatcherd beat up the culprit and though he may have caused the man's death, even the victim's devoted brother, Dr Thorne, thought that the attack was justified. When he was sent to gaol, Scatcherd bore his punishment as stalwartly as he did everything else. Just as thoroughly as Scarborough ignored the niceties of law, Scatcherd managed to ignore the ordinary requirements of physical health and made fools of his doctors even on his deathbed. Nevertheless Dr Thorne found Sir Roger Scatcherd unfit to meet his bastard niece, Mary Thorne.

What disqualifies Scatcherd from being a gentleman is not the roughness of a stone mason but his lack of self-sufficiency. That he named his son, Louis Philippe, reflected the ruling idea in Scatcherd's life – his ambition to rub shoulders with the great. Everything that he did was designed to bridge the distance that he believed to exist between himself and those whose good opinion he yearned to have. Having made his money and got his title, he bent all his efforts on getting a seat in parliament because it seemed to him that his life would be made worthwhile once he had 'the power of walking into that august chamber, and sitting shoulder to shoulder in legislative equality with the sons of dukes and the curled darlings of the nation'.[39] When he failed to get that seat, his life was over.

Success made Scatcherd too grand to be accepted by working-men but did not qualify him to live with gentlemen. As he had no resources within himself, he felt that he could not do or be anything that he wanted and took to drink. 'Such a life as mine makes a man a fool,' he said to Dr Thorne. 'When a man has made three hundred thousand pounds, there's nothing left for him but to die. It's all he's good for then.' Scatcherd needed 'to be kept in a groove'.[40] Once his ambition was satisfied and he left the groove into which he had been born, he had no idea of how to live. His eccentricity was merely the defiance of a weak man, who lacked the self-sufficiency to find his own way.

What distinguishes Mr Scarborough from both Mr Prosper and Sir Roger Scatcherd is that his eccentricity was inspired by a superabundance of the qualities that they lacked. But there is a danger attached to such superiority. No one knew better than Trollope how easily eccentricity slides into obsession, and else-where, as we shall see, he explored the fine gradations of such a descent. His account of what Scarborough's solicitor had to endure suggests also how unbearable life might be if there were many eccentrics like Mr Scarborough. Nevertheless a Scar-borough is a valuable reminder of what lies beind a gentleman's respect for the formalities established by convention and law.

*   *   *

That a gentleman's honesty is one with his individuality is the moral of the story about a liar, Lizzie Eustace (*The Eustace Diamonds*). Though she has been likened to Thackeray's Becky Sharp, Lady Eustace lacks the essential qualifications for an adventuress because 'as an independent young woman she was perhaps one of the richest', having inherited from her husband a fortune, a title, and a castle.[41] This has suggested to other readers that Lizzie lied only because she was an innocent lost among nasty people, and they see her as a victim desperately trying to keep her head above water in a world full of disorder and ruthlessness. But this view cannot account for the character of Lizzie's lying.

When the family solicitor, Mr Camperdown, first asked her to restore the diamonds, she had no fixed policy. She remembered well enough that when her husband had handed her the necklace for a special dinner party in London, he had told her that they were 'family jewels' which, he hoped, would one day be worn by their daughter-in-law. But she 'did not exactly see how her own interests would be best served' by granting the lawyer's request.[42] She had the daimonds valued only to learn that she could gain little by selling them; she had a strongbox made, which exposed her to ridicule from her servants and which she never used for storing the diamonds; and she continued to ignore Mr Camperdown's letters.

Within a short time, however, the diamonds acquired a new significance: 'How can a woman give up such a present – from a husband – who is dead? As to the value, I care nothing. But I won't do it.' And her recital always ended fittingly in tears. She was frightened by her aunt's warning that keeping the jewels was tantamount to stealing and would land her in prison. But her fear soon turned into a conviction that as there were 'so many points in her favour', it would be 'a cruelty that any one should grudge her the plunder'.[43] By the time that she retold the story to her companion, she had discovered a new reason for keeping the diamonds – that the family had made her pay for the furniture in her castle and the diamonds would compensate her for the loss. The truth was that she had tried to get the family to pay for furnishing her own country house and had never thought of the diamonds in this connexion. But her right to compensation was bolstered by another reason, a fine, public spirited reason – that the diamonds had been given to her as a present and it was important to protect the right of people to give and keep presents.

When after her engagement to Lord Fawn, he insisted that she return the diamonds, Lizzie looked up into his eyes with a tear in her own and related a moving love story: Sir Florian had put the diamonds into her hands and had said to her, 'There, those are yours to do what you choose with them,' and it was only her dear dead husband's manner of giving them, Lizzie assured his would-be successor, that made them so valuable to her. In fact, her husband had come to hate her before he died and her marriage to him had been founded on the fact that he was titled, rich, offered an excellent settlement, and showed every promise of dying soon after the marriage, which he duly did. At other times, Lizzie explained that Lord Fawn's objection was inspired by jealousy of her dead love and that only her dislike of such male tyranny kept her from yielding. Though Lizzie made it clear to everyone that she would not dream of wearing the diamonds, at the height of the scandal she appeared at Lady Glencora's party in the full blaze of diamonds around her neck. By the time that she left London for her castle in Scotland, she could not decide whether to leave or take the diamonds, and wished that 'she had never seen' them – but not altogether: 'She hated the box, and yet she must cling to it now. She was thoroughly ashamed of the box, and yet she must seem to take a pride in it. She was horribly afraid of the box, and yet she must keep it in her own very bedroom.'[44]

When the iron box was stolen, Lizzie neglected to mention that she had kept the diamonds elsewhere and still had them. Once it became known that the box had been empty and the police were searching everywhere, she did not dare to reveal the truth. The idea of holding the key to a mystery which the whole world was trying to solve gave her much pleasure, but she could not decide where to put the diamonds. Flinging them into the sea from her castle seemed appropriate but, as she was on the way back to London, was hardly possible. A hole in the ground would do the job, Lizzie thought, but where to find the ground or opportunity to dig was far from obvious. She considered whether a jeweller could be persuaded to buy them from her if she accepted a low enough price, fell asleep clutching the diamonds in her hand, and when she awoke, could think of nothing better than to lock them in her desk drawer. When her cousin, Frank Greystock, who was acting as her legal adviser, asked her about the theft, she told him how the loss had broken her heart, even though she 'felt that her heart was bursting rather than being broken, because the ten thousand pounds' worth of diamonds was not really lost'.[45] Only her fear of being seen, she kept telling herself, prevented her from throwing away the necklace; yet she kept running to her desk drawer to see if the diamonds were still safe and, when the police came to search the house, she refused to let them and fainted away.

Nevertheless, once the diamonds were truly stolen, Lizzie quickly forgot about them and worried only about being exposed and punished. As long as the police were unable to find the thieves, she congratulated herself on being at last free of the great burden. But when compelled to tell the 'story in all its nakedness' before her old enemy, Mr Camperdown, Lizzie managed it beautifully: 'I did not know what I was doing,' she told the lawyer: 'You had been persecuting me ever since Sir Florian's death, about the diamonds, and I didn't know what I was to do. They were my own, and I thought I was not obliged to tell everybody where I kept them. There are things which nobody tells . . . When Sir Walter Scott was asked whether he wrote the novels, he didn't tell.' Everyone in the courtroom was on her side – 'Poor, ignorant, ill-used young creature; and then so lovely!' And her brother-in-law, John Eustace said: 'She is a very great woman, a very great woman: and, if the sex could have its rights, would make an excellent lawyer.'[45]

The oddity of Lizzie's lying is summed up by Lord George's remark: 'It has been uncommonly clever, but I don't see the use of it.'[47] Great though the battle was, at no time did Lizzie stop to think of what she hoped to gain; one lie led to another, without plan or purpose, and each only added to Lizzie's difficulties. All this might suggest that she fell into an unfortunate predicament out of carelessness and lacked the wit to disentangle herself. Against it, however, there is not only Trollope's repeated emphasis on how very clever Lady Eustace was, but also the fact that the diamonds were not the only subject about which Lizzie lied.

With her lovers, she was just as indifferent to truth. She became engaged to Lord Fawn while waiting for a proposal from Frank Greystock. But her engagement did not stop her from playing many touching love scenes with Frank. She told him that he was as a brother to her, and fell into his arms – in a way that allowed her to rise with marvellous rapidity when they were interrupted. She took Frank around the grounds of her castle, sprang lightly among rocks which she otherwise shunned – exclaiming on how often she came there alone. She assured Frank repeatedly

that she would never give up her betrothal to Lord Fawn, but also
declared that she could not bear the sight of Lord Fawn and had
no intention of marrying him. She told Frank that his betrothed,
Lucy Morris, was 'a hypocrite', trying to trick him into a marriage
that would ruin him, confessed that she herself was pining away
for love of him, and when Frank tried to comfort her, she pro-
tested tragically: 'I cannot stand picking my words when the
whole world is going round with me, and my very brain is on fire
. . . You know my secret, and I care not who else knows it.'[48]

In between these scenes with Frank, there were others, played
in a different style, with Lord Fawn. When he suggested that
perhaps she would not mind ending their engagement because
she had received attentions from others, she was outraged:
'Attentions; – what attentions? . . . If you mean, sir, . . . to throw
it in my face now, that I have, – have in any way rendered myself
unworthy of the position of your wife because people have been
civil and kind to me in my sorrow, you are a greater dastard than
I took you to be.' And it was done so effectively that Lord Fawn
'quailed before her'.[49] At the same time, Lizzie wooed the 'pinch-
beck lord', Lord George de Carruthers, confessed to him her
perjuries, and begged him to protect her against the cruel world.
But that did not keep her from letting others know, and encouraging even the police to think, that she suspected Lord
George of having arranged the burglary of her diamonds.

Yet Lizzie did not know which, if any, of these men, she wanted
to marry. When she dreamt of risking all with a brave corsair,
who would be heartless and make her deliriously unhappy by his
reckless adventures and abuse of her, Lord George was her ideal.
At other times, she revelled in the glory of being an impeccably
respectable wife of a peer of the realm and minister of the government, so grand that everyone bowed to her as she rode past in her
grand coach. With her cousin, Frank, she used 'every wile she
knew, straining every nerve to be victorious, encountering any
and all dangers' to make him yield, but 'she had no definite aim
before her'. She neither wanted to break her engagement with
Lord Fawn nor to make her cousin her lover – 'in the ordinary
sense of love', and she had reason to know that he would have
given her all the help that she wanted without any tender
passages, indeed more usefully, if she had told him the truth. In
her greatest love scenes. Trollope says, 'she herself did not know
what she would be at'.[50] To her lovers, as about her diamonds,

Lizzie lied for no obvious reason and succeeded only in hurting herself. Instead of becoming the wife of a peer, she was reduced to marrying a squint-eyed, foreign preacher who was a murderer as well as fortune-hunter.

As Lizzie's lies were so pointless, should she perhaps be regarded as an unworldly poetic creature, lost in a beautiful world of her imagination? It might be argued that only a prig could fail to be grateful for the amusement that she provided by creating a world more interesting than the real one, as Lady Glencora suggests when she says: 'I call that woman a perfect God-send. What should we have done without her?'[51]

How poetic Lizzie's imagination was, Trollope lets us see in his account of her delight in reading Shelley's 'Queen Mab', while looking out upon 'her dear wide ocean with its glittering smile'. The morning after arriving at her castle, she went off immediately after breakfast, with Shelley in her pocket, to her beloved rocks by the sea. But in fact, she settled herself about fifty feet above the shore, which even at its worst had hardly any rocks. After half a minute on her 'rocky' perch, Lizzie found the sun too hot and retired to the shade of the summer-house in her garden. For it was, of course, impossible to read 'her darling "Queen Mab"' in the 'coarse, inappropriate, every-day surroundings of a drawing-room'.[52]

Though she had often talked about how deeply the poem affected her, she had not actually read it before. Now that she did, the lines, 'Sudden arose Ianthe's soul; it stood all-beautiful in naked purity' made a great impression upon her: 'The name of Ianthe suited her exactly. And the antithesis conveyed to her mind by naked purity struck her strongly.' When she got to 'Instinct with inexpressible beauty and grace/ Each stain of earthliness/ Had passed away, it reassumed/ Its native dignity and stood,/ Immortal amid ruin,' she was not quite sure 'which was instinct with beauty – the stain or the soul', but she felt that it was all terribly true and precisely how she felt and it suggested to her a happy time when she would be free of the trouble of the diamonds and of bills for the stables. Then the idea of the ruin and the stains pleased her almost as much as the idea of immortality and purity and led her to reflect on higher things: 'As immortality must come, and as stains were instinct with grace, why be afraid of ruin? But then if people go wrong – at least women – they are not asked out anywhere!'[53]

Having learned 'a bit to quote', she stopped there. She had not yet discovered, Trollope says, that it was wiser, if one memorized only one passage in a poem, to pick one closer to the end because 'the world is so cruelly observant nowadays' that no one will 'give you credit for a page beyond that from which your passage comes.' What she lacked in understanding she made up for by studying her gestures and modulating her voice with such care that she knew that she could 'be effective'. When she described how long and lovingly she had studied the poem, 'she actually did not know that she was lying'. Nor did she remember how she had been troubled by the sun when, later that day, she told her companion: 'Ah, I love the full warmth of the real summer. With me it always seems that the sun is needed to bring to true ripeness the fruit of the heart.' But she made good use of her morning's work. The line, 'It stands all beautiful in naked purity', proved to be suitable for describing Sir Florian's soul. But in recalling the glories of their love, Lizzie improved on Shelley: 'I see him now,' she said and quoted the lines that reminded her of her beloved husband's soul: 'It reassumed its native dignity, and stood Primeval amid ruin.' She did not mean to deny immortality to poor Sir Florian. It was just that 'primeval' seemed such a 'very poetical word'.[53]

In his detailed account of how Lizzie read poetry, Trollope spells out the quality that distinguished all her thinking – the lack of any steady connexions. Her consciousness came close to being merely a bundle of random thoughts and feelings. An immediate discomfort provoked her to say whatever seemed useful for relieving it, but with no thought for what she had said yesterday. She was never surprised by the consequences because she had no expectations. Her emotions never lasted. She was easily frightened, but as easily comforted. When thwarted, she could become angry and 'snap and snarl', but she was incapable of 'a sincere, true, burning wrath'.[55] Because her ideas succeeded one another rapidly, she was 'clever' and could always grasp the immediate problem and produce a new stratagem. But a coherent understanding was beyond her.

Lizzie's only steady idea was that of winning a battle. The one time that we see Lizzie being natural is in a hunt because that allowed her to engage in a genuine contest – once the run was on, she was wholeheartedly engaged in what she was doing. But away from the hunting field on a good day, real battles were sadly wanting. Her possession of a title and fortune eliminated the obvious sort of battle. And as she was incapable of following a complicated train of thought, she was unable to invent elaborate plots in the fashion of Becky Sharp. The only way in which Lizzie could be sure of having a battle worthy of her wit and courage was by trying 'to make things seem to be other than they were'. What made life interesting to Lizzie was lying 'readily and cleverly, recklessly and yet successfully'. She found delight in whatever was 'not compatible with humdrum truth'. Mr Emilius's love-making pleased her just because she knew that there was not a word of truth in his speeches. That gave him 'a dash of poetry'.[56]

Saying that she had been living entirely on the grapes out of her hot-house or that Shelley was her only solace gave her pleasure just because there was not a grape in sight on her estate and she had never read a line of Shelley. That her companion, Miss Macnulty, had an unshakeable sense for the difference between truth and falsehood and knew the sordid truth about her married life, challenged Lizzie to try to persuade Miss Macnulty that the marriage had been idyllic. In lying to Mr Camperdown, Lord Fawn, or Frank Greystock, she saw herself as engaged in a battle. It was not the battle seen by ordinary eyes, for property, a husband or a lover, but a much grander and simpler battle – to get them to believe what was not true.

In order to 'make things seem to be other than they were', Lizzie was always looking for an audience to confuse and a stage on which to perform. She thrived on the fuss about the diamonds and all the subterfuges that it provoked because it offered such scope for acting. It gave her an opportunity not just to deceive the world about the diamonds but to persuade everyone that she was to be pitied, that 'no woman had ever been so knocked about in her affections' or endured so many hardships – 'left an early widow, persecuted by her husband's family, twice robbed, spied upon by her own servants, unappreciated by the world at large, ill-used by three lovers, victimized by her selected friend ... driven out of society because she had lost her diamonds ...'. Of course, having to appear before the lawyers and in court inspired her greatest performances. When the affair of the diamonds was over, she found a new challenge in trying to teach the world that none of it had happened or meant what it had seemed to mean – 'she was not going to give up the battle, even now ...'.[57] And just in case the world yielded too easily, she acquired in Mr Emilius a husband who showed every promise of providing an adversary worthy of her.

In Lizzie Eustace, Trollope drew the perfect antipode of a gentleman – someone who is almost wholly devoid of integrity. Whatever she did was a performance which lasted only as long as there was an audience to see it. When she took pains to let a carefully curled lock hang down carelessly, it was not her artfulness that constituted the deception. Madame Goesler's appearance was also the product of great art. But whereas Madame Goesler's art was a natural expression of what she was, whatever Lizzie did was bound to be an affectation because she had no coherent self to express. It is the absence of selfhood, rather than her deviations from truth, that makes Lizzie 'a bundle of deceit'.

She was held together by the force of her will to survive and to give one more performance. The only intractable, objective reality which she recognized was money. Much as she admired Mr Emilius's talent for lying, she took care not to let him get hold of her fortune; she haggled over pennies and watched her expenditures. And because she clung to the reality of money, she remained sane and safe.

But apart from money, there was nothing in the world that she hesitated to manipulate. Other people were merely material for her changing fancies. They were what a teddy bear is to a child – something to be endowed with whatever imaginary life the owner finds amusing at the moment, which becomes more valuable the more it loses its shape because it has less to fix attention upon itself. Its charm lies in its shapelessness, in its offering so little resistance to its possessor, in its being just something that he can do things with. Some people may like being treated as a teddy bear but there is no greater disrespect to a human personality. Lizzie is inhuman in the strict sense of having no conception of human personality.

Her lies as such do not explain why Trollope described Lizzie as dangerous as well as bad, but what the lying indicated about her – that she was an unbound will. Whereas Mr Scarborough lied to make others aware of the reality which they had mistaken, Lizzie lied to destroy any sense of reality. She did so in a relatively harmless fashion by remembering events that never happened, and in a more lethal fashion by telling Lucy Morris that her lover had deserted her. But the worst of it is that there was no knowing what she might do. She herself could not know because there were no limits to her imagination. That was why Lord George, though he was unscrupulous, wanted her fortune, and admired her beauty, decided against marrying Lizzie: 'he did not dare to share – even his boat with so dangerous a fellow-passenger'.[58]

How differently Lizzie Eustace can be judged provides a telling summary of the contrast between the morality of a gentleman and that of the self-divided man. According to the latter, the fact that Lizzie is wholly indifferent to truth and consistency and that her life consists of gratuitous acts makes her a model of individuality. To a gentleman, her inability to respect any limits or order makes her as nearly devoid of individuality as any sane person can be, and as tiresome as she is dangerous.

6 Manners

If what distinguishes a gentleman is an inner moral quality, it would seem that the outward appearance and deportment of a man, his voice, carriage, or dress, can have no bearing on whether he is a gentleman. Is it not wrong then to say that manners make a gentleman?

Like so many others who have written about gentleman, Trollope might seem to be in two minds about the answer. On the one hand, he takes great pains to tell us how people look and speak and seems to connect it with their characters. The fact that Isabel Boncassen, despite being an American descended from a dock labourer, speaks without the nasal twang often found in American voices is part of the evidence for her being a lady fit to be the mother of dukes. And it is just as evident that Louis Scatcherd, baronet though he was educated at Eton and Cambridge, is not a gentleman from the fact that his voice 'had a Yankee twang, being a cross between that of an American trader and an English groom'.[1] We are told that the wives and daughters of gentlemen are careful to 'invest themselves' with a 'brightness of apparel' that gives them that 'sheen of high-bred womanly bearing'.[2] And anyone with eyes to see, Trollope makes it plain, would not mistake that unrelenting warrior, Mrs Proudie, in full battle dress, for a discreet, compliant, modest lady: 'She was gorgeous in a dark brown silk dress of awful stiffness and terrible dimensions; and on her shoulders she wore a short cloak of velvet and fur, very handsome withal, but so swelling in its proportions on all sides as necessarily to create more of dismay than of admiration in the mind of any ordinary man. And her bonnet was a monstrous helmet with the beaver up, displaying the awful face of the warrior, always ready for combat, and careless to guard itself from attack. The large contorted bows which she bore were as a grisly crest upon her casque, beautiful, doubtless, but majestic and fear-compelling. In her hand she carried her armour all complete, a prayer-book, a bible, and a book of hymns.'[3] Other kinds of detail in the appearance of Mr Samuel Prong make it obvious that though he was devout, sincere, hard-working, he was not a gentleman: 'there was about his lips an assumption of character and dignity which his countenance and body generally failed to maintain; and there was something in the carriage of his head and in the occasional projection of his chin, which was intended to add to his dignity, but which did, I think, only make the failure more palpable'.[4]

But, on the other hand, Trollope seems to deny that outward polish is essential to the gentleman. He compared Lord Chesterfield unfavourably with Cicero, pointing out that whereas Chesterfield warned his son against laughing, Cicero disdained to concern himself with such matters, and told his son just to walk 'simple and upright'. 'I feel sure', Trollope says, 'that Cicero would laugh and was heard to laugh; and yet he was always true to the manners of a gentleman.'[5] Certainly many of the ladies and gentlemen whom Trollope especially commends would fail Chesterfield's tests. The fastidious lord could hardly have approved of Miss Dunstable who was endowed by nature with red cheeks, a large mouth, big white teeth, a broad nose and bright small black eyes, and managed to heighten the far from gentle effect with crisp, strong, bright, black ringlets, loud laughter, and blunt remarks. Dr Thorne was no more notable for gentle deportment. He announced that he wished to be paid the inelegant fee of seven and six and felt no embarrassment when he had to 'lug out half a crown from his breeches pocket and give it in change for a ten shilling piece'; he did not in the least mind being seen at the coarse work of 'putting together common powders for rural bowels, or spreading vulgar ointments for agricultural ailments'; and he regularly offended the sensibilities of his neighbours and patients by tart utterances and abrupt actions.[6] Lord Chiltern is worse than Dr Thorne – red, growling, rough, and fierce, he is hardly an adornment for elegant drawing rooms. Yet Trollope never suggests that he is therefore not a gentleman. And when the Rev Josiah Crawley feels that he is unfit for the company of gentleman because he has grown so shabby and rough, he is found to be showing false pride.

How can Trollope be both so indifferent and so attentive to manners? The answer is an entirely coherent, but not at all simple, conception of the relation between manners and morals.

In *The Belton Estate*, in connexion with Clara Amedroz's suitors, Captain Aylmer, MP, and Will Belton, farmer, Trollope explores the relation between inner and outer refinement. Captain Aylmer was everyone's idea of a gentleman. He was a Member of Parliament, wrote a pamphlet every two years, talked about literature and history, read Dante critically in the recess, laced his conversation with poetry, could accommodate to the austerity of his pious aunt and yet be perfectly at home in the salons of London. He was also punctilious about keeping promises – having promised his aunt, on her deathbed, to marry Clara, it was a matter of course with him to do so; he was generous – though he hoped to be his aunt's heir, he advised her to leave something for Clara; and he was sensitive – his proposal to Clara came only after meeting her at his aunt's over some years and having spoken many 'soft words' to her.

Will Belton had none of Aylmer's refinement. He had no interest in literature or politics, indeed looked and lived very much like a ploughboy. His house was barely furnished, he happily dined on beans or on nothing, and had to be told to change for dinner. When Clara's brother committed suicide, Belton unexpectedly became the heir to the Amedroz estate, which meant that upon her father's death, Clara would be left penniless. Yet soon after he became the heir, though he had never before met the Amedroz's, Belton invited himself to visit them and showed no awareness of the awkward circumstances as he went bustling about the place, proposing to rearrange things without making any apologies, all of which convinced Mr Amedroz that he was a heartless man. And Belton's proposal to Clara followed the the same harsh pattern. He asked for her hand within three days after meeting her, and when she refused him, he showed no sign of disappointment, from which Clara concluded that he was not a man likely to be 'deeply sensitive in such matters for any long period'.[7]

But as the story unfolds, Aylmer and Belton exchange characters. Aylmer's gentlemanliness turns out to be the plated kind that comes off with rubbing. The time that he took before coming to the point with Clara was not due to delicacy – he had played with the idea of marrying her but waited to see how his aunt would dispose of her money. The loving words that he had spoken to Clara had been inspired by vanity – it pleased him to lead her to rely on him. In advising his aunt to leave something to Clara, he wished to behave like a man who is generous and trusting, but as to the amount, his counsel had been 'well-balanced'. He willingly fulfilled his promise to his aunt because, as he thought that Clara would be difficult to conquer and that her name counted in the eyes of the world, it would be a mark of success to capture her. But when she foolishly responded with immediate enthusiasm, she lost her value for him, much as 'the fruit that falls easily from the tree, though it is ever the best, is never valued by the gardener',[8] and Captain Aylmer's thoughts began to dwell on the fact that she was penniless and wholly dependent on him. Despite his long acquaintance with Clara, he had no idea of what sort of person she was, nor any interest in finding out. When his mother, who wanted a grander alliance, took to persecuting Clara, the captain did not object. When Lady Aylmer ordered that Clara cease seeing her one friend, Mrs Askerton, because there was gossip about an impropriety in her life, the captain ordered that his mother be obeyed, without thinking about Clara's loneliness or the decency of driving a woman into isolation on the strength of a rumour. When Clara withdrew from the engagement, Aylmer worried only about whether his reputation would be damaged.

Though Captain Aylmer behaved correctly and did not want to hurt others, he was a cad. And it is because he regarded his behaviour as a set of signals to establish a certain identity for himself. The motive for his correctness was a desire to get from others the deference normally granted to a gentleman. When Belton made a scene in the hotel and charged the captain with behaving like a blackguard, Aylmer did not feel disgraced by being accused of unkindness to Clara, but he felt strongly the shame of being seen with a man who did not care whether the servants overheard him.

What is wrong with the captain's understanding of manners is made more obvious in connexion with his mother. When the captain brought Clara to meet her for the first time, Lady Aylmer took care not to be in the hall to receive her because, Trollope explains, 'Lady Aylmer was too accurately acquainted with the weights and measures of society for any such movement as that. Had her son brought Lady Emily to the house as his future bride, Lady Aylmer would probably have been in the hall when the arrival took place; and had Clara possessed ten thousand pounds of her own, she would probably have been met at the drawing room door; but she had neither money nor title .... Lady Aylmer was found stitching at a bit of worsted, as though she had expected no one to come to her. And Belinda Aylmer was stitching also, – by special order of her mother.'⁹ Trollope makes it plain here that, for Lady Aylmer, manners were coins with which to register her power relative to others. The captain was only a more subtle version of his mother. As he found it pleasant to move among gentlemen, he tried to do whatever would make him acceptable. The refinement of his manners and tastes, like his observation of promises, was a performance by an acter who knows that lines he has to speak in order to stay in the show. He is a pure example of someone for whom being a gentleman consists in conforming to a 'code', and he is therefore not a gentleman, but a cad.

An abundance of the moral quality that Aylmer lacked gave Will Belton an appearance of roughness. Because Belton knew instinctively what was more and less important, he was impetuous and disposed to forget that others might misinterpret his behaviour. His sudden visit was inspired by his fear that the Amedroz's affairs were in a bad shape and by his feeling that he had a special responsibility for helping them. As he was not a man who could easily explain what he was doing under such awkward circumstances, he pursued his projects without worrying about what impression he made on the Amedroz's – 'I don't mind a little dislike to begin with.'¹⁰ What did worry him was how to avoid humiliating them by his help. He therefore made his plans for improving their estate as a business arrangement that profited him as well as them so as not make them objects of his charity and he never expressed nor felt a consciousness of being their benefactor.

The same delicacy governed his conduct to Clara. He did not wait before proposing to her because he felt sure at once about his feeling for her. When she refused him, he recognized that he had rushed in as if he were buying a horse and concealed his disappointment, because he was anxious not to impose his difficulties on others and would not allow himself to indulge in self-pity. But if when Clara was in full possession of herself, he had not worried about being impetuous, later when there was a danger of exploiting Clara's gratitude and dependence on him, he took care not to talk of love until he had been given good reason to think that it would be welcome. When he learned that Clara was engaged to marry the captain and saw the danger that she was running because of her poverty and the captain's character, he determined to turn the estate over to her, in spite of the legal difficulties and Clara's refusal to have it. And he showed the same thoughtfulness in connexion with Clara's friend who meant nothing to him. He looked into Mrs Askerton's story only because he wanted to make certain that she would not bring harm to Clara. But he made his enquiries discreetly, and when he discovered that Mrs Askerton's furtiveness was due to a small irregularity in her marriage, Belton dismissed the matter. Here as elsewhere, he distinguished, as the captain did not, between virtue and propriety.

In addition to these positive qualities, Belton had a gentleman's attitude to his deficiencies. He recognized himself to be an ill-educated farmer, who had never read a French novel nor spoken to a duke, but he neither felt ashamed of lacking such accomplishments nor resented Clara's appreciation of them. He knew that he had other virtues and did not belittle them any more than his deficiencies. His feeling about himself was of a piece with his attitude of farming: 'When he threw his seed corn into the earth with all such due appliances of agricultural skill and industry as his captial and experience enabled him to use, he did his part toward the production of next year's crop, and after that he must leave it to a higher Power to give him, or to withhold from him, the reward of his labour.'[11]

Even the apparent abrasiveness of Belton's behaviour turns out to have the quality expected of a gentleman. Of course he could not inspire the tenants with awe as did Mr Amedroz, who sat in the family pew with such dignity that he seemed to be 'one of God's nobler creatures'. But in a different style, Belton had the pleasing and commanding presence of a gentleman – he seemed to add to the pleasure of being alive; his voice spoke of 'cheery days and happy friends, and a general state of things which made life worth having'. Though at first this was not noticed by the Amedroz's or Mrs Askerton, as they learned to read his deportment more accurately, they discovered that for all his lack of refinement, Belton looked 'very much like a gentleman'.[12]

In the contrast between Belton and Aylmer, Trollope makes it clear that the relation between manners and morals is not that of appearance and reality. Manners are not a mask that hides the truth nor a rigid social form imposed on a chaotic personal reality. There is no 'inner man' covered more or less effectively by 'outer clothing', no 'core of brutishness' disguised by a 'mask of civilization', no unruly passions being tamed by the forms of society. The bearing of a man, his voice, his dress, the way in which he enters a room and takes his leave are as intrinsic to him as how he earns his living, or spends his money and energy, or thinks about politics. In all of his actions, whether they are utterances or gestures or choices, a human being expresses his personality. And that is why manners make the man.

But manners are a language, not a code. The same gesture may have different meanings in different contexts because what people say and do are their chosen responses and not mechanical reactions. Just what particular performances display the manners appropriate to a gentleman depends on the person and the circumstance. Reserve may indicate either self-possession or a desire to conceal one's true character. Amiability can be inspired by a servile desire to flatter or a ruthless desire to exploit others, while awkwardness and ferocity may spring from unusual honesty. Clothes can be rough when perceptions are delicate, and phrases can be fine when sentiments are crude. It is therefore easy to mistake the roughness of a Belton for a lack of sensitivity and the delicacy of an Aylmer for the thoughtfulness of a gentleman.

Manners are also a matter of fashion. To interpret them correctly one must be acquainted with what is taught in the community to which the person belongs. When Miss Stanbury insisted that a young woman who wears false hair cannot be a lady or that no gentleman would take up smoking, she had failed to notice that these expressions no longer carried the significance that they had when she was young.

Nevertheless the significance of manners is not wholly erratic. Though chignons were no longer the mark of a tart, when Arabella French wanted to establish her naturalness, she stopped wearing her false hair. In the same way, the character of a voice may reflect conventional standards and yet reveal personal qualities. Because a nasal twang is common among Americans, a twang is likely not to mean the same in an American voice as in Sir Louis Scatcherd, who had been educated at Eton and Cambridge among people who used their voices differently. But, on the other hand, Trollope points out that a nasal twang imparts to the voice a certain self-assertive quality which may be connected with a disposition in Americans to admire vigour and action: 'let the reader go into the closet and talk through his nose for awhile with steady attention to the effect which his own voice will have, and he will find that this theory is correct'. As Miss Wallachia Petrie was a woman who went through life fighting dragons on all

sides, she was especially addicted to 'this intonation, which is so
peculiar among intelligent Americans ... Her ears had taught
themselves to feel that there could be no vitality in speech without
it, and that all utterance unsustained by such tone, was effemi-
nate, vapid, useless, unpersuasive, unmusical – and English.' Miss
Petrie's friends, Caroline and Olivia Spalding, brought up in
much the same circles, were of a more yielding temperament and
accordingly modulated their voices differently, which led Miss
Petrie to complain 'that they debased their voices, and taught
themselves the pulling British mode of speech'.[13]

One can therefore say something general about the manners of
a gentleman. There are good reasons, for instance, why a gentleman is likely to be reserved. His awareness of what it takes to
understand and be understood by others will inhibit him from
speaking to everyone as he does to friends. With friends, he can
make his meaning clear by a word or a syllable or a glance;
others, he knows, are likely to misinterpret even the plainest
words, and therefore he will not speak of delicate matters to mere
acquaintances. His respect for the privacy of others will make him
reluctant to impose his conversation on strangers.

There are many other such connexions between the manners
and the morals of a gentleman. Taking careful notice of others
enables one to adapt easily to different people in a variety of
circumstances and so to fit in readily with new company. Recognizing the importance of fine distinctions makes a man more
likely to take the trouble to acquire a richer language for
expressing himself, and a repertory of more subtly discriminated
gestures allows him to express himself tactfully in a variety of
circumstances and to speak the truth without giving offense.
Freedom from self-preoccupation keeps people from assuming
that they are the objects of everyone's attention, and therefore
prevents them from taking offence readily or supposing that their
small failures are so important to others as to require apology.
Listening is no less enjoyable than commanding attention to those
who are genuinely interested in others. An aversion to deceiving
others and to betraying oneself makes affectation and pretentiousness unlikely. If a man does not think more of himself than of
what he is saying, he is unlikely to have the over-precise pronuni-
cation of a *parvenu*. In all these ways, the manners associated
with a gentleman flow from the moral quality that defines him.

But on the other hand, it is impossible to say what are the

manners of a gentleman because interpreting a man's expressions requires a highly complicated judgement. In a well established community, there are likely to be certain uniformities of expression. But the uniformity is at most rough and there may be deviations for any number of reasons. A gentleman always judges an expression in terms of its context.

It is not John Caldigate, but his gardener, who has a fixed notion of the dress suitable for a gentleman. When an Australian thug came to blackmail Caldigate and presented himself at the door, the gardener reported that the gentleman was a gentleman because 'he had been driven over from Cambridge in a hired gig ... and was dressed quite accordingly and genteel'. But when Caldigate saw the caller, he noticed other features of the man's appearance: 'The coat and hat and gloves and even the whiskers and head of hair might have belonged to a gentleman; but not, as he thought, the mouth or the eyes or the hands. And when the man began to speak there was a mixture of assurance and intended complaisance, an affected familiarity and an attempt at ease, which made the master of the house quite sure that his guest was not all that Carvell had represented.' On another occasion, Caldigate noticed something even in the clothing of the blackmailers that betrayed them – they seemed to be 'not quite at home in their clothes'.[14] Not just the fact that their clothes appear to be 'ready-made' determines Caldigate's judgement. He took the adoption of ready-made clothing to indicate an indifference to whether their clothing belonged to themselves, and a willingness to assume an appearance prepared by other people. Because their dress seemed to signify a readiness to pass for something other than they were, Caldigate concluded that the Australians were not gentlemen. But this does not establish a universal connexion between ready-made clothing and a lack of integrity. At other times and in other places, a man such as Caldigate might notice instead the differences in the way that ready-made clothing is chosen and assembled, or he might even regard clothing that is not ready-made as an affectation. The crucial question for a gentleman is always why the form of expression has been adopted.

Although Trollope said that there was no need to explain why Mr Prong was not a gentleman because 'most men and most women' would understand what he meant, he drew a host of men and women who believed that they could tell a gentleman when they saw one and were mistaken. They go wrong because they fail to explore sufficiently the connexions between the traits that they have noticed. For what distinguishes the deportment of a gentleman is how his traits fit together to constitute his personality. Character may be manifested in many ways and any manifestation may have different meanings. The manners of a gentleman are not a set of choreographed movements and they cannot be found in a code or a manual. But nevertheless, there might be good reason for saying – 'he looks like a gentleman'.

7 Occupations

That only some occupations are fit for gentlemen seems to be as much taken for granted in Trollope's world as in all the literature about gentlemen. The distinction appears at first sight to be like the ancient one between the liberal and the servile arts, between activities which exercise the higher, spiritual, rational faculty and those which, being concerned with material things and requiring physical labour, make those who practise them base. This ancient distinction belongs to the morality of the self-divided man, and it explains why honest manual labour has been considered inferior to the work of a hack who wields a pen.

Trollope seems to endorse the ancient idea when he refers to brewers as models of vulgarity; when he exludes Neefit, the breeches maker, from the order of gentleman; and speaks of the church and parliament as the natural occupations for a gentleman. And it is true that gentlemen draw a line between noble and servile work. But the distinction does not rest on a repugnance to contamination by matter and leads to different judgements about the moral significance of a man's occupations.

It is possible to be both a brewer and a gentleman. Indeed the fact that Luke Rowan (*Rachel Ray*) chose the 'contamination of malt and hops', when he could easily have avoided it, helps to make him a gentleman. He had been well educated, articled to a lawyer in London, and might have exchanged his inherited share in the brewery of Bungall and Tappitt for a considerable sum of money. The quality of its beer left something to be desired: the 'sour and muddy stream' that flowed from their vats was a 'beverage disagreeable to the palate and very cold and uncomfortable to the stomach'. But it was nevertheless a 'fat, prosperous, money-making business' which supported the Tappitts in comfort. Rowan noticed both the badness of the beer and the abundance of the profits, and found the combination irresistible. He not only preferred the rivers of Devonshire to the dingy chambers of Lincoln's Inn Fields. He liked brewing because it was a business in which one could see 'a clear line between right and wrong'. No man could brew bad beer or sell short measure without knowing it, and a brewer, unlike a lawyer, did not have to wait for others to put things right. The fact that the beer produced by Bungall and Tappitt was a disgrace challenged him to make the 'fatness' in brewing go together with the 'honesty'.[1]

Tappitt found Rowan's interest in brewing nothing short of sinister. Tappitt knew that the beer was 'too bad to be swallowed', but he saw no reason why a man should not 'employ himself, openly and legitimately, in the brewing of bad beer, if the demand for bad beer were so great as to enable him to live by the occupation'.[2] He had conveniently forgotten that half of his firm belonged to Bungall's heir, and regarded Rowan as an intruder. When it became clear that Rowan meant to claim his share and would not marry any daughter, Tappitt made great scenes, spread calumnies, and never for a moment doubted that he was right. And this was in accordance with the general pattern of his behaviour. Tappitt went through life as through a battlefield, never considering the reason for the struggle, bent only on staying ahead. His sense of his own worth depended entirely on how many people he could look down on, and on the fact that the lady from the big house came to his ball. In short, he valued himself in the same way as he valued his beer – by what price others put on him. And therefore he had the soul, and not just the occupation of a tradesman.

Rowan took a different attitude to everything. He acknowledged that just who should get what in the division of the brewery was a matter about which there might be reasonable disagreement. He even felt that something more than legal right was due to a man who had for long been his uncle's partner. He denounced no one but persisted quietly and hopefully. And he was not ashamed to settle down with the vats and beer barrels right under his nose. Though the Tappitts were not just what he would have preferred for his most intimate friends, Rowan was anxious not to be 'above his trade'. His attitude was not inspired by a doctrine of equality or any desire to see the 'degradation of nobles, the spoilation of the rich, or even the downfall of the bench of bishops'.[3] But just as deference to either queen or earl could not affect his sense of his own worth, so the society of tradesmen could not make him feel degraded. He had decided to take up his share in Bungall and Tappitt because that was how he preferred to make his life, and he accepted the conditions that his choice entailed, without worrying about whether he was higher or lower than someone else.

Because a disposition to reduce all of life to the calculation of profits and losses is usually found among tradesmen, they are commonly thought not to be gentlemen. Gentlemen hold that: 'Buying and selling is good and necessary; it is very necessary, and may possibly be very good; but it cannot be the noblest work of man ...'[4] But a gentleman recognizes also that the character common among tradesmen is not necessarily to be found in every tradesman. Luke Rowan and Tappitt were both brewers, but they went about their work and their lives in very different manners, and therefore one was a gentleman and the other, servile.

The story of Luke Rowan makes it plain that there is nothing whatever in the idea of a gentleman incompatible with his earning a living in business. Indeed, as in the case of Rowan, like that of Will Belton, the farmer, he might be more of a gentleman just because he engages in business and runs it well and profitably. Rowan displays the attitude of a gentleman not in any indifference to profit but, on the contrary, in the serious sense of craftsmanship with which he approached the business of brewing.

There is, however, more to be considered. A sense of craftsmanship may be carried too far, and that is the grain of truth in the popular belief that a gentleman must never be so serious about his work as to become a professional. But that belief is a crude way of recognizing the importance of how a gentleman's sense of craftsmanship is related to his sense of himself. What different roles a care for craftsmanship can play in a man's life, and which are suitable for a gentleman, is illustrated in the differences among the lawyers.

Mr Chaffanbrass (*Orley Farm, Phineas Redux*), was a renowned barrister whose gift for cross-examining a witness made the Old Bailey tremble before him. He considered it a betrayal of a client to think of anything else. Nevertheless Chaffanbrass was not a cynical man. He was capable even of reflecting dispassionately on the nature of the testimony that he used to win his cases, on 'how impossible it was for a dull conscientious man to give accurate evidence as to what he himself had seen'.[5] There was probably some truth in his claim that he had done a 'deal of good' by preventing unnecessary bloodshed, by saving the country 'thousands of pounds' in the maintenance of men 'who've shown themselves well able to maintain themselves', and by making the Crown lawyers 'very careful as to what sort of evidence they would send up to the Old Bailey'.[6] He was undoubtedly very hard working and wholly devoted to giving the best possible service for his pay. But Trollope says also: 'we may give the same praise to the hired bravo who goes through with truth and courage the task which he has undertaken. I knew an assassin in Ireland who professed that during twelve years of practice in Tipperary he had never failed when he had once engaged himself. For truth and honesty to their customers – which are great virtues – I would bracket that man and Mr Chaffanbrass together.'[7]

What makes Chaffanbrass an ignoble character is not just his indifference to the truth of what he tried to establish in the courtroom. A lawyer is obliged to accept a degree of such indifference. What is wrong with Chaffanbrass's attitude is something more subtle. It is the same flaw that appears in a more obvious form in another kind of lawyer, Mr Dove (*Eustace Diamonds*).

Mr Dove never descended to appearing at the Old Bailey. He was renowned solely for being so learned in the law that there was no question that he could not answer: 'If he had a case in hand, though the interest to himself in it was almost nothing, he would rob himself of rest for a week, should a point arise which required such labour.' His learning, coupled with his lack of concern for the money that his labours brought him, makes him a model of the vulgar conception of a gentleman as someone who never dirties his hands. But in fact, the very trouble that Mr Dove took to be right, regardless of the money; is what keeps him from being a true gentleman. He worked with the wrong motive. He was 'fond of law, but fonder, perhaps, of dominion; soft as milk to those who acknowledge his power, but a tyrant to all who contested it . . . It was the theory of Mr Dove's life that he would never be beaten.'[8] So concerned was he with victory, that he never undertook anything where there was a risk of failure. Nor did his thoughts ever stray beyond his law books. In short, the motive for Mr Dove's devotion to the law is the same as that of the Tappitts' operations in Bastlehurst, their desire to be first, and therefore it has the same moral quality.

In Mr Dove, as in Mr Chaffanbrass, the good craftsmanship is not an expression of the man's personality but a substitute for it.

Both lack that sense for the connexion between his work and his understanding of himself that distinguishes the brewer, Rowan. They wear their wigs into the drawing room and think of themselves as 'lawyers', not gentlemen. In other words, though they deal with legal matters, they do so in an ignoble, mechanical spirit.

Something closer to the integrity of a gentleman is displayed by Mr Furnival (*Orley Farm*), who often worked with Chaffanbrass but never considered meeting him socially. Furnival had made his way up from poverty and humble origins to a large income and a great name through very persistent labour, but had not reduced himself to a legal mechanic. Though he did not wholly approve of Felix Graham's deserting a case when he ceased to believe in its truth, Furnival respected the young man's concern to preserve his honesty. He himself defended clients without enquiring too closely into their innocence because he recognized complexities about a legal system that Graham failed to see. And Furnival was sufficiently aware of what he was doing to take care, when he doubted Lady Mason's innocence, not to express his doubts, because then he would have found it difficult to stand up before all the world to say the opposite. His readiness to spend his valuable time and talents on helping Lady Mason, for no reason other than a disinterested devotion to her, helps to establish Furnival's freedom from a servile professionalism and strengthens his claim to be considered a gentleman.

A complete gentleman among the lawyers is the modest family solicitor, Mr Grey (*Mr Scarborough's Family*). He attended Mr Scarborough through all his strategems to outwit the law, with both the imagination to appreciate his client's peculiar honesty and the integrity not to lend his legal services for everything that Scarborough demanded. The distinction of Mr Grey comes of his seeing a case as part of a larger context of obligations, not just to his clients but also to the client's ancestors and descendants and perhaps to others, and not just to observing the letter of the law, but to upholding the law. That made every case for Grey a subject to be reflected on and he astonished his partner, who was immune to such speculation, by the 'searching justness' with which he would, after a matter had already been debated for a day or two in the office, take the question home to discuss with his daughter.[9] Although there is a suggestion that Grey might be outwitted by lawyers of the Chaffanbrass variety, what makes him a gentleman is not any indifference to success in his work. He is nothing like solicitors such as Slow and Bideawhile, who equate gentility with inefficiency and an unwillingness to exert themselves and are ridiculed by Trollope. Grey is a gentleman because he does not think of himself as 'a lawyer'. His personality is neither determined nor exhausted by his occupation.

Nevertheless there is something to be said for the commonplace notions about noble and servile occupations. But a gentleman's reasons have to do with a respect for personality rather than an ambition to escape from mortality. An independent income makes self-sufficiency easier to sustain because it enables one to ignore the whims or good opinion of others, and to do what one believes to be right without any danger of offending the source of one's bread. Education helps to make a man more aware of the variety of responses open to him, gives him an ear for finer distinctions and for precision in the use of words, a realization of how much he owes to what other people have thought and done in the past, and fills his mind with ideas that can be enjoyed in solitude. That is why men in occupations requiring education are more likely to be gentlemen. In politics or in the church, where a man is supposed to devote himself to serving his country and his God, there is a greater incentive to preserving integrity. Farming has the same advantage because the natural demands of soil and animals make it difficult to cheat.But a shopkeeper or business man is more suspect because he may easily succeed by providing mechanically whatever anyone will buy, and men who spend their days in getting more for less may get so used to counting money, that they have an eye to business in everything.

There is some justification, too, for thinking that a care for integrity may interfere with success. A man whose first concern is with the quality of his life may go about his work with an eye to different considerations. He might spend less time or effort on keeping everything as trim and productive as does the farmer who has nothing else in his life. He might employ men because of a personal regard for them even when others might do the job better. He might engage in a less profitable business or take work with lower pay simply because he enjoys it. He might prefer the risk of being cheated to becoming aware of every dodge that will occur to a crooked mind, or rather be robbed than bothered.

But on the other hand, gentlemen feel an obligation to recognize that some skills are rarer than others, require more time, discipline, or talent to acquire, are in greater demand and therefore may be rewarded more than others. They feel obliged to recognize also the changes that occur in the affairs of men. Only in the gentleman's world, differences in reward, whether they take the shape of money or esteem, are not taken to indicate moral worth, because it is recognized that there are many reasons for rewarding men differently and various kinds of esteem. A man may be unusually skilled in doing something which others especially want, and yet less admirable morally than someone doing an utterly ordinary job. People may work hard, or very little, for a great variety of reasons, some admirable and others not. The fact that a man does a job which few people want done and therefore earns very little money does not in itself make him better or worse.

The right conclusion to draw from all this is not that a gentleman is indifferent to efficiency and success or incapable of achieving it. It means rather that he has more than money to think of deciding how he will work. The requirements that he tries to fulfil may be difficult to reconcile with one another, and no simple formula will do. A disdain of success may reflect nothing better than a genteel pretentiousness, whereas the shrewdness of a farmer, who gets the best out of his land, may display an admirable readiness to deal with the world as he finds it. Even in occupations where there is a strong temptation to violate integrity, it is possible to conduct oneself otherwise. A concern to make one's investments pay neither requires nor justifies lacing declarations of love with talk of money. What reading does for some men, farming or brewing may do for others.

In occupations, as in manners, there is some regularity in the connexion between what a man does and what he is. But the connexion is contingent and therefore facile generalizations are misleading. One thing only can be said with assurance – that the mark of a gentleman is not idleness but an ability to work conscientiously without losing himself. And he would not mind being found planting cabbages.

8 Birth and Rank

If gentlemen are made, not born, and if one has to learn to be a gentleman and it is not like blue eyes passed on by genes, why is there so much talk among Trollope's gentlemen and ladies about ancestry? What is the relation between an aristocrat and a gentleman? Why should a gentleman respect the social hierarchy?

Many of the people whom we meet in the novels believe that the quality of people is determined by their ancestry and that superior people, like winning horses, are to be found in good breeds. The Duke of Omnium talks of the blue blood of his family and argues that to be born of a long line of peers means that one has inherited the best blood in the country and that those born into such a rank have a duty to protect it against dilution by bad blood.[1] The distinction between the hereditary aristocracy and the mere possession of a title appears to be important. When the American democrat, Wallachia Petrie (*He Knew He Was Right*), says to Lady Rowley, 'I believe that in London the titled aristocrats do hang pretty much together'. Trollope makes it clear that it had never occured to Lady Rowley, 'since the day in which her husband had been made a knight in order that the inhabitants of some island might be gratified by the opportunity of using the title' that she was the equal of a peer of ancient lineage.[2] In the story of *Lady Anna*, a 'theory of blood' dominates the life of Countess Lovell. When her daughter proposed to marry the tailor whom she had loved since childhood, the Countess described him as 'infinitely beneath' one who had an earl's blood in her veins. And her belief is shared by a close friend and admirer of the tailor who tells him that as Lady Anna is of the Lovells, who were 'noble and of an old nobility, among the few hot-house plants of the nation', and Daniel Thwaite, tailor, is but 'one of the people – a blade of corn out of the open field', a marriage between them would constitute too violent a 'grafting'.[3] There are also commoners who pride themselves on 'blood', and no man plumed himself more on 'good blood' than Dr Thorne.

He took inordinate pride in 'his genealogical tree, and his hundred and thirty clearly proved descendants from MacAdam' and believed that whereas the other doctors in his country had 'ditch-water in their veins', he could 'boast of a pure ichor, to which that of the great Omnium family was but a muddy puddle'.[4]

But on the other hand, as the stories unfold, they seem to show that 'blood' does not count. The Duke of Omnium acknowledges that a descendant of an American labourer is fit to be a duchess. When the American, Caroline Spalding (*He Knew He Was Right*), was persuaded by her democratic friend that it would be improper for her to marry an English lord, the lord, though he was one of England's highest nobles, told her curtly that she had been misled by 'some misty, far-fetched ideas respecting English society . . . and by the fantasies of a rabid enthusiast'.[5]

In *Lady Anna*, the arguments for concluding that blood does not count are developed at length. Though Daniel Thwaite was a journeyman tailor, he had not only spent his fortune on helping the Countess win her right to her title and wanted nothing for himself but was also widely read and reflective. Ordinary conventional people found it difficult to believe that a tailor could possess such qualities, but the Solicitor-General, Sir William Patterson, who had lived all his days 'with people of the right sort', declared that Thwaite would fit perfectly into the position that Lady Anna brought him.[6]

The arguments against Thwaite are ridiculed by Trollope. He describes as 'a young female Conservative with wisdom beyond her years', the girl who informed Lady Anna that she must not think of marrying the tailor because 'a girl who is a lady should never marry a man who is not a gentleman . . . Otherwise everything would be mingled, and there would soon be no differences. If there are to be differences, there should be differences.' Nor does Trollope show any more respect for the high-flown argument produced by Mrs Bluestone, who told Lady Anna that a 'well-preserved and exclusive aristocracy' was divinely ordained because 'God Almighty has chosen that there should be different ranks to carry out His purposes, and we have His word to tell us that we should all do our duties in that state of life to which it has pleased Him to call us'. The echo of Burke in Mrs Bluestone's exhortation does not save her: 'The excellent lady was somewhat among the clouds in her theology, and apt to mingle the different sources of religious instructions from which she was wont to draw lessons for

her own and her children's guidance; but she meant to say that
the proper state of life for an earl's daughter could not include an
attachment to a tailor . . .'⁷

All this might seem to suggest that Trollope endorsed Daniel
Thwaite's view that earls and countesses are no better than those
'senseless, over-grown brutes' which perished 'in the general progress' because the 'big things have all to give way to the intellect of
those who are more finely made'. In the refinements of the earl
who was his rival for Lady Anna, Thwaite saw only the marks of
an aristocrat's debased nature – the earl's hands were soft because
they 'could never help him to a morsel of bread'; he was 'sweet
with perfumes' because he was idle and never knew the sweat of
labour; and all in all, he was 'an excrescence . . . produced by the
evil habits and tendencies of mankind' and the sooner eliminated
the better. The tailor felt infinitely superior to the earl because he
was 'the working bee' and the earl was a mere 'drone', hardly
conscious of the mental faculties given to him, always 'consuming
and never producing'.⁸

But this view of the aristocracy finds no favour with Trollope.
Thwaite's opinions were due, he says, to 'half-knowledge', ill-
gotten and ill-digested information', and reading which 'had all
been on one side'. The case for the aristocracy is all the more
forceful because it is made by the same Solicitor-General, who
defends the tailor's right to marry Lady Anna. Sir William told
Thwaite that he was wrong in 'not having perceived that the best
men who come up from age to age are always migrating from that
pole which you say you prefer, to the antipodean pole to which
you are tending yourself'. The conversation ends on a theme
which appears repeatedly in the novels – 'the theory of equality is
very grand . . . But could you establish absolute equality in
England tomorrow, as it was to have been established in France
some half century ago, the inequality of men's minds and
character would re-establish an aristocracy within twenty years
. . . It is the fault of many patriotic men that, in their desire to
put down the evils which exist they will see only the power that is
wasted, and have no eyes for the good work done. . . .'⁹

It looks as if a gentleman is obliged to hold inconsistent
opinions about the aristocracy, to believe both that 'blood' matters and that it should be ignored. Certainly that seems to be true
of Dr Thorne. He was proud of his lineage, but proud also of
'repudiating the very family of which he was proud' as well as of

'keeping his pride silently to himself'. He took care to 'let a lord walk out of a room before him' and never assumed 'familiarity with bigger men than himself'. But he was also ready to hate a lord on sight, and made it evident to the Earl de Courcy that 'the privilege of dining at Courcy Castle was to him no greater than that of dining at Courcy Parsonage'.[10] His niece, Mary Thorne, was a bastard fathered by his brother on the sister of a stonemason who certainly was not a gentleman, and the doctor recognized that she was not, by blood, fit to marry a squire's son. Nevertheless the doctor was also sure that his bastard niece was more of a lady than the daughters of the Earl de Courcy.

How contradictory were the doctor's beliefs, we are shown in the dilemma that they produced for his niece. She had been educated as a lady, first at a school and later with the daughters of the squire, where she learned 'how to speak and talk as other young ladies do; how to dress herself, and how to move and walk'. And she believed, as did the doctor, that 'God's handiwork was the inner man, the inner woman, the naked creature animated by a living soul; that all other adjuncts were but man's clothing for the creature; all others, whether stitched by tailors or contrived by kings'. She held this opinion with the 'stern, unflinching antagonism, the antagonism of a democrat, to the pretensions of others . . . blessed with that of which she had been deprived'. But she also had as much respect for the position of the Greshams as they did themselves and a belief in blood according to which her own was tainted: 'she knew that were she a man . . . nothing should tempt her to sully her children's blood by mating herself with anyone that was base born'. Consequently, when the heir to Greshamsbury proposed to make her his wife, her mind went to 'war with itself'. At first, her belief in blood won out and she refused him. But after he persisted in his suit, Mary thought again and concluded that there was no 'real reason . . . founded on truth and honesty, why she should not be a fitting wife to Frank Gresham. – Francis Newbold Gresham, of Greshamsbury, though he was, or was to be'. She was undoubtedly as 'basely born as any lady could be', but in character and upbringing she was as suited to being his wife as if she had been 'the legitimate descendant of a score of legitimate duchesses'. And therefore, in refusing Frank, she was sacrificing the happiness of two people who loved one another to what she now dismissed as 'a theoretic love of pure blood'.[11]

Dr Thorne, however, never denied the importance of blood. Throughout Mary's trials and deliberations, he remained faithful to all of his convictions. He thought that the Greshams were justified in their opposition, and also that Mary might do very well as the wife of a Gresham. And Trollope treats the doctor's attitude as wholly reasonable. The explanation for this, as for the other apparent contradictions in how gentlemen think about ancestry, is that there is a myth associated with the aristocracy, and with 'good lineage' generally, which has a complicated relation to reality.

According to the myth, the aristocracy consists of gentlemen who possess qualities which their nation especially esteems, and have received their titles, possessions, and privileges because of this distinction. Because an aristocrat is a member of an order which has been, or will be, continuous over many generations, he is peculiarly conscious of his family connexions. He may describe this connexion as 'good blood', but in doing so, he is using a shorthand for both a genetic and cultural inheritance, for breeding in the sense of both nature and nurture.

Of reverence for 'blood' in the strict, genetic sense, a gentleman is incapable. The crude certainties of those who suppose that there are breeds of human beings as there are breeds of horses are alien to him. He does not deny that dispositions, talents and defects are genetically inherited and will open or close certain possibilities to their possessors. But he believes that, because human beings transform whatever is presented to them, it is impossible, even if one were certain of what gifts a man possessed, to predict how he will develop, use, or deform them. For the same reason, he denies that education can iron out all differences because what is taught can as easily be converted into a multitude of unexpected consequences as what is transmitted by genes. Cultural inheritance is no more fixed than genetic inheritance and the interaction between the two makes the outcome of all breeding, whether by nature or nurture, uncertain.

But if there are no certainties, there are greater and lesser likelihoods. Those who, in the nursery, or in the drawing room, have heard nothing coarse or sordid, who have had the opportunity to converse with the cultivated and wise and have possessed the books with the leisure for reading and reflecting, are more likely to be fit to live on an eminence and serve as a model to their fellows. If such people have taken care over many generations to

hand on their achievements and not to adulterate their inheritance, they will form a class who consistently display the virtue of a
gentleman in its most polished form.

A further reason for the peculiar grace of an aristorcrat is that
he has the character of a custodian. As the inheritor of an estate,
it is his special obligation to maintain and to pass it on. He does
not regard what belongs to him as his own to do what he wills with
it but as a bequest of which he is, for his lifetime, the custodian,
just as his father and grandfather were before him. And this sense
of having a duty to perpetuate something that is impossible to
create deliberately and easy to destroy distinguishes the attitude
of an aristocrat. He has an air of leisure, and the refinement that
goes with leisure because his job of custodianship releases him
from the whirl of his contemporary world and allows him to be indifferent to the demands of the moment. An aristocrat consequently has none of the brusqueness that characterizes the man
whose job it is to turn out something for here and now. But, on
the other hand, an aristocrat does not feel free as an ordinary
gentleman might, to retire from the world. His job as custodian
obliges him to play an active role in public life.[12]

The refinement that belongs to custodians of culture is what
Lady Anna notices when she goes to live with her noble cousins –
'The softness, the niceness, the ease, the grace of the people
around her. The pleasant idleness of the drawing room, with its
books and music, and unstrained chatter of family voices . . . She
seemed to live among roses and perfumes.'[13] What attracts Lady
Anna is that perfection in the art of living produced by the
existence of a set of people who have for many generations
devoted themselves to elaborating refinements on an inheritance
already far from primitive. Thwaite's antagonism to the aristocracy reflects ignorance of what it takes to make an art of living.

An aristocrat's special consciousness of building on what was
created in the past makes him the contrary of a *parvenu*.
Whereas a *parvenu* believes that he has sprung complete with his
virtues and skills out of his mother's womb or his own will, an
aristocrat reveres ancestors, age, and tradition. Whereas the
parvenu's characteristic emotion is envy, an immunity to envy distinguishes the aristocrat, not because he is confident of being at
the top, but because he regards it as his special task to cultivate
what is given to him rather than to outdo others. The distinction
that he seeks is that of a conscientious custodian.

An aristocrat is the contrary of a *parvenu* also in his attitude to his inferiors. Whereas a *parvenu* rejoices in looking down on others, an aristocrat is no more inclined to despise even those who are genuinely and not merely formally inferior, than a father, his children. Although his inferiors may be weaker and coarser, less discriminating, less able than he to endure hardship and to enjoy the achievements of civilization, they are not for an aristocrat, any more than for other gentlemen, a breed of monsters, but intelligent beings like himself who happen to be less able than he, or perhaps less fastidious, in finding their way. Consequently they are never an outlet for his powers of contempt. An aristocrat may feel that his inferiors will be better for being governed by him, whether as their ruler or their model or both, but he recognizes their dependence on him to be of the same character as his own dependence on many generations of illustrious ancestors.

That is the myth of the aristocracy as it appears in the morality of the gentleman and it should not be confused with other conceptions of aristocracy. These come in two varieties, each attached to the perfection of the different parts of man conceived of as a compound of reason and passion. On the one hand, there is an aristocracy of Reason, for which the model was drawn by Plato, whose perfection of intellect divorces them from ordinary human life and makes them wholly indifferent to the pleasures of a material existence. This is an ascetic, self-denying aristocracy, who regard the rest of mankind as clay for the potter, material for being moulded by the few who know the pattern for perfection because they, and they alone, have insight into it. On the other hand, there is an aristocracy defined by a Will to Power, by a superior ruthlessness or egoism, by the highest development of those 'instincts' of the lion in the jungle which are dormant or weak in ordinary people. To the aristocracy of Will, such as Nietzsche celebrates, their inferiors are but instruments to be used, suppressed, or perhaps indulged just as their masters please, and an uninhibited readiness to command, to command arbitrarily according to no rule or reason, is what distinguishes an aristocrat. As always in the conclusions drawn from the morality of the divided man, the common opinions about aristocracy are an incoherent mixture of both these models, to be found as much among those who profess to be 'egalitarians' as among avowed 'élitists', and all are as alien to the morality of a gentleman as the conception of man as a 'rational animal' on which they rest.

A gentleman not only subscribes to a different myth. He also recognizes an inescapable discrepancy between the myth and the reality, without being tempted either to discard the myth or to deplore the reality.

In reality, of course, not all nobles have received their titles for the same reasons. Even when they possessed the qualities stipulated by the myth, their heirs may have been wanting in either the biological or the cultural breeding. Aristocrats may be indifferent to the duty of custodianship and may squander their estates carelessly or sell them cold-bloodedly. Their refinement may consist in nothing more than the useless, soft hands despised by Daniel Thwaite. Lord Grex is only one of many stupid, silly, mean, far from noble aristocrats who populate Trollope's novels. The Marquis of Brotherton is a reprobate; the elder Duke of Omnium is hardly a model of virtue; the duke's heir is clearly inferior in gifts to the commoner whom the duke considered unfit for his daughter. There are not only commoners, but utter strangers, Americans and Jews, descended from no one knows whom, at least as good as the most splendid duke or duchess, and far better than most. Why then should a hereditary aristocracy be venerated?

It is a symbol of certain admirable qualities and a readiness in the nation to defer to those who possess them. The grandeur and the privileges of those of high rank, even when they do not signify what they should, stimulate the imagination and keep alive a capacity for reverence which might otherwise be lost. For as men are not spirits, they need a visible token of what they believe.

The privileges may not be wholly deserved, but they need not be repudiated by a conscientious aristocrat. A gentleman will take the view of Tregear who, despite being rejected as a son-in-law by the duke, urged the duke's son to accept the seat offered to him because of his name: 'Take the goods the gods provide you. Of course all these things which our ambition covets are easier to Dukes' sons than to others. But not on that account should a Duke's son refuse them.'[14]

That good birth means the possession of ancestors who were recognized to be gentlemen is a further reason why it should be respected. It is a sign that a man was intended to be a gentleman. Such an intention is significant in the same way as the intention of an artist to produce a work of art. He may fail, but if we take his intentions seriously, we feel obliged to give his creation careful consideration. It is just because gentlemen are made, not born, just because one ordinarily learns how to be a gentleman from those who know, that ancestry is important. Of course the teaching or the capacity to benefit from it may fail, and those born into the most unlikely circumstances may somehow discover for themselves how to think and behave like a gentleman. In this as in all other matters, there is no limit to the variations that may arise. But the give and take of social life rest on the possibility of regularly connecting certain signs with a certain reality, and as mortals lack the time to discover the essence of everyone whom they encounter, and often lack even the capacity or will to make such an exploration, a man's ancestry or rank permits a quick identification.

The reliance on such signs has its drawbacks. It introduces a certain rigidity and falsity into social life. For once the labels are affixed as the signs dictate, reading labels may become a substitute for judging. Even at best, a social hierarchy will be at odds with the fine gradations in personal reality, and not infrequently the quick identification may mislead because it relies on a regularity in connexions that may at any moment disappear and will certainly be absent in particular instances. Nevertheless the regularity is not altogether lacking and the rigidity is not altogether undesirable. Men who live together do acquire certain resemblances and therefore conventional generalizations about the meaning of birth and rank are not altogether wide of the mark. Despite all the silly and deplorable aristocrats that he drew, Trollope did 'not scruple' to admit that he preferred the society of the well born and wealthy. He never, he emphasizes, 'toadied any one' or acquired the 'character of a tuft-hunter', but he did believe that 'the son of a peer is more likely to rub his shoulders against well-informed men that the son of a tradesman. The graces come easier to the wife of him who has had great-grandfathers than they do to her whose husband has been less, – or more fortunate, as he may think it. The discerning man will recognize the information and the graces when they are achieved without such assistance, and will honour the owners of them the more because of the difficulties they have overcome; – but the fact remains that the society of the well-born and of the wealthy will as a rule be worth seeking.'[15]

It is reasonable to believe that the country will be better governed if the descendants of certain families are prominent among its rulers because such men are more likely to be disinterested and brought up to the art of ruling. Barrington Erle speaks with the approval of Trollope and of all gentlemen when he says: 'I do believe in the patriotism of certain families. I believe that the Mildmays, FitzHowards, and Pallisers have for some centuries brought up their children to regard the well-being of their country as their highest personal interest, and that such teaching has been generally efficacious. Of course, there have been failures. Every child won't learn its lesson however well it may be taught. But the school in which good training is most practised will, as a rule, turn out the best scholars. In this way I believe in families.' But as aristocrats do not always and are not the only ones to acquire such patriotism, it is reasonable also for the same Barrington Erle to promote the career of Phineas Finn, the son of an Irish doctor: 'You have come in for some of the teaching', he tells Phineas, 'and I expect to see you a scholar yet.'[16]

The portion of the genuine quality in those conventionally supposed to possess it will vary. But it does not follow that deference should be granted only after investigation. The inquiry can go wrong; life is too short; and less harm is generally done by treating a duchess who is not a perfect duchess as if she were, than by an effort to keep the labelling perfect. A gentleman will give the labels their due without putting undue faith in them.

The pride of the de Courcy's, who had no notion of an aristocratic virtue, will seem to him as ridiculous as the conviction of egalitarians that a great gulf separates them from the titled. A gentleman has too much self-esteem for either such arrogance or such servility. But it does not prevent him from deferring to formal as well as to real superiority. He will not feel demeaned by the deference or become confused about its significance.

A social hierarchy, with or without a hereditary aristocracy, has the value of a standing reminder that some kinds of conduct and character are more worthy of esteem than others, that the equal worth of men as God's creatures does not make them equally worthy of men's esteem. Deference to those of distinguished ancestry keeps people from forgetting that whatever virtues may be possessed by their contemporaries who are amassing wealth and power here and now, there are also distinctions of another kind. And for those who are not strong or perceptive enough to rely on their own judgement, a social hierarchy provides a rough guide to whom they will find compatible. It is one of the ways of marking paths through the wilderness of a mortal life that few are able to find for themselves. The duke's daughter had the discernment to ignore the conventional signs and to choose a husband outside her own class, without falling prey to an adventurer, but had her mother been left free to run outside the conventional grooves, she might have been destroyed. Conventional judgements may be defied, but anyone who has the wisdom and strength to do so will also recognize their value.

There is something to be said for dreaming of a day when all tailors will possess the graces of a duke. But the dream should not be mistaken for a reality. It can be made easier for a tailor to acquire those graces if he should choose to do so. But if a tailor like Daniel Thwaite can muster the stamina to marry Lady Anna, or if a conventional squire's son like Frank Gresham can find the courage to marry a bastard like Mary Thorne, that is better than having no constraints at all. For that way, the good – the bridging of the distance between the grand and the humble, the recognition of superiority wherever it may arise, and the constant renewal of the higher orders – is achieved subtly and indirectly without destroying the virtues of a hierarchy.

After all, Dr Thorne's attitude is not inconsistent. And there was no one better able to appreciate the profundity hidden by the apparent perversity in the doctor than Miss Dunstable, the heiress who had no ancestors to boast of but the wit to respect the myth about ancestry, and yet to be amused by her own role as the target at which needy aristocrats might shoot their arrows.

When her sponsor in the drawing rooms of the aristocracy indicated doubt about her hard, black curls, Miss Dunstable assured her that, 'They'll always pass muster when they are done up with bank-notes.'[17] To have her fling at high life, she bought a house which she called affectionately 'Ointment Hall', and just because it was a monstrous thing, built by an eccentric millionaire at great cost and 'deficient in most of those details which, in point of house accommodation, are necessary to the very existence of man', the preposterous mansion was as appropriate for Miss Dunstable as the gem in Park Lane for Madame Goesler. Nor did Miss Dunstable mind when it was reported that Mrs Proudie accused her of plagiarizing the 'conversaziones' in the bishop's palace. She made no pretence of having invented everything for herself: 'I copy everybody that I see, more or less . . . If Mrs Proudie has any such pride as that, pray don't rob her of it.'[18] To an outstandingly bogus proposal from George de Courcy – 'if ever a man loved a woman truly, I truly love you', Miss Dunstable answered without resentment: 'I am sorry to say that I had not perceived from your manner that you entertained any peculiar feelings towards me ... but I am in too humble a position to return your affection; and can, therefore, only express a hope that you may be soon able to eradicate it from your bosom.' But when Frank Gresham, whom she took to be a better man, seemed to join the horde of greedy suitors, Miss Dunstable spelled out for him the unpalatable facts about herself: 'I am neither young nor beautiful, nor have I been brought up as she should be whom you in time will really love and make your wife. . .'[19] And when Mr Moffat, who was distinguished even among the de Courcy's for his servile adulation of both money and rank, chose the money and offered to break his engagement with the earl's niece on the ground that he and Miss Dunstable were two of a kind, having both 'risen from the lower class' and induced 'the highest aristocracy of England to admit them into their circles', Miss Dunstable 'understood his object as well as she had that of his aristocratic rival' and sent him packing.[20]

Then, having had her taste of life among the great, she decided that she would like to be the wife of an untitled, undistinguished, prickly country doctor who considered her money a great defect and whose proposal was hardly flattering: 'If it be possible that you can think that a union between us will make us both happier than we are single, I will plight you my word and troth with good faith, and will do what an old man may do to make the burden of the world lie light on your shoulders ... I can hardly keep myself from thinking that I am an old fool: but I try to reconcile myself to that by remembering that you yourself are no longer a girl.'[21] In marrying Miss Dunstable, who had floated into the society of aristocrats on the oils of Lebanon, Dr Thorne had not in the least betrayed his pride in his genealogical tree and his hundred and thirty ancestors descended from MacAdam.

Part III
The Conduct of a
Gentleman

9 Love

A good test of how a morality regards mortal existence and especially human individuality is its attitude to love and sexuality.

The essence of the attitude common to all moralities of the self-divided man appears in Plato's *Symposium*. There Diotima explains to Socrates that those who think of love as a pursuit of the other half of a whole are right, but they mistake the character of the whole. They fail to recognize that love is a completion of the soul, not the body. Although the first impulse to love arises at the sight of a beautiful body, if a lover is properly educated and his reason succeeds in keeping passion under control, he ascends through increasingly abstract perceptions of beauty until he learns to appreciate the unchanging beauty that belongs to the whole from which his soul has been alienated by earthly existence. Union with this eternal whole is what the lover truly desires. In short, love is attached to the spiritual element in man and sexuality to the base animal part, which means that sexual desire is necessarily an impediment to perfecting the higher self and cannot be reconciled with virtue.

Their acceptance of some such picture of human sexuality made it difficult for the early Christian theologians to explain how God could bid men to multiply without at the same time commanding them to sin. Aquinas found an ingenious solution – that sexual relations between a Christian husband and wife can be virtuous if they both remain utterly free of emotional disturbance. But as C. S. Lewis pointed out, this good Christian relationship resembles nothing so much as 'the cold sensuality of Tiberius in Capri'.[1] Yet there is no better way of reconciling respect for a human condition with the Platonic idea of *eros* because that has no place for humanity. Its true object is neither a human being nor a human quality, but the divine spark in all men, which the lover, who has learned to see the truth, can discern. The pursuit of love consists in freeing this uniting divinity from the adulterating human vessel which imposes the distinctions that separate lovers.[2] Consequently, love is always at war with earthly existence. It can be truly consummated only by giving up the world, and the models of such lovers are Tristan and Isolde, who slept with a dagger between them and found joy in death.[3]

Their story, however, encapsulates only one strand in the tradition of romantic love that rests on the ancient idea of *eros*. We are more familiar now with another, opposite implication of that same idea. If a soul is not in good order, it will seek an illusory kind of wholeness, which is described in the *Symposium* as the pursuit of the 'common Aphrodite'. In this kind of love, reason has lost control and passion pulls the soul from one pleasure to the next, but each pleasure achieved is only a spur to seeking another. There is no stopping because the object pursued is an illusion instead of the good for which the lover's soul really craves, and therefore the lover can never be satisfied. Because the governing role of reason has been usurped by passion, such a lover is disordered and frenzied, indeed mad.

Such madness is the sign of true love, according to what is called the 'modern romantic ideal', of which the classic exposition is Stendhal's treatise, *De l'Amour*. There, the 'beloved', is described as something that, like the grit that irritates an oyster into producing a pearl, stimulates the lover's imagination to conjure up dreams of desires and satisfactions. The association of the beloved with pleasures enjoyed in the past, along with the hope of enjoying more in the future, constitutes 'being in love'. As long as his imagination continues to be stimulated to invent new desires, the lover remains constant because he continues to hope for new satisfactions in the same quarter. Fear is essential to love because the possibility of losing a pleasure enhances it, and success that comes with effort is more gratifying to vanity. Reason is incompatible with love because, by introducing considerations such as regard for truth and goodness, submission to conventions, concern with the business of life, it intrudes reality on the dreams that constitute love and so threatens love.

Stendhal's idea of love is supposed to be the apotheosis of modern individualism. And there is a good reason for this belief. The classic source of modern individualism is Hobbes, whose description of felicity reads like a paraphrase of what appears in Plato as a description of a disordered soul and in Stendhal as the definition of love: 'Felicity is a continual progress of the desire, from one object to another; the attaining of the former, being still but one way to the latter.'[4] But an individual understood as a pursuer of Hobbes's 'felicity' is merely a separate bundle of desires; his individuality has nothing to do with personality. And the same is true of Stendhal's lover. The individuality that he recognizes is only the capacity of someone to give him more or less satisfaction. The real object of his love is the pleasure that he happens to associate with some human being. Although Stendhal's lovers are not required to repudiate their separateness, neither do they appreciate it because they take no interest in each other's personalities; they merely use one another. They still seek unity, just as in the ancient picture, only they achieve it through sexual possession. That is why the relationship of such lovers is described as a traffic between tyrants and slaves, and why they are said to eat one another. They certainly cannot be self-possessed.

The model of such a lover is Emma Bovary, for whom things had significance only in proportion to the satisfaction that they brought her. The object of her love was always a dream of desires fulfilled to which attached the name of a man. And her lovers had no more understanding of her. They tire of her, not because they become aware of her shallowness, or mind her blindness to them, but because Emma regularly fell into the error against which Stendhal warned – of killing fear by the eagerness of her transports, as a result of which possessing her lost its value because it could no longer gratify her lovers' vanity.

Both the agonies and the transports of Emma Bovary are foreign to gentlemen because their love has nothing to do with unity of any kind, is not a desire for either completion or possession, is destroyed rather than enhanced by fear and vanity, and is entirely rational. Love in the gentleman's sense is a kind of relationship that was never conceived of by pagan philosophers or their modern disciples.[5] But this kind of relationship has been a preoccupation of Christian theologians because they have devoted themselves to explaining how there can be a communion, distinct from obedience or fear, between man and God.[6] For according to Christian doctrine, God loves men and men should love God, but this love cannot be based on similarity, or fusion, or possession because the Christian God is a Creator, who made men out of nothing, which means that men do not share in God's nature and having nothing in common with him. The object of

God's love cannot then be resemblance to himself. Nor in loving God, may men seek to perfect or complete themselves by becoming one with him, because they would be aspiring to the immortality, omniscience, and omnipotence of God. It remains then to explain how there can be a relationship other than fear or obedience between beings who are separated by an infinite chasm.

Such a relationship is possible, at least some Christians have argued, because God wills to love men for what they are in themselves. And men will to love God only in order to love him. The character of such a relationship, and how it comes about, necessarily is a mystery, which can only be symbolized by the paradox of the death of Jesus – the God who died on the Cross, because only a relationship based on a similarity can be understood. In other words, Christian love is a relationship between beings who recognize one another to be irrevocably different. They do not see themselves as members of the same class, instances of the same species or incarnations of the same universal principle. They do not use one another, desire to possess or fuse with the other. They remain wholly separate and unlike, and their appreciation of one another does not depend on any common element.

Lovers in the gentleman's world also do not lose, or wish to lose, their separate and distinctive identities. One of the earliest portraits of such a lover appears in Chaucer's Wife of Bath.[7] It is the love celebrated in Donne's lines: 'If ever beauty I did see/Which I desired and got, 'twas/but a dream of thee', and the love of which Shakespeare's Imogene is a model. Such love has nothing to do with either cannibalism or a repugnance to the human condition because it is a peculiarly profound appreciation of another human being, of the personality that is revealed in all his attributes, bodily as well as mental, and is therefore truly the apotheosis of a regard for individuality. That is why the severest test of a gentleman is his conduct in love.

*   *   *

Because such lovers are neither satyrs nor saints, it is easy to misunderstand how their bodily life affects their relationship. Trollope pays a great deal of attention to details of physical appearance and even emphasizes that beauty will work its magic on almost everyone. It is only natural, he says, that men should be more disposed to fall in love with pretty girls[8] than with ugly ones and to find comfort in having a pretty woman by their side. And it is equally natural for women to prefer handsome men. But Trollope also makes it plain that no pattern of beauty is certain to win love, and that love may find beauty in unlikely features, and that the impression of beauty may not be produced by any physical attributes. No description of Isabel Boncassen's figure and face, he says, could convey the impression she made because it was 'the vitality of her countenance . . . the command which she had of pathos, of humour, of sympathy, of satire, the assurance which she gave by every glance of her eye . . . that she was alive to all that was going on, that made all acknowledge that she was beautiful'.[9] When Dorothy Stanbury blossomed into a beauty, Trollope attributes the change in her to the development of her talent for 'a keen sense of humour, a nice appreciation of character, and a quiet reticent wit'.[10]

All this suggests that physical features may be irrelevant to love. But the same might be said of moral and intellectual qualities. Not even the highest admiration and gratitude, Trollope shows in *An Old Man's Love,* add up to love. Mr Whittlestaff had given Mary Lowrie a home when she had no other resources and had shown her impeccable generosity and kindness; he was capable of passionate love, having come near to suicide when he was disappointed; he was a man of considerable charm, who won the devotion of all who knew him; and he possessed, in addition to a good name and fortune, a cultivated intellect which Mary appreciated. Indeed she was convinced that 'he was of all human beings surely the best' and worshipped him as 'something almost divine'.[11] Still, even when she had brought herself to believe that she ought to marry him, she remained certain that she did not love him. And he, too, acknowledged that her feeling for him was not to be confused with the love that he wanted from a wife.

The distinction between love and affection or admiration is drawn still more finely in the story of Mary Lowther and Mr Gilmore. She acknowledged that she 'liked him, his manners, his character, his ways, his mode of life, and after a fashion she liked his person'.[12] For long, she struggled unsuccessfully to find Gilmore acceptable and felt that he deserved to get what he wanted. When, however, Captain Marrable declared his love, she knew at once that she could promise 'to be his wife without the least reserve or fear'. She did not, as with Gilmore, 'dread the time in which he would have to put his arm round me and kiss me', but took great pleasure in his physical presence. Yet she could no more explain her desire for one than her hesitation about the other. She could only say, 'I don't know why it should be so; but it is.'[13]

Mary Lowther and Mary Lowrie are typical of the many girls who say about a man whom they admire and like: 'I do not feel for him what a wife should'. Only a reader blinded by the cant about Victorian prudery could fail to recognize that Trollope is insisting on the sexuality of love. Diatribes against teaching women that there is something to fear and abhor in the sexual desires of men appear throughout his novels. Far from suggesting that women are or should be any more indifferent to sexual desire than men are, Trollope denounces those who 'tell us that no pure-minded girl should think of finding a lover'.[14] In his *Autobiography*, he commends the love-making in *Framley Parsonage* for being 'downright honest love – in which there was no pretence on the part of the lady that she was too ethereal to be fond of a man, no half-and-half inclination on the part of the man to pay a certain price and no more for a pretty toy. Each of them longed for the other, and they were not ashamed to say so.'[15] There can be no doubt of Trollope's hearty dislike for coy lovers. The most admirable of his gentleman and ladies welcome and enjoy 'the right true end of love'.

It is true that there are no explicit descriptions of love-making in Trollope's novels. But what explains it is the opposite of prudery – the fact that his lovers see each other as distinctive personalities. The difficulty of putting what is intensely personal into words is repeatedly pointed out by Trollope in remarks about things 'which can be spoken but which cannot be written', which happen in a day but would take a life-time to explain.[16] Only indifference to 'the proper powers and limitations of words'[17] makes it difficult to see that Trollope's reticence was no more inspired by an aversion to the sexuality of love than Swift's explicitness about the human body was meant to celebrate and commend it. The sexuality anatomized in manuals, whether ancient Oriental or modern, is that of an animal body devoid of personal quality and therefore easily captured in universal formulas. The explicitness of Lawrence's descriptions of sexual encounters reflects his conception of sexual union as a means of liberating human beings from their individuality and dissolving them into the unity of humanity.[18] But as the sexuality of the love that concerned Trollope is one with the deepest appreciation of individuality it is so quintessentially personal as to elude words altogether. Although poets can sing of it, lovers, who try to explain, produce the absurdity mocked in Lucy Robarts's peroration on why she loved Lord Lufton:

> I'll tell you what he was: he has fine straight legs, and a smooth forehead, and a good-humoured eye, and white teeth. Was it possible to see such a catalogue of perfections and not fall down, stricken to the very bone? But it was not that that did it all, Fanny. I could have stood against that. I think I could at least. It was his title that killed me ... What is it that I feel, Fanny? Why am I so weak in the body that I cannot take exercise? Why can I not write two sentences together? Why should every mouthful that I eat stick in my throat? Oh, Fanny, is it his legs, think you, or his title?[19]

*   *   *

The impossibility of explaining love does not, however, mean that love is at war with reason. The error of associating passionate love with frenzy and madness, with irrationality, is exposed in the story of Alice Vavasour's difficulties (*Can You Forgive Her?*).

Her troubles might appear to be, as many have supposed, due to a struggle to give up romantic love for a prudent marriage. The difference between Alice's two suitors accords perfectly with the images that Plato has taught us to connect with reason and passion. John Grey was fair, elegant, and scholarly; lived quietly in the country, and could plead for the love of his life without a quiver in his voice. George Vavasour had all the traits of a romantic hereo: black hair, bright dark eyes, a black moustache and a scar that became livid when he was strongly moved, as he often was; throughout his life, he had tamed wild horses both literally and metaphorically; he embarked on a political career without means or patronage and of course as a Radical. Grey was regarded as a model of a gentleman and George was condemned as a reckless adventurer. George had been Alice's first love, but she had broken her engagement to him when she discovered that he was unfaithful to her. And when she became engaged to Grey, it was generally felt that she had wisely chosen safety.

But as Alice thought about her coming marriage, she found the idea increasingly distasteful: she would be reduced to an 'upper servant', immured on a dreary country estate with a dull, cold, tyrannical husband, with whom she would have nothing to talk about; she would have to pretend that she was made of 'milk and honey' when she was really a woman of 'fire', who ought to live on 'brandy' with a dashing knight who would brave any danger from 'Moscow to Malta'.[20] Her cousin, George Vavasour, appeared to be that dashing knight. The more she was told that he was reckless and dangerous and would leave her penniless, the more she was enchanted by the dream of saving him. To risk all in heroic service to George would mean a life of passion, freedom and action, such as Grey's estate in deadly Cambridgeshire could never provide. So Alice jilted Grey and became engaged again to George.

But the truth about Grey was very different from Alice's picture of him. Far from being a dessicated stick of a man he had unusual physical beauty – even Vavasour found him 'uncommonly handsome'; he was so strong and agile that when Vavasour attacked him Grey easily threw him down the stairs; and he was exceptionally lively and amusing. When Grey and Alice met, he behaved as a passionate lover should and at his touch, 'the fibres of her body had seemed to melt within her . . . so that she could have fallen at his feet'.[21] Instead of being tyrannical, Grey loved her, Trollope says, 'with the perfect love of equality', and took great care never to intrude on her – when she proposed suddenly to go to the Continent with George and his sister, he responded 'with a pleasant joke . . . abstaining even from expressing anything that might be taken as a permission on his part'. His love was so free of possessiveness that, even after she broke their engagement, he tried unobtrusively to protect her against Vavasour's villainy. Grey's estate was not grim and isolated but very pretty, within easy reach of Cambridge and Ely, possessed of one of the country's most distinguished and handsome private libraries and a glorious garden, and in any case, Alice had little use for London as she rarely and reluctantly went into society, took no interest in the shops, and disliked the noise and bustle. Conversation with Grey came easily and was nothing like the talk of a master to 'an upper servant' – he had discussed with her questions like 'the conduct of the Girondists at the time of Robespierre's triumph' and the fate of Rome.[22]

In short Alice had wholly deluded herself. She had translated Grey's self-sufficient life in the country into imprisonment, his forbearance into indifference, his compliance into conceit, his calmness into arrogance. And she was just as wrong about George. Far from being a bold hero, he was reckless, selfish, cowardly, indeed a villain, who wanted her money and had no thought for her. Worst of all, she had mistaken her own feelings. Whereas she longed for the physical presence of Grey, she found George repulsive: 'he had come to her and asked for a kiss, and she had shuddered before him, when he made the demand'.[23]

Alice had been misled by her romanticism. The essence of romanticism is summed up in George Vavasour's declaration that he would not climb the mountains that he saw in the distance because he cared too much about their beauty: 'In this world things are beautiful only because they are not quite seen, or not perfectly understood . . .'.[24] In the same spirit, Alice could find glory only in the unknown, and the greater the threat of danger, the more she was attracted because she associated clarity, calmness, and order with a lack of life, depth of feeling with turmoil and danger and delights that are present and secure with boredom. As a result, when she supposed herself to be reflecting carefully, she was in fact converting an entirely congenial reality into an illusion worthy of romantic agony, and the more she thought, the more she compounded her errors. Lady Glencora went to the heart of Alice's weakness when she said: 'I know that it is quite a misery to you that you should be made a happy woman of at last. I understand it all, my dear, and my heart bleeds for you.'[25] Nothing but Alice's romantic illusions prevented her from enjoying her true, passionate love for Grey.

*   *   *

The model of a true lover is a girl difficult to associate with either cold reason or desperate passion – the light-hearted Violet Effingham, who is beautiful, rich, and flirtatious. And her most persistent suitor is even further from the romantic ideal – Lord

Chiltern was red and scowling; while he pined, he hunted; in between hunts he proposed marriage to Violet, with a highly unpoetic bluntness, and each time that she refused him, he swore it was the last and then tried again (*Phineas Finn*).

The romantic dream of love made in heaven, to which there could be no alternative and which was impossible to resist, was firmly rejected by Violet. From the fact that she had known Lord Chiltern all her life, and that she had loved him as a child, nothing followed, she insisted, about whether she should marry him. When Chiltern charged her with reducing love to a matter of calculation, she agreed that it was ridiculous to calculate about love, but that did not dispose of the matter. She remembered perfectly the pleasures of the days when they had been playmates, but now that they were both grown up, things were different: 'These disagreeable realities of life grow upon one ...'. When told that she could save Chiltern from his bad ways by marrying him, Violet replied: 'I don't know that I have any special mission for saving young men. I sometimes think that I shall have quite enough to do to save myself.' That Chiltern was regarded as reckless and dangerous was a very good reason for not marrying him, even though she liked improper men. At no time did Violet see herself as a helpless victim of 'society', 'conventions', or even of her uncomprehending guardian. Madame Goesler described her as 'the most independent girl I ever knew in my life'.[26]

Every accused Violet of a different vice. Her friend, Lady Laura, charged her with a cowardly prudence that kept her from marrying the man she really loved; to her guardian, Lady Baldock, it was obvious that Violet would throw herself away on a boot-black, if not on a murderer; and Violent happily provided support for every accusation. When taxed with a plan to marry Lawrence Fitzgibbon, she explained 'that it was not quite settled; but that as I had only spoken to him once during the last two years, and then for not more than half a minute, and as I wasn't sure whether I knew him by sight, and as I had reason to suppose he didn't know my name, there might, perhaps, be a delay of a week or two before the thing came off'. She confessed that she flirted with many men, and liked some better than others. But that had nothing to do, she insisted, with wanting to marry him. Yet she also declared that 'a husband is very much like a house or horse. You don't take your house because it's the best house in the world, but because just then you want a house. You go and see a house, and if it's very nasty you don't take it. But if you think it will suit pretty well, and if you are tired of looking about for houses, you do take it. That's the way one buys one's horses, – and one's husbands.' It was not an exact description of how Violet thought about love but neither was it altogether beside the point.[27]

She had a very accurate understanding of all her suitors. Mr Appledon, she knew, dyed his whiskers and his love was a rural malady, against which he was proof while he remained among his clubs. She appreciated the liveliness and perfect manners of Phineas Finn, but she was also aware that she was just the heiress needed to put a poor man on his feet, and that he wore the bonds of love loosely. Nor did Violet ignore what was said to her by people like Lady Baldock. When Phineas requested that she try to love him, she told him, 'I wound try rather not to love you. Why should I try to do that which would displease everybody belonged to me?'[28] But when Lady Baldock warned her that Phineas was an adventurer, Violet replied – 'If Mr Finn asked me to marry him to-morrow, and if I liked him well enough, I would take him – even though he had been dug right out of a bog.'[29] And it was all perfectly consistent. Violet recognized in obligation to take into consideration the opinions of others, but insisted on deciding for herself how or whether they were to count, because she alone could know what another person meant to her.

When at last Violet decided that she would risk loving Chiltern, 'though the threatened evil might be fatal' – her decisive conduct after their engagement was entirely of a piece with her conduct beforehand. Their engagement was no sooner settled than they quarrelled and parted. To Lady Laura, Violet said that 'though they loved one another', they were 'not fit to be man and wife'. To Lady Baldock, Violet announced, with stunning effect, that she had given up Chiltern because he was 'too good' for her.[30] The truth was that Violet had considered it her duty and her privilege to tell Chiltern that he was wrong to remain idle. But if he had borne being told that his life was 'discreditable' without exploding, she would have felt that he was not worthy of her love. She was able to see both aspects of the event because, when she had accepted Chiltern, she had decided that she loved him complete with his ferocity.

The love of Violet Effingham could hardly be further from romanticism. She knew that she had kept her early feeling for

Chiltern. But her refusals were not due to wilfulness, indecisiveness or coyness. She distinguished between a disposition and a readiness to love.

This distinction is part of a gentleman's obligation to recognize what his inclinations are and to decide whether to encourage them. In doing so, he is not imposing the cold discipline of reason on the frenzy of passion, but teaching himself to respond to a particular experience in a different, preferable way. Governing a disposition to love is a choice about whether to become absorbed in one way of seeing another person. It does not exclude spontaneity and has nothing to do with repression because it is not like pulling the strings of a purse to shut in the disorder. It is an effort to interpret experience in one fashion rather than another and to find satisfaction in a different quarter. To say that one can and should govern one's love assumes that life is not a jigsaw puzzle, which can be solved only by finding the one right piece for each place, but a picture that can be made in a variety of ways. Concentrating so completely on a single piece as to lose sight of other possibilities shows a lack of both imagination and realism. That 'there are things that should not be thought of' is therefore a constant refrain in Trollope's novels and in connexion with all activities and being 'unable to help what one thinks' is a sign not of a passionate nature but of moral ignorance and weakness.

Violet Effingham's love is an enchantment without illusion, a rational passion. She had discovered in Chiltern something that was really there, even though she could not communicate what she saw to others. Her love takes its strength from her clarity of thought. But she never added up Chiltern's paroxysms, habits, promises and devotions. Just what the risk connected with loving Chiltern meant for her could neither be calculated by herself nor judged by others.

Not only her clear-headedness, but also her humour makes Violet a surprising romantic heroine. The commonplace, that nothing spoils a romance so much as a sense of humour in a woman, does not belong in the gentleman's world. Violet's humour springs from her seriousness. It expresses her awareness that everything in the human world can be seen from different standpoints, that each can render the other absurd, and that none of this makes everything absurd nor renders it impossible to stay with one's own standpoint and to enjoy the difficulties of doing so as part of the sport of living. Such an awareness is essential to a gentleman. In a less complete form, it may not take the shape of humour. His lack of humour reveals the flaw in Plantagenet Palliser, though his efforts to compensate for it make him heroic. In Violet, as in Madame Goesler, her humour is the mark of her sound good sense.

*   *   *

A man who cannot keep his thought straight cannot be a true lover. That is the moral of Phineas Finn's history (*Phineas Finn, Phineas Redux*).

Phineas was the son of an Irish doctor in modest circumstances. Though he had come to London to read for the bar, instead of going on to practise law, he was launched on a political career by patronage. To continue in politics, he had to acquire an income, either by becoming a member of the government or more secure-ly, by marrying an heiress. With this set of requirements, he made his way through four relationships that he called 'love'.

Before coming to London, he had thought of himself as being in love with Mary Flood Jones, and had spoken 'soft words' to her. But by the time that he returned to Killaloe, he had become an intimate of Lady Laura Standish, who had opened the way to a political career. Of course he told Mary about Lady Laura and there was nothing distinctly false in his account of her, but it represented his impression of Lady Laura at the moment rather better than what he had felt in London. There, Phineas had been struck by Lady Laura's stateliness; to Mary, though he dutifully made his bow to truth by declaring that Lady Laura was 'hand-some', he said that she looked 'six feet high' and had 'an appear-ance of power', hardly enhanced by 'lumpy hair', 'large hands' and a 'straggling figure'.[31] Back in Killaloe, he took and got a kiss from Mary as well as a lock of hair, and given all that had passed between them, Mary might reasonably have concluded that he was in love with her. But that was not how Phineas remembered Killaloe in London.

He often asked himself questions, as a gentleman should, about his feeling for Lady Laura and for Mary. But the asking was hardly of that searching kind with which the Duke of Omnium plagued himself, and the answering was even more casual.

Phineas supposed that 'he was in love with his darling little Mary, – after a fashion'. But he went on to tell himself that 'Of course, it could never come to anything, because of the circumstances of his life, which were so imperious to him.' About Lady Laura he was also of two minds: he was not in love with her 'and yet he hoped that his intimacy with her might come to much'. He had even wondered 'how he would feel when somebody else came to be really in love with Lady Laura . . . but this question he had never been able to answer'. The pertinent points were duly raised but, as soon as they threatened discomfort, dropped. If he could not marry 'his darling little Mary', why did he persist in thinking of her as 'his darling'? What were the 'imperious circumstances' that put marrying her out of the question? If he was not in love with Lady Laura, why was he wondering about her 'other lovers'? But instead of risking the discovery of disconcerting answers to such awkward questions, Phineas reflected that 'it was his fate to walk over volcanoes. "Of course, I shall be blown into atoms some fine day," he would say; "but, after all, that is better than being slowly boiled down into pulp." '[32]

The pattern of well-intentioned dishonesty is the same in Phineas's thinking about whether to take up a political career. When offered the chance to contest a seat, he had found it 'a beautiful dream, a grand idea . . .'. When his mentor in law, Mr Low, tried to persuade him to consider the drawbacks of entering politics without any independent resources, Phineas supposed that he was seriously weighing the alternatives. But he soon lost sight of Mr Low's uncomfortably convincing arguments by advancing to heroism: 'If he did this thing the probability was that he might become utterly a castaway, and go entirely to the dogs before he was thirty . . . But then, would it not be better to go to pieces early than never to carry and sail at all?' When, in order to make progress in his political career, Phineas was obliged to take further risks, he went so far as to recognize that, 'At every turn the chances would of course be very much against him; – ten to one against him.' But he soon moved on to telling himself that 'it was his lot in life to have to face such odds'. As his thinking proceeded, the drama deepened and 'He expected to be blown into fragments – to sheep-skinning in Australia, or packaging preserved meats on the plains of Paraguay', until he found for himself a glorious fate that was irresistible: 'But when the blowing into atoms should come, he was resolved that courage to bear the

ruin should not be wanting. Then he quoted a line or two of a
Latin poet, and felt himself to be comfortable'.[33]

Before long, Phineas succeeded in blending his reflections on
love with his reflections on politics to produce an even more
satisfactory conclusion. He began by thinking that if he followed
the advice of Mr Low, he 'must make up his mind never to see
Lady Laura Standish again'. But that, he discovered, was impossible because he was in love with her, and 'for aught he knew,
Lady Laura might be in love with him'. In this fashion, Phineas
persuaded himself that he was obliged to give up law for politics
in order to pursue his passion for Lady Laura. The romance was
fortified by another set of arguments in which the order of events
was given somewhat differently: 'Simply as an introduction into
official life nothing could be more conducive to chances of success
than a matrimonial alliance with Lady Laura. Not that he would
have thought of such a thing on that account! No; – he thought of
it because he loved her; honestly because he loved her . . . But,
loving her as he did, and resolving that in spite of all difficulties
she should become his wife, there could be no reason why he
should not, – on her account, as well as on his own, – take advantage of any circumstances that there might be in his favour.'[34]

There was no obvious fault in Phineas's behaviour, but he let
his thoughts run on a slack rein. When Mr Kennedy invited him
to join the party of distinguished politicians at Loughlinter, it
pleased Phineas to realize that Lady Laura had taken the trouble
to secure the invitation for him; then he moved on to noticing
that there was some mystery about why he should have been
invited; and finally he arrived at the encouraging discovery that
perhaps Lady Laura 'really loved him'. Any sensible observer
might have predicted that he would reach this conclusion, but to
Phineas it came as a surprise. Although Lady Laura had told
Phineas that her fortune was no greater than his, he assured
himself that he would work for both. He had no idea of how he
would do that, but her influence among politicians was not far
from his mind, and without much effort, all the reasons against
proposing marriage to Lady Laura were deftly wrapped away in
the thought 'that it was incumbent on him to persevere'. Who or
what made perseverance 'incumbent' was certainly very obscure,
but that did not trouble Phineas. Nor did he find it difficult to
dismiss the memory of the kiss exchanged and the lock of hair cut
in Killaloe, because he had forgotten it.[35]

Throughout all his earnest reflections about Lady Laura, Phineas never gave any serious consideration to her feelings. He sprang to the conclusion that she might marry him from a surmise about why he had been invited to Loughlinter. How that matched with what he knew about her fortune, her concern for her brother, whether her manner to him might not be compatible with a feeling very different from love, he never stopped to ask. Of course, when Lady Laura announced her engagement to Kennedy, Phineas was shocked. But it took him no time to discover a completely new set of truths: What a fool he had been to imagine 'that his poverty could stand a chance against the wealth of Loughlinter! ... How he wished that he were now grinding, hard at work in Mr Low's chambers, or sitting at home at Killaloe with the hand of that pretty little Irish girl within his own!'[36] It was a quick shift, but such changes were a frequent experience for Phineas.

Whereas before he had not been altogether certain of his passion for Lady Laura, now that he had lost her, his love was overwhelming. He meant every word when he said: 'It will weigh very heavily, but I will struggle hard that it may not crush me. I have loved you so dearly!' To complete the drama of their separation, he pleaded: 'As we are parting give me one kiss, that I may think of it and treasure it in my memory!' The possibility, that the woman who gave the kiss might treasure the memory more than he, never worried Phineas. No more now than before did he think seriously of how his words and actions might affect Lady Laura. He was 'of course' wretched, 'as wretched as a man can be; there were moments in which he thought that it would hardly become him to live unless he could do something to prevent the marriage of Lady Laura and Mr Kennedy'.[37] But in the midst of his unbearable distress, Phineas enjoyed the pleasure of recollecting that Lady Laura Standish, the daughter of the Earl of Brentford, had not been offended by his confession of love, that she had kissed him, and that probably her husband would not be told of that passage in their conversation. What Phineas regarded as his great anguish was really absorption in contemplating himself as the forlorn but not despised lover of a great lady.

As a disappointed lover, Phineas behaved with the same coarse blend of decency and thoughtlessness. He served Lady Laura faithfully as a friend, but he failed to notice how he hurt her when he confessed his love for Violet Effingham. He sincerely tried to heal the breach between Chiltern and his father that seemed to stand in the way of Chiltern's success with Violet, and did not try his own luck until Violet refused Chiltern for the third time. But he was not too distraught over Violet's refusal to enjoy the good repute of having been injured – not too seriously – in a duel with Chiltern.

When, upon returning to Killaloe after his disappointment over Violet Effingham, Mary Flood Jones kept aloof from him, it was 'a natural consequence of this', Trollope says, that Phineas should be 'more in love with her than ever'. He confided his woes to her, enjoyed her sympathy, and asked her to marry him. Of course he confessed that he had been 'inconstant' for he 'could not speak of a new passion' until he had at least 'told the story of that which has passed away'. But once he returned to London, Phineas enjoyed the idea of his 'passionate' proposal to Mary Flood Jones more than the prospect of marrying her. Besides, his impressionable mind was strongly affected by the perfection of Madame Goesler's drawing room. When, however, Madame Goesler offered to help him with money he refused, and when she offered herself to him, he found the strength to say: 'It cannot be . . .'. He could not betray an explicit promise.[38]

Phineas's conduct in love is of a piece with his conduct in politics. When Mr Monk came to Ireland, Phineas insisted on accompanying him to political meetings, and when Monk was acclaimed for advocating tenant-right, Phineas found it impossible to remain silent; in the excitement of speaking to an admiring audience, 'the old pleasures of the debating society' turned Phineas into a champion of Irish tenants and a rebel in his party. And just as easily the joys of rebellion wore off. By the time he returned to London, Phineas wished that he had been 'a little less in love with independence, a little quieter in his boastings that no official considerations should ever silence his tongue'. But once having declared himself, he remained true to his word when it came to voting and paying the price for doing so.[39]

Whether Phineas Finn is a gentleman is a nice question. Certainly he lacks the quality that distinguishes Madame Max and Plantagenet Palliser – a hard sense of how things are as opposed to how he would like them to be. He was not tormented by an instinct for facing the truth and accepting responsibility. Instead he regularly allowed himself to interpret people and events in a manner that lessened his responsibility for choosing. His memory suffered from convenient lapses and his imagination readily endowed questionable conduct with a distant glory. Though he often chose the riskier path, in both love and politics, it was hardly done with full awareness. He heedlessly let himself be drawn into a course of action until he found himself committed to what he had never before considered. Though his equanimity looks like fortitude, it sprang from a talent for avoiding discomfort, because whenever he set out to reflect on his conduct, Phineas had an instinct for dodging the nasty turns. In all these ways, Phineas lacks the qualities of a gentleman.

It is conceivable that someone who is not a gentleman might be a true lover. There is no doubt, for instance, that the bootmaker, Ontario Moggs, truly loved Polly Neefit (*Ralph the Heir*). Polly was not the best but the only possible girl for him and he remained faithful to her simply because he was incapable of being anything else. It is equally clear, however, that Moggs lacked the self-awareness of a gentleman, and that defect allowed him to combine a degree of fantasy about some aspects of his life with utter clarity in his love. But where there is greater self-consciousness, such a combination is more difficult. Because Phineas was more of a piece than Moggs, his lack of awareness about what he was doing was as marked in love as in politics. He could as easily love one pretty girl as another because in each he saw only another assortment of attractive qualities. That scrupulous sensitivity to the person before him that makes it impossible for a gentleman to be equally friendly with everyone was absent in Phineas. The only faithfulness of which he was capable depended on his feeling obliged to keep a promise. But faithfulness maintained by discipline betrays an incapacity to love. A deeper faithfulness was impossible for Phineas because, as Violet Effingham said, he lacked 'something in individuality' and was accordingly 'too much a friend to everybody'.[40] Phineas was both too little and too much of a gentleman to be a true lover.

What nevertheless keeps him within the fold of gentlemen is not just that he is incapable of breaking a promise, but that he is restrained by self-respect rather than fear of the consequences. For all his self deception, he knew what falseness was and abhorred it as such and not just because other people disapproved of deceit. And he was sufficiently conscious of his failings to recognize that there was something false in his position. Though his notion of truthfulness was hardly profound and often confused, an aspiration to be honest was steadily present to his mind. Though he regularly failed to notice how far he had strayed into dangerous territory, when he came to the boundary of decent conduct, he would not cross it even for something that he badly wanted. Phineas comes very close to the line that separates cads from gentlemen, but never crosses it because of his rightly motivated aversion to falsehood. When his susceptibility to influence and his good fortune enabled him to be guided by Madame Goesler, he was, as the end of his story shows, capable of learning to become more surely a gentleman.

*   *   *

Though a lover like Phineas cannot suffer real disappointment, true lovers can. The possibility of disappointment is intrinsic to love because it is, in a sense, an unconditional acceptance of what the beloved is. But what that acceptance implies is, for a gentleman, a complicated judgement.

A true lover who becomes inconsolable does not behave like a gentleman. Mr Gilmore (*The Vicar of Bullhampton*), who found it impossible to understand that love is not a reward for virtue, who persisted in his courtship to the point of persecution, and when disappointed became nearly insane, is a fallen gentleman rather than a heroic lover because he forgot that 'a man shouldn't stake his happiness on a thing beyond his reach'.[41] Yet some lovers in Trollope's gallery are all the more admirable for being ready to risk disappointment. It was entirely reasonable to Will Belton to persist in his suit, even though there was a great risk of disappointment, because he was a man who had the strength to bear it. Sir Roger Carbury (*The Way We Live Now*) is a model of a persistent and disappointed lover. He refused to retire from the field until Hetta had firmly engaged herself to marry another man, and although he then became 'what I suppose people call broken-hearted', in time he learned to acknowledge that he should never have allowed himself 'to get into such a frame of mind'. He remained devoted to Hetta but rearranged his ideas about how to find satisfaction in life: 'After all, though love is a wonderful incident in a man's life, it is not that only that he is here for. I have duties plainly marked out for me; and as I should never allow myself to be withdrawn from them by pleasure, so neither should I by sorrow.'[42] Those who play the tragic lover, far from being heroes, are condemned for indulging themselves with the pleasures of performing in a melodrama. To be able to conquer disappointment is a sign not of weak passion but of the strength that a gentleman ought to possess, what Trollope calls 'manliness'.

Though Trollope suggests that women are more disposed than men to love once and forever, he condemns 'dying for love' in women as much as in men. He is fairly harsh with Emily Hotspur (*Harry Hotspur*) and Emily Wharton (*The Prime Minister*) for finding it impossible to forget and to love again. Emily Hotspur is described as the victim of a spell – 'He was to her as a thing abominable, and yet necessarily tied to her by bonds which she could never burst asunder. She felt like some poor princess in a tale, married to an ogre from whom there was no escape.'[43] That she continued both to love and to despise, and died of grief, indicated not heroism but weakness. That Emily Lopez, after the death of her villainous husband found it impossible to think of marrying her former suitor is put down to an inability to admit that she had chosen the wrong man, and to recognize that 'there are passages in our life which one cannot forget, though we bury them in the deepest silence', but which need not therefore blacken all our lives.[44] The same point is made in *The Vicar of Bullhampton,* when Janet Fenwick writes to Mary Lowther: 'If you encourage yourself to feel that, because you have loved one man from whom you are necessarily parted, therefore you should never allow yourself to become attached to another, you will indeed be teaching yourself an evil lesson ... The Indian, indeed, allows herself to be burned through a false idea of personal devotion; and if that idea be false in a widow, how much falser is it in one who has never been a wife.' The argument in favour of forgetting and loving again is presented not as a counsel of prudence but virtue. To suppose that one can never love again is an 'evil lesson'.[45]

But on the other hand there is Lily Dale (*The Small House at Allington*), who never gave up her love for the man who jilted her, who refused her ever faithful suitor, Johnny Eames, and lived on happily without marrying. The last conversation between Lily Dale and Johnny Eames is a vignette of eternally constant lovers: 'I think, Johnny, you and I are alike in this, that when we have

loved we cannot bring ourselves to change. You will not change
... Nor can I ... I want nothing from him ... But I move
through my little world thinking of him, and I shall do so to the
end.' And yet Lily gets praise and affection from Trollope
because she had tried to love Johnny Eames and did not go about
draped in gloom. When the blow had first struck her, her friends
thought that she would never stand again, but less than a year
after her disaster, she was the brightest guest at a wedding:
'Though she was as a man whose right arm had been taken from
him in battle, still all the world had not gone with that right arm.
The bullet which had maimed her sorely had not touched her
life, and she scorned to go about the world complaining either by
word or look of the injury she had received ... So she resolved
that she would be happy, and I here declare that she not only
seemed to carry out her resolution, but that she did carry it out in
very truth.[46]

How disappointment should be borne cannot be prescribed.
That Lady Hartletop, in all the ugliness of her old age, retained
so strong a memory 'of those forty years' that she rushed to see the
Duke of Omnium before his death, was entirely to her credit. The
ability of Roger Carbury and Lily Dale and Johnny Eames to
remain unchanged in their love is undoubtedly something 'on
which our nature should pride itself'. An enduring attachment is
admirable. But the noble constancy of an Imogene must not be
confused with the destructive romanticism of a Juliet. There are
many different ways of loving and losing but none justifies
turning life into a tragedy. Here, as elsewhere, what matters is
recognizing that a mortal existence is a gift which men have a
duty to enjoy.

*   *   *

The pattern of marriage is no more uniform that that of
disappointed love. Lovers may sometimes dream that their
marriage was made in heaven and say that they have found their
second half. But such musings are not to be taken literally.
Husband and wife are neither halves of a whole, nor images of
one another.

Violet Effingham and Lord Chiltern are undoubtedly as true a pair of lovers as any to be seen in the world, but when we see them installed as an unusually happily married couple there is no suggestion that they have melted into one. Violet has not in the least come to share Chiltern's preoccupation with hunting. He is just as choleric as before and she just as unperturbed.

Although more profound differences divide the Rev. Josiah Crawley and his wife, they have a good claim to being considered the most touching pair of married lovers in literature. He was as trying a husband as a man can be without deliberately intending to be cruel – he subjected his family to severe and unnecessary hardships; he was often awkward and even harsh; and there is no doubt that his wife was driven nearly to distraction by his odd ways. Besides, Crawley was a man of intellectual distinction and serious scholarly interests which were foreign to Mrs Crawley. Nevertheless, there can be no doubt that 'As had regarded all the inner life of the man, – all that portion of his life which had not been passed in the pulpit or in pastoral teaching, – she had been crown, throne, and sceptre all in one.'[47] What is more, though she was not his intellectual mate, she understood what she described as the 'workings of his mind' better than he did himself. Her conviction that her husband could not be guilty of theft rested on her profound certainty about what he was capable of intending. This highly unromantic, and far from happy, couple have a profound communion that bears no resemblance to that of friends sharing common interests (*The Last Chronicle of Barset*).

Only in tyrannical marriages is the unity, so markedly absent from the life of the Chilterns and Crawleys, all too present. The tormenting efforts of Mrs Proudie to be bishop with her husband were, like the attempts of Mr Kennedy to turn Lady Laura into a strict and ascetic Christian like himself, inspired by a romantic ideal that requires husband and wife to be one in all that they think and do. When Trollope says that a woman thinks of a man as a 'staff to lean on' or that men know more about how to conduct worldly affairs, he is referring to a division of labour between men and women or to the peculiar reliance of lovers on one another; he is not saying that women are instruments for the service of men. Indeed the leaning is often in the other direction – Plantagenet Palliser became so dependent on Lady Glencora that life without her was unthinkable for him. Trollope sometimes also suggests that a good wife should be, as Plutarch said, a looking-glass to her husband's feelings – merry when the world is pleasant for him and sad when he sorrows. But Fanny Robarts is a good wife precisely because she does not always rejoice in what her husband finds pleasant. Archbishop Grantley and his wife are remarkably well matched but Mrs Grantley often persuades her husband to think differently, and it is plain that her husband had good reason to be, and was, grateful for it.

That two people be required to have the same interests, tastes, or occupations to live together harmoniously is regarded by gentlemen as both ridiculous and tyrannical. When Trollope speaks of a man and wife as becoming 'one flesh' or being of 'one mind', he means a much more abstract and profound sympathy than similarity of opinion or occupation. Such sympathy consists in being tuned to play in the same orchestra, not in striking the same notes.

*   *   *

There is a place, too, for marriages resting on a bond that only assumes the name of love. The marriage arranged for his daughter by the Dean of Brotherton (*Is He Popenjoy?*) was not a love match in the sense of the Chilterns. The Dean liked the idea of having his daughter marry someone as splendid as Lord George Germain, and recognized that his daughter's money and beauty would suit the lord. Though the daughter had pictured her knight somewhat differently, when her father made it clear that 'the great business of her life' was to fall in love with Lord George, she worked at it successfully. As a wife, too, she followed her father's sage advice to remember that a man might tell his wife he wished she were dead, and be restored to being a loving husband by a drop of magnesia in his beer. And the result was that apart from a brief difficulty, the two became truly devoted to one another, in the fashion of people with modest imaginations. Had they been compelled to blaze their own trials, they would have managed nothing better, possibly something worse, and certainly with considerably more labour and anguish.

Mrs Greenow's marriage to Captain Bellfield provides another variation in Trollope's gallery of married couples bound together by a feeling other than love. Mrs Greenow decided to marry the captain with a clear understanding of what she might expect of him:

Men and women ain't like lumps of sugar. They don't melt because the water is sometimes warm. ... He'll always be wanting my money, and, of course, he'll get more than he ought ... And he'll smoke too many cigars, and perhaps drink more brandy-and-water than he ought. And he'll be making eyes, too, at some of the girls who'll be fools enough to let him ... But, my dear, marriage is a comfortable thing. And then, though the Captain may be a little free. I don't doubt but what I shall get the upper hand with him at last. I shan't stop his cigars and brandy-and-water, you know. Why shouldn't a man smoke and have a glass, if he don't make a beast of himself? I like to see a man enjoy himself. And', she added, speaking tenderly of her absent lover, 'I do think he's fond to me, – I do, indeed ... Of course, I shan't let any of the money go into his hands, ... I know a trick worth two of that, my dear ...[48]

That Mrs Greenow managed the captain to the satisfaction of both seems certain.

There is even room for marriages which are a business arrangement. When Lord Fawn, who is typical of men who are unlikely to care about love, goes about getting married in a business-like way, he gets no reproof from Trollope. When he proposed to Lady Eustace, he spoke about love but both he and she understood perfectly well that the words indicated no more than a willingness to be a faithful and pleasant husband. It was that sort of love which means that husband and wife are careful of one another's interests and live in what amity is possible to them. Keeping to the bargain is of the essence of such a marriage, as of any contractual arrangement. And therefore Lord Fawn was in the end rightly persuaded that the evidence of Lizzie's dishonesty released him from his proposal.

But though it may be prudent to marry without love, there may also be too much thought of prudence. Lady Laura Standish (*Phineas Finn*) and Julia Brabazon (*The Claverings*) supposed that they were sacrificing passion for reason when they married. Lady Laura married Mr Kennedy in order to maintain her high position socially and politically and to find money for assisting her brother. Julia Brabazon married Lord Ongar for his money because she felt that she could not bear poverty. Both gave up the men they loved in the belief that they could do without love. But they misjudged themselves as they misjudged the men whom they married. In choosing what they took to be the 'prudent' way, they committed the gross imprudence of failing to recognize that they were people who could not be content with a marriage of convenience.

Co-habitation without marriage is not unthinkable. Paul Carbury (*The Way We Live Now*) and John Caldigate (*John Caldigate*) lived with a woman as man and wife without being married. In both cases, it was outside of England – in the far West of the US, and in Australia – and the women were accustomed to such relationships. Reasonable people did not share the outrage of prigs and saints at the thought of such a liaison. The rules that govern the relations between men and women are conventional rather than sacred.

Frivolous love-making, in the sense of flirting, is also permissible. But the players must be quite sure that they have the strength to keep a proper control over their hearts so as not to attempt to do what is beyond them, and they must take care to notice as well whether the other players are equally fit for the game. Trollope recognizes, too, that there is likely to be a special quality about the friendship of a man and woman because of their sexuality. All those possibilities are treated as part of the joys of life for which we should be grateful.

About a love such as that of Anna Karenina and Vronsky, there is nothing in Trollope's novels. But had he written it, his stress would have fallen on how Anna and Vronsky came to indulge in a love which they were incapable of bringing to life. He would have said more about Vronsky's heedlessness in seducing Anna and more also about how he changed from a fashionable gallant into a true lover. He would have told us just how Anna came to marry a man so alien to her as Karenin and the connexion of that blindness with her subsequent conduct, how she managed to remain for so long unaware of her feeling for Vronsky and why she failed to guard herself against it, how she allowed herself to dodge serious thought about the possibility of divorce and the fate of her child, how she failed to think about what Vronsky would do with himself and succeeded in deluding herself into believing that she could compel conventional people to accept her status, and why she could not resign herself to the fate that she had chosen. In short, whereas for Tolstoy, Anna's self-destruction is the inevitable consequence of violating the laws of God and man, what matters from the standpoint of a gentleman is the indifference to knowing herself and others and her unwillingness to recognize the constraints of a mortal life that led her first to marry where she could not love, then to break her marriage vows, and finally to pervert her love into an obsession.

The fact that a variety of relationships is acceptable to gentlemen does not reflect either confusion or the absence of a sharp line between right and wrong. It shows rather that the gentleman's world is not governed by a 'code' which automatically tells one to do this and not that. There are conventions, which provide rituals for certain situations, but the precise meaning of any action depends on who is performing it, under what circumstances, with what tone of voice and turn of phrase. Some may be too obtuse to recognize that; others may be ready to exploit such obtuseness; but those who do either cannot qualify as gentleman.

*   *   *

Some things, however, are unequivocally ruled out. Gentlemen may not behave like alley cats. The notion that human sexuality is a 'natural drive', which demands satisfaction that can only be denied by repression, has no more place in the gentleman's world than the notion that men have a natural need to commit violence. What human beings feel inclined to do is taken to depend on what they have learned, and how they respond to their inclinations is regarded as a choice that might be other than it is. Sexuality may not be divorced from respect for personality.

Nor is it ever permissible to deceive oneself or others about the character of a relationship or to forget its connexion to the whole of the personalities involved. The less noticeable such exploitation or heedlessness, the worse it is. Love-making such as that of Colonel Osborne (*He Knew He Was Right*) is intolerable. The colonel was a member of parliament, a man of fortune and highly cultivated tastes. There was nothing 'fiendish in his nature' and he was not 'a ravening wolf going about seeking whom he might devour'. But he liked the pleasant things of this world – books, pictures, china, and in the same way he liked collecting pretty and clever women. When, for the moment, he found no woman 'so pleasantly pretty' and so 'agreeably clever' as Emily Trevelyan, he found excuses to visit the Trevelyans frequently, wrote business-like notes to Emily with hints of a special tenderness, encouraged little secrets between them, pressed her hand warmly and pronounced her name tenderly, in short, indulged in all the gestures that intimate love without having any intention or even disposition to love.[49] He is the sort of man whom Trollope condemns when he contrasts the 'downright honest love' in *Framley Parsonage* to relationships in which the lady is 'too ethereal to be fond of a man' and the man has an inclination 'to pay a certain price and no more for a pretty toy'.[50] Colonel Osborne is neither light-hearted nor passionate, but a parody of both because he plays at love. And there is no more or less excuse for the female of the species, Mrs Adelaide Houghton (*Is He Popenjoy?*), who worked to confuse Lord George into believing that they were in love just for the pleasure of seeing the fish rise to the bait.

But if some kinds of behaviour are always wrong, just what conduct is required by respect for personality in a sexual relationship is not obvious. It certainly will be different from what is required in commercial dealings, because what respect for personality entails varies with the character of the relationship, yet it cannot be deduced from any first principles. To answer such questions, a gentleman relies on the traditional insights of his community. His conception of tradition is, however, highly complicated. It requires recognizing that traditional ways of doing things can be violated without causing the heavens to fall, that conforming to them need not produce a rigid uniformity, and that nevertheless, although the human world is wholly distinct from the natural world, tradition is a second 'nature'. How all this should and can be acknowledged at once is illustrated in Trollope's treatment of the condition of women.

He firmly rejected the view that women have a natural obligation to be more chaste than men. In the story of the miller's daughter (*The Vicar of Bullhampton*) who, when seduced by a ruffian, found that she liked it, Trollope roundly denounces the injustice of blaming the girl but not the man, and he regularly dismisses the notion that a man who trifles with a girl's affections may be excused because 'men are not like women'.

Nevertheless, Trollope also says that women have to govern themselves more carefully than men because they are more vulnerable to disappointment. This is partly because, in the society that he describes, the explicit proposal is expected to come from the man, and whereas he may repeat his suit, she can only wait. It is due also to the difference in the occupations of men and women. Whereas a man can hunt, dine at his club, fill his life with 'rough work' which can 'rub away' the affliction of disappointed love, the woman has quiet, solitary occupations that leave her all too free to dwell on what she has lost and to feel like 'a thing broken, a fragment of humanity . . . never to be used'. But that is not the whole story.[51]

The expectation that men speak first may also make things easier for women by providing a clear signal of where they stand; a man also exposes himself to disappointment when he speaks without having been given reason to believe that his words will be welcome; the speech of the man may have been contrived by the woman in all but utterance; generally, lovers have come to an understanding which the words only serve to make formal and public; a woman may choose to behave unconventionally – Madame Goesler's offer of her hand and fortune to Phineas is treated as a display of the discernment and courage that makes her such a perfect lady. Nor is it always the woman who finds it more difficult to bear disappointment. When Mary Lowther's engagement to Captain Marrable was broken, things went more easily for him than for her because he went out into the world. But whereas, in time, she 'resolved that she would not be lugubrious' and recovered her self-possession, the man whom she had refused, who had endless rough work on his estates to occupy him, nearly lost his wits.[51]

In short, traditional constraints do not operate in any simple uniform fashion. A great deal depends on how people choose to observe them. What makes life difficult for women, Trollope points out, is not the expectation that they should marry, but the pretence that they are indifferent to finding a husband. In any case, he emphasizes, men also have good reason to seek marriage. Indeed feminists would do better, he tells them, to remind men of the joys that they miss without a wife and family than to urge women to look for new careers.

In all of this, Trollope walks a fine line between denying and asserting that the traditional distinctions between men and women reflect a natural order. He does not dismiss constitutional differences between the sexes as irrelevant for how they should make their lives and he frequently remarks on what is foreign or native to 'a woman's nature'. Yet many of his men and women do not conform to a generic division, and they are not presented as either monstrous or deplorable. In this as in other respects, Trollope accepts what has long been the way of doing things as somehow 'natural' without inquiring too closely into what that means or forbidding departures from it. Anyone who makes a dogma of either is condemned for the sin of pride, because he is attempting to know and decide more than any man should. If a judicious individual prefers an unusual mode of life and can manage it without becoming a hermit or a rebel, there is no reason to condemn him, and there might be good reason to admire his independence.

But if common preferences should not be elevated into a universal law, neither should eccentrics try to impose their innovations on everyone else. The serious Flaw in a feminist like Miss Petrie (*He Knew He Was Right*) is her certainty that she knows how to put the world right: 'Wallachia Petrie, in her heart of hearts, conceived that she had fairly discussed her great projects from year to year with indomitable eloquence and unanswerable truth, – and that none of her opponents had had a leg to stand upon.' One 'fatal triumph of a lecture on the joint rights of men and women' had rendered her 'unfit for ordinary society'.[53] Of course, changes are bound to be made. But changes that come as the result of choices made by people going their own ways are a very different matter from remaking the world to fit the dreams of a Miss Wallachia Petrie.

Miss Petrie's doctrinal opposition to marriage is silly. But it is true that women can live very satisfactorily without marrying. Lily Dale is one example, and Mary Lowther's aunt, Miss Marrable, (*The Vicar of Bullhampton*) is another. At seventy, Miss Marrable had never known a day's illness; she was 'very pretty, quite a woman to look at with pleasure'; and far from being dry or narrow in outlook, she was a great reader – 'Pope, Dryden, Swift, Cowley, Fielding, Richardson, and Goldsmith, were her authors ... It is certain that she had Smollett's novels in a cupboard up-stairs, and it was said that she had been found reading one of Wycherley's plays.' So well satisfied with her fate was Miss Marrable, that, although she very much wanted Mary to become the wife of Gilmore, she insisted that it was better to remain unmarried than to acquire a husband who was 'not fitting'.[54] Miss Stanbury (*He Knew He Was Right*), who had once been engaged to marry, continued to wonder whether the joys and risks of married life were better than the safety of spinsterhood in which she has found contentment. But other women, like Priscilla Stanbury, feel sure that they are not suited to being a wife: 'I should make any man wretched, and any man would make me wretched.'[55] Why women should differ in this fashion is a mystery, but no more so than that there should be men who prefer to live alone. There is no single 'healthy' pattern for all human beings from which deviation signifies inferiority or misery.

Women who desperately pursue marriage as the only way to survive are portrayed not as victims but as mean-minded, ruthless exploiters. The same poverty of mind, that made it impossible for Georgina Longestaffe (*The Way We Live Now*) to imagine that, even though she cared nothing for love, others might, led her to think that without marriage she was lost. Trollope leaves us in no doubt about the baseness of her attitude: 'That ultimate failure in her matrimonial projects would be the same as drowning she never for a moment doubted. It had never occurred to her to consider with equanimity the prospect of living as an old maid. It was beyond the scope of her mind to contemplate the chances of a life in which marriage might be well if it came, but in which unmarried tranquillity might also be well should that be her lot. Nor could she understand that others should contemplate it for her.'[56] Lady Arabella Trefoil (*The American Senator*), for whom trying to making a good marriage had become a martial campaign in which she was perpetually engaged, is treated with contempt. Everything about her is shown to be false: in describing her carriage, Trollope does not say that she moved gracefully but that 'she never allowed an awkward movement to escape from her'; to believe even in friendship or trust was beyond her; only for a moment, when the man, who had behaved magnanimously to her and whom she had treated shamelessly, lay dying, was she brought 'back to humanity'.[57]

The twisted view of the world that prevented Lady Arabella and Georgina Longestaffe from seeing any alternative to marrying is explored more fully in the story of Lady Carbury (*The Way We Live Now*). Despite her own disastrous marriage for money, Lady Carbury remained convinced that 'a woman . . . if she were unfortunate enough to be a lady without wealth of her own, must give up everything, her body, her heart, – her very soul . . . to the procuring of a fitting maintenance for herself'.[58] But Lady Carbury's talk about the helplessness of women is blatantly contradicted by her success in making a career for herself as a writer.

She was in difficulty only because, in her blind devotion to her son, she had allowed him to impoverish her. And when a man who was truly devoted to her offered to remove her troubles by marrying her, she found it difficult to believe him.

The ability to recognize that marriage is not the only recourse for a woman, however poor or gentle, is one of Trollope's tests of a lady. Grace Crawley, Lucy Robarts, Lucy Morris, Mary Thorne, Mary Bonner, Mary Lowther, are all penniless, welcome the prospect of marrying a man whom they love, and are not immune to the comforts of money and rank. But when they suspected that their lovers might prefer to be released from their vows, they not only volunteered to do so but took care to do it in a manner that allowed him to escape without discomfort. Lady Mabel Grex (*The Duke's Children*) is the most striking refutation of the notion that gentle women are driven into marriage by their circumstances. She suffered from a most inconvenient combination of high rank, no money, and a taste for luxury, and renounced the man whom she loved because she could not bear living on what he earned. She succeeded in getting a proposal from the duke's heir, whom everyone wanted her to marry and of whom she was very fond. But though he believed himself to be in love with her, she rejected him in order to give him a chance to learn his own heart. And then, bitter as she felt about the bleak prospects before her, after she had reduced the duke's son to remorse for not having offered his hand again, she had the generosity to relieve his distress by confessing that she had never loved him.

What distingishes the true ladies from their false counterparts is nothing very lofty. There are neither saintly nor ascetic. They simply refuse to consider any one satisfaction essential to their lives. Ladies do not think of themselves as helpless victims when they cannot have what they want. And they do not feel compelled to follow any one pattern. Traditional ways of doing things offer a clearly marked trail to follow. But wandering off is not impossible, though it may be perilous, and even those who keep to the trail can walk in different ways.

*   *   *

In love as in other pursuits, both their circumstances and the people among whom they live, with all their convictions and expectations, are a reality to which gentlemen feel obliged to accommodate. And yet, as love is so utterly private, others cannot know what lovers should or should not risk for their love. How then can we tell whether lovers who insist on going their own way are justified or are being unreasonable? Or to put it another way, how do we distinguish the steadfastness of a gentleman from an unfitting intransigence? And this question, pushed further, becomes a question about how to distinguish between sanity and madness. Is the madman called so only because he refuses to conform to what others believe and expect of him, or can he be distinguished objectively from the rebel, the eccentric, the man of unusual individuality? Is a man of staunch individuality obliged to deny that anyone can judge another to be mad? These questions are explored in *He Knew He Was Right* where Trollope drew a rich assortment of characters whose refusals to yield to the opinion of others range from steadfastness, through several varieties of obstinacy, to madness.

If a gentleman's steadfastness consisted merely in refusing to change his opinions to agree with prevailing beliefs, Miss Jemima Stanbury would be the model of it. She had a great collection of convictions which had remained unaltered at least since her 'twenties and had put her at odds with almost everyone. She knew that a girl who wore false hair was no better than a slut; that afternoon tea was a bad thing but tea and buttered toast at half-past eight in the evening splendid; that port cured everything, but that sherry was dangerous; that the Church of England began to decline when it substituted rents for tithes; that it was useless to post a letter in the new pillar boxes (introduced by Trollope's reform of the postal system); that a penny newspaper was incendiary and could not possibly be a steady course of income. She had fought and quarrelled for all her convictions, and there was a number of people with whom she would not speak only because they were related to others with whom she had quarrelled. Far from holding up Miss Stanbury as a model of steadfastness, Trollope describes her as 'ignorant, prejudiced, and passionate'. But she is undoubtedly sane.

The most obvious sign of her sanity is her ability to acknowledge that others disagreed with her, and to change her mind. Her maid could contradict Miss Stanbury without giving offence, and was even invited to do so. When Miss Stanbury received a strong letter refuting her charges against her niece, her 'imagination painted to her' all that the girl had suffered and she altered her opinion, and when her niece decided to marry the man who had been forbidden to her, Miss Stanbury came to recognize that this was a matter on which she had no right to demand obedience.[59] By the end of her life, Miss Stanbury had eaten a great many of her words and become reconciled with her greatest enemy. What made this possible was that, for all her stubbornness, Miss Stanbury never slipped into thinking that her believing something to be true made it so. Because she recognized that her thought ought to conform to some objective order which was not subject to her will, she could be brought to acknowledge a mistake. Moreover, though she was headstrong, her mistakes were not mere acts of wilfulness – they belonged to a coherent outlook. And consequently, though her ideas were odd, her responses were consistent and she never ceased to notice and consider the effect of what she did both on herself and on others. These are the traits of sanity.

How their absence produces a state of mind fundamentally different from extreme obstinacy, Trollope shows in the story of Louis Trevelyan. The quarrel with his wife that ended in his madness began with a request that Colonel Osborne should visit his wife less often, which was reasonable because everyone but Mrs Trevelyan knew that the Colonel was an 'ancient Lothario'. But in his manner of speaking about the matter to his wife, Trevelyan suggested much more anger than was warranted or felt, and insulted her. He was so well aware of having done so that immediately afterwards, 'he almost made up his mind to go up-stairs and to apologize'. Nevertheless, he kept putting off the apology, and the longer he put it off, the more difficult it became for him. So the disastrous quarrel began.

Though at first Trevelyan 'was quite sure' that his wife was innocent, and told himself that he was not in the least jealous and that any such feeling 'would be a monstrous injury' to her, he continued to dwell on such feelings. He ordered his wife both to see and not to see the Colonel and his behaviour became so erratic that it was impossible for her to discover what he wanted her to do. But with each shift, he came to feel his sense of wrong more strongly. He moved from believing that his wife had been imprudent to believing that she had committed some grievous fault for which she ought to apologize, though what the fault was he could not say. In this frame of mind, he broke up their home.

Everyone whom Trevelyan had previously regarded as a friend and mentor told him that he was wrong. But in asking for advice, he wanted only to be 'encouraged . . . to do that which he was resolved to do on his own judgment'.[60] He listened only to his hired detective whose every characteristic offended Trevelyan's sense of decency, and who told him only what he wanted to hear. Whereas at the beginning, Trevelyan had considered it his duty to apologize, he moved on to discovering a duty 'to be firm'. Whereas before he had acknowledged that his words had been too strong, now he hardly recognized the force of the language which he used to his wife. Everywhere he saw slights and injuries and became a hunted man. Though his wife wrote him a plain letter declaring her innocence and enclosed all her correspondence with Colonel Osborne, though she wrote entirely in a tone of supplication and offered to do whatever he ordered, Trevelyan became convinced that he had received proof of his wife's guilt, and all of his efforts were directed to making his condition more wretched.

He settled in an isolated house in Italy, and demanded that his son be sent to him. If the boy cried, Trevelyan knew at once that his wife had deliberately taught their son to hate him. He was full of pity for himself, prayed that his wife might not descend into utter depravity, yet rather hoped that she would. Of any responsibility for what happened, he wholly absolved himself. The recent events of his life were described by him 'as though they had been governed by an inexorable Fate which had utterly destroyed his happiness without any fault on his part.' He saw himself as a helpless victim of malign forces.

Inconsistency pervaded his life. He was miserable and dirty, but dressed in elaborate, gaudy clothes, quite unlike what, in happier times, he had thought appropriate to himself. He made a great pretence at nonchalance but 'the affected air of ease, the would-be cynicism, and the pretence of false motives, all told the same story'.[61] He kept longing to be reunited with his wife, but every action that he took was designed to keep them apart. In short, he was as much at war with himself as with the rest of the world. The only thing that remained steady in his life was the conviction that he had always been right.

Trevelyan's madness consists in his incapacity to consider whether what he believed might be wrong, and to judge consistently by some objective standard. Such a standard might be

found in the opinions of a few or many people, in some immediate experience such as reading the words on a page, or in the
absence of contradictions in one's thinking. What matters is that
there should be some criterion for the rightness of one's opinions
which cannot be changed at will. Miss Stanbury often refused to
consider evidence against her prejudices, but as she did not re-
construct everything that was presented to her into a confirmation of them and as she preserved consistency, it was possible to
get along with her by accepting certain conditions. Therefore,
demanding as she was, those who lived with her were not compelled to become slaves to her whims. But slavery was what Trevelyan demanded. His fixed idea was in essence a demand for
unlimited submission.

His intelligence was exercised solely on constructing justifications for whatever he did. In the false justifications he found a
sanction for wilder behaviour. And his increasingly outrageous
behaviour inspired ever more fantastic justifications. Since the
trivial folly, which he at first supposed his wife to have committed, could not justify his intransigence, he came to believe
that his wife had done something which did justify him. So his
bubble grew and he became entirely enclosed in the fantasies that
he constructed. It is not the fixity of Trevelyan's intransigence
that makes it mad, but the way in which his intransigence affected the rest of his thinking, the fact that it deprived him of
anything fixed by which to steer himself.

How the genuine steadfastness of a gentleman makes him both
more firm and more adaptable is illustrated in the perfect antipode to Louis Trevelyan, his wife's sister, Nora Rowley. She had
made it the rule of her life that she would not marry a man without means. That was the only sensible course, she believed, because 'the lot of a woman . . . was wretched, unfortunate, almost
degrading. For a woman such as herself there was no path open to
her energy, other than that of getting a husband.' Nevertheless,
Nora twice refused the heir to a great title and fortune even
though she found him highly congenial; and then, against opposition from her sister and parents, she married a journalist
whose income was small and precarious and whose occupation
was hardly respectable. Although Nora totally reversed herself,
Trollope asks us to believe that she was 'like a rock; – nothing can
move her'.[62]

What explains Trollope's judgement is the manner in which

Nora arrived at the change in her views. It was due partly to her coming to know herself better, and partly to her learning from new experience. In her sister's misfortune, Nora saw how a marriage that seemed to be entirely free of risk produced the utmost wretchedness; as a result of being forced to live in straitened circumstances by the Trevelyans' separation, she had discovered that doing without luxury was not so unthinkable as she had supposed. She did not change her attitude to marriage in the romanticist manner of Alice Vavasour but slowly connected one revised idea with another. That she felt a twinge of regret, when shortly before her marriage she saw her rejected suitor in his full glory on his estate, indicates that she had not deluded herself by just repressing her desire for grandeur. Nora could acknowledge even his many virtues as well as that she regretted the absence of luxuries that she liked without wavering in her decision because her conversion had been genuine.

The final proof of how genuinely independent was Nora's intransigence is that she ceased to think of herself as a victim, as an instance of a class of women all doomed to the same unhappy fate. Though she had witnessed and suffered from the tyranny of Trevelyan, far from concluding that men 'always marry to get a slave',[63] she saw that Hugh Stanbury was not to be confounded with Trevelyan. Instead she felt that it had been given to her 'to choose' and she took pride in having chosen 'to make shirts and hem towels for her husband if he required it'.[64] Because she had come to be aware of possibilities that she had earlier been unable to see, she enjoyed a new sense of independence that came of recognizing that she was responsible for how she lived and that she could do so in more than one way.

Her ability to stay with her determination to marry the man she loved went hand in hand with flexible responses in other questions. To different people, on different matters, Nora acknowledged a different sort of obligation. When her sister and her aunt tried to prevent her from writing to Stanbury, she denied their right to do so. But she agreed that Stanbury should not visit her while she was staying in her aunt's house. When her father was outraged by her engagement, she acknowledged her parents' authority over her and felt obliged to make every effort to get their consent. But if she could not do so before they left England, she proposed to marry without their approval because, 'There is a time when a girl must be supposed to know what is best for herself just as there is for a man.[65] Whereas Trevelyan could see only a simple choice between having his way and yielding, Nora commanded a finely modulated range of responses and therefore could be both steadfast and accommodating.

But if Nora Rowley's decision to marry Hugh Stanbury was a thoroughly considered judgement, why does Trollope describe her decision as a 'leap in the dark' which is at odds with 'a sterner prudence'? The answer is that the 'sterner prudence' which Nora and Hugh ignore is not identical with true prudence. Their decision to risk 'love in a cottage' was a 'leap in the dark' because love eludes explanation in words. Neither the recognition that constitutes love nor the lovers' capacity to endure hardships can be assessed by others. But this does not absolve lovers from distinguishing truth and falsehood, right and wrong, more and less important considerations. Even if lovers choose to ignore the conventional wisdom of 'sterner prudence', still they are making a rational judgement.[66] In love, as in other things, it is impossible to arrive at perfectly comfortable and indisputable answers. Gentlemen do not convert this uncertainty into an excuse for yielding to illusion or obsession. They can love and remain self-possessed.

10 Ambition

The desire to get ahead or what is called, ambition, is supposed to be the motor of civilization. But there has always been disagreement about whether it should be deplored or admired. The issue has been put in many different ways – whether it is nobler to sit and dream under an olive tree or to go out to conquer the world; whether the practical statesman or the contemplative philosopher is superior; whether it is better to emulate the merchant's opulence or the friar's poverty. Most recently, the argument about ambition has taken the shape of a dispute about competitiveness and equality, about whether men should strive for a larger share of good things or should consider it wicked to seek eminence over others. And in all ages, the argument about ambition has appeared as an exhortation to give up 'materialism' for a higher 'spirituality'.

These different attitudes to ambition are reflected in its two opposed meanings. One, derived from the Latin word, associates it with canvassing for votes and therefore, servility, and the other with a lofty love of honour, a selfless passion for doing something grand. Both these meanings accord with the attitude to worldly success implicit in the morality of the self-divided man according to which a concern with anything so material as money must be base, and only the pursuit of some object beyond the human world can be truly noble. From this it follows that the man whose ambition takes the form of 'idealism', who attempts to transcend ordinary human desires to do what others say is impossible, is an admirable hero even if he fails, while an ambition which takes careful account of what is possible in this world should be despised.

The stereotype of a gentleman rules out for him ambition in its worldly sense either because a gentleman is supposed to have everything that he could want or would not dirty his hands with money or effort. That Trollope denies this is clear. There is no end of talk about money in his novels, and not least among landed gentlemen and clergymen: Squire Gresham is preoccupied with money; Archdeacon Grantley knows, down to the last penny, the value of everything that he owns; money is ever-present in both the Crawley and Robarts households. Sermons on the dangers of falling into debt are a regular feature. And any doubts about whether the prominence given to money in the novels should be taken seriously are disposed of by Trollope's tart denunciation, in the *Autobiography,* of that 'high-flown doctrine of the contempt of money'.[1] He himself never admired it, Trollope declares, and he goes out of his way to insist that whether men are doctors or clergymen, artists or authors, they may 'without disgrace follow the bent of human nature, and endeavour to fill their bellies and clothe their backs, and also those of their wives and children as comfortably as they can ... They may be as rationally realistic as the butchers and bakers ...' It is all very well, he says, for clergymen to preach against the love of money, but they must know that it is 'so distinctive a characteristic of humanity that such sermons are mere platitudes called for by customary, but unintelligent, piety'.[2]

Not only money, but reputation, too, is a reasonable object to pursue. Trollope did not hesitate to declare his own ambition to stand well in the eyes of others: 'I have certainly always had also before my eyes the charms of reputation. Over and above the money view of the question, I wished from the beginning to be something more than a clerk in the Post Office. To be known as somebody – to be Anthony Trollope if it be no more – is to be much. The feeling is a very general one ... It is that which has been called the "last infirmity of the noble mind". The infirmity is so human that the man who lacks it is either above or below humanity.'[3]

The difficulty about Trollope's attitude to ambition comes of his seeming to make just as strong a case for the other side. Men like John Grey or Sir Roger Carbury, who prefer to live quietly in the country, and care neither for money or fame, are presented as admirable; fortune hunting is as certainly condemned; and *The Way We Live Now* is supposed to be a sustained attack on the pursuit of money and advancement. Indeed the novel has often been cited as a resounding denunciation of Victorian capitalism and the rewards it gave to people who strive for material success. Nor can it be denied that the hero of the novel, Mr Melmotte, who came from no one knew where and engaged in financial swindles on a worldwide scale, is presented as a far from noble character, as are those who become connected with him in the hope of making their fortunes.

But there is no contradiction between Trollope's remarks in his *Autobiography* and his judgements in *The Way We Live Now*. For he does not attribute Melmotte's corruption to his pursuit of worldly success or money.

We meet the great swindler at his first ball. Melmotte's house in Grosvenor Square had been wholly reconstructed in just the way that Plantagenet Palliser called 'vulgar'. Everything had been made to look like something else. Not only the furnishings, but also the guests had been bought for the occasion. The guest of honour was not known to the host, nor was the host permitted to meet his royal purchase during the party. It had all been arranged by Melmotte's impoverished aristocratic servitor who distributed his money and despised him for it. Melmotte's progress proceeded so rapidly that at his next ball, his guest of honour was the Emperor of China and the host was seen to address some words to the 'brother of the Sun' as he balanced his chopsticks. This time the guests, instead of being bought, had scrambled to pay for invitations. Melmotte no longer felt that he had to depend on his daughter's marriage to rise but hoped to become a Member of Parliament and to receive a baronetcy.

The 'world at large,' as Trollope puts it, knew that Melmotte was a great man and had unlimited money at his disposal. But just who knew what was by no means clear. The shareholders in Melmotte's enterprises kept asking one another, without finding any answers, what they owned or might expect to gain. Melmotte's wife and daughter, who were not perfectly certain that they were wife and daughter, knew only that their fortunes seemed to go up and down with great suddenness. Indeed, the great man himself did not know on what ledge in the world he was perched. For the facts were that he had bought houses that he had not been able to pay for and had mortgaged them in order to meet other debts, had forged a signature, and might, at any moment, be ruined financially and convicted of a serious crime.

Although Melmotte used everyone around him, Trollope does not speak of the wrong that Melmotte does to others, or show us anyone whom Melmotte destroys. On the contrary, there are suggestions that his swindles may have brought wealth to many others besides himself, and we are encouraged to believe that his wife and daughter would otherwise have lived less comfortably and are not much affected by his occasional roughness to them. The emphasis falls on Melmotte's unlimited confidence in his own will, on how nothing could discourage or frighten him. He had been jailed in Hamburg for fraud and had come out without a penny, but had risen again to be a member of the British Parliament. When he knew that everything was collapsing under him, he could brazen out the most uncomfortable questions and still smile. When he was nearly certain that he was ruined and had publicly lost control of himself, when damaging and true rumours about him were circulating in the City, he still moved among the electors in Covent Garden as if nothing were wrong and gave, on the spur of the moment, the only successful speech of his life. Even when he was alone, burning incriminating papers behind locked doors, he remained fully armed, taking care not to 'betray himself by the working of a single muscle, or the loss of a drop of blood from his heart'. Whatever had to be done, he could do without 'a sign of shrinking', remaining throughout 'the blandly triumphant Merchant Prince'.[4] But though Melmotte's self-control is real, it is not the courage that it seems to be.

Of some things that he did, Melmotte had a perfectly clear understanding. In his head, he kept an account book where all his transactions were recorded with complete accuracy down to the pennies he had given last Tuesday to the crossing-sweeper. He knew precisely what he owed and had not paid to the Longestaffes for the purchase of their house. He knew that he was sailing very close to the wind, and he kept a safe store to protect himself in case of a fall. He was even able to recognize that he had been too arrogant, and would have done better to bind people to him 'by a feeling of kindness as well as by his money'.[5] In all these ways, Melmotte's sense of reality was sound. What was missing was something subtler and more profound.

When it came to the purpose of his operations, this sense of reality deserted him. It was a great thing, he felt, to entertain a Chinese Emperor. After the party was over, Melmotte sat 'looking out on his own magnificent suite of rooms from the armchair which had been consecrated by the use of an Emperor,' and told himself that whatever happened to him, 'the grand dinner which he had given before he was put into prison would live in history'. But he had not intended to make his name 'live in history'.[6] It had all happened without his having meant to play so high a game.

He had started with a dim sense that having been born in a gutter, without father or mother to look after him, it was a good thing to rise and to go on rising. At first, a titled son-in-law seemed to be his object. Having heard that a marquis was higher than a baronet, he preferred a marquis for a son-in-law. But getting the marquis ceased to matter when an offhand remark turned his ambition to becoming a Member of Parliament.

But the object of his ambition had so little reality for him that he never troubled himself to learn about the procedures of Parliament, and when the great moment came, his achievement turned into a farce. Melmotte arrived at the door of the House of Commons without any arrangements having been made to introduce him as a new member. While he was trying to bluster his way in, the leader of his party arrived and took pity on him, so that Melmotte appeared to have been introduced in a glorious fashion. But Melmotte did not know enough to appreciate either the appearance of honour in his arrival, or its real absurdity. Having entered the House, he became fired by an ambition to make a speech, and against all precedents he managed to be recognized. But when it came to speaking, Melmotte could only repeat that 'Mr Brown was wrong', without being able to understand the request that he address the Speaker, or to hear the reminders to remove his hat. In his next and last appearance in the House, he rose to his feet, could not utter a word, fell over, and then, picking his steps so as not to stagger, he made his exit. Although he knew that he was doomed, and that everyone knew it, still he went through the motions to demonstrate that his will could triumph even over brandy before going home to kill himself.

That a pointless crime ruined him is the clue to the moral of Melmotte's story. His fortune had truly been very great, and his adversities were temporary ones that might have been overcome. If only he had been able to stop climbing, he might have stayed on the heights that he had achieved. But he brought disaster upon himself by attempting to buy the Longestaffe house when he could not afford it, and then trying, by forgery, to secure the property that he could not pay for and that did not matter to him. Melmotte himself recognized 'that the fault had been not in circumstances, not in that which men call Fortune ...'.[7] But what constituted the fault was not, as Melmotte believed, his tactical errors, nor even his readiness to cheat ever more brilliantly. Melmotte's indifference to committing fraud is merely part of a larger indifference to how things really are.

The reason for his downfall, as his German associate said, was that Melmotte 'vas blow'd up vid bigness . . . he bursted himself . . .'. As he grew bigger, he became increasingly vulgar and offensive because he became more sure of his power to achieve anything. His ruthlessness had a kind of innocence – he had no awareness of trying to override law and morality, because there were no such realities for him. He had a small boy's belief in the power of a title – if only he had one, he thought, he would be safe from the law. He vastly exaggerated the value of his entertainments: 'A man who had in very truth had the real brother of the Sun dining at his table could hardly be sent into the dock and then sent out of it like a common felon.'[8] Even when he realized that his frauds had been detected, he went on believing that their very enormity would make it impossible to punish him. Each of his ambitions, whether to acquire a royal guest, a titled son-in-law, or a place in Parliament, became all important as it gained ascendancy over the object that had preceded it, and none inspired him to take a serious account of his circumstances. He supposed that audacity would serve him just as well in the House as it had in his so-called boardroom, and therefore he felt none of the diffidence that saves a parliamentary novice from making a fool of himself. When, to insure himself against calamity, he had set aside money in the name of his daughter, it did not occur to him that she might be unwilling to sign the necessary papers when he commanded her to do so. At every turn, his belief that he was not vulnerable, as other men were, infected all that he did with fantasy.

The result was an ambition shaped neither by any sense for what is desirable, nor by any consideration of what is possible, but driven by a belief that determination can conquer all. Melmotte had kept moving without knowing what mattered to him or on what scale he measured his achievements. As his projects had no real object, there was nothing that once achieved could satisfy him, and the more he achieved, the more he believed in his power to go further. Devoid of any content or limit, his ambition was simply a relentless urge to climb ever higher. His boldness only served to remove the restraint that fear might have placed on his disposition to lose sight of the real world. His capacity for endless illusion, the very unreality of what he tried to achieve protected him against the boredom of Macbeth. But for the same reason, the higher he climbed, the more certain he was to lose his bearings and fall.

Melmotte is a character who is familiar enough when he appears in the role of a general or ruler, as a Hitler. But Trollope showed how this phenomenon might appear in ordinary life and escape recognition because it is associated with such trivial events. Melmotte's achievements rested wholly on his mystifying those around him by an audacity so fantastic that they believed it to be real power. The story of Melmotte is not about the wickedness of ambition, but about the impossibility of achieving an ambition without limits.

The Way We Live Now does not condemn worldliness or the pursuit of money any more than ambition. Financial speculations are at the centre of the story because the lack of realism, which is the real object under attack, more easily escapes detection in such activities than in farming. But Trollope is just as critical of Mr Longestaffe, whose fantasies are inspired by his inherited estate, while, on the other hand, one of the few admirable characters in the novel is a financier and associate of Melmotte, the Jew, Brehgert (cf. Chapter 13).

*   *   *

But if an ambition with no real object is ruled out for a gentleman, a definite aim may be just as unsuitable. A well defined project of the sort pursued by so-called idealists is the worst of all.

The folly of having a humanitarian blueprint to follow is satirized in *The Fixed Period*. It has been acclaimed as an admirable proposal for euthanasia and also as a literary experiment, which ingeniously leads us into ridiculing the narrator only to find that we have failed to see the moral of the story – that death is too important a matter to be left to God. But anyone who believes that can believe that Dean Swift dined on Irish babies.

The story is set in 1980, in a former British colony, which had become an independent republic and passed a law providing that at sixty-seven, citizens were to be 'deposited' for a year of honourable seclusion in a 'college' before being painlessly put to death. The president of the republic, Neverbend, writes the history of his great reform.

In no sense is Neverbend a despot. He is anxious only to be of use to others; he loves his family and is devoted to his friend, who happens to be first candidate for 'depositing'. Law and parliamentary procedure are sacred to him, the only difference between the constitution of his republic and that of England being the abolition of capital punishment and the institution of the 'fixed period'. It had been enacted not only in a perfectly legal and democratic manner, but with great rejoicing: 'young men and women called each other brother and sister, and it was felt that a great reform had been inaugurated . . . for the benefit of mankind at large'. To objections from abroad, they had replied staunchly that they would 'stand and fall by the new system'.[9]

The strength of Neverbend's arguments for his reform is essential to the moral of the story. It is quite likely that Trollope said to his friend, as the reviewer in *Blackwood's Magazine* reported, 'It's all true – I *mean* every word of it'.[10] Who can deny, even now, what the Fixed Periodists asserted – that life beyond sixty-eight may bring afflictions, 'slippered selfishness' and 'senile weakness', and that the old can be a burden on the young? But the conclusion drawn by Neverbend is another matter.

He prided himself on how thoughtfully all the details had been arranged. There was careful provision even for amusing the old during their year in the College, while they were preparing themselves for their 'great departure'. Neverbend had himself seen to the details of all the necessary machinery. He had even thought of testing it on especially fat hogs because the old were often stout and he trusted no one but himself to supervise the tests in order to make sure that the machinery was adequate for disposing of the entire population of the capital – 'as I hope we shall some day and not a living soul would know anything about it'.[11] He recognized that there might be some practical difficulties: perhaps a few faint-hearted people would have to be prevented from trying to leave as their time approached or from preparing for an escape by removing their property to another country. He himself kept a careful record of everyone's period in case someone attempted to cheat. But he abhorred the idea of using force. The perfection of the system, as Neverbend saw it, required a willing acquiescence, and he felt certain that as reason came to prevail, which it was bound to do as the system flourished, the wisdom of the Fixed Period would be recognized by everyone.

Of course it might happen that an odd individual had to 'depart a year or two before he was worn out', but he would have the inestimable compensation of departing 'before he had ever known the agony of a headache'. When it was pointed out that the first candidate was far more able to look after his property than the young man who would inherit it, the president was outraged: 'The whole system was to be made to suit itself to the peculiarities of one individual constitution?' Only someone who could see 'nothing of the general beauty of the Fixed Period' could raise such an irrational objection. The Fixed Period had been chosen with reference to the community at large. It was founded on an undeniable philosophical truth, and had been translated meticulously into a practical scheme which would make humanity 'prosper and be strong, and thrive, unpolluted by the greed and cowardice of second childhood'. Anyone who could see reason, whatever his personal condition, would say happily when his time came: 'Lead me into the College and there let me prepare myself for that brighter life which will require no mortal strength.'[12]

The essence of Neverbend's project, Trollope keeps reminding us, is that in order to perfect the 'life of humanity' men must learn to welcome death. But Neverbend allowed no talk of death. Even in private, he disliked references to 'victims', 'executions', 'putting an end to', or 'making away with' people – 'What language in which to speak of the great system!' The correct phrase, he insisted was 'mode of transition'. He had opposed giving the name, 'Necropolis' to the establishment where the Fixed Period was enforced because he 'had never wished to join with it the feeling of death,' and preferred a name that would suggest 'an approach to good things to come'. For the same reason, he planned a beautiful avenue leading up to the crematorium which he called 'the temple', and had refused to plant cedars and yew-trees, as some had wished, because 'our object should be to make the spot cheerful, rather than sad'. At the gate, he hoped to see a 'smiling hamlet' which would be 'inhabited by those who would administer to the wants of the deposited'. His thoughts often dwelled on how splendid the College would look when it would be a 'whole township of old men and women, as in the course of the next thirty years they might come hurrying on to find their last abode in the College'. He so looked forward to his own time in the College that he had already selected rooms for himself and his wife.[13]

The reality was not quite as Neverbend imagined it. Instead of the 'smiling hamlet', a desert surrounded the College because no one wanted to live so near to those 'awful furnaces'. The curator of the College, though he was enthusiastic about 'the system' and was feeble and worn out ten years before his period, found his job unbearable. No girl, he said, would work for them because young men refused to call there: 'They say they'll smell dead bodies . . . that when you tried the furnaces there was a savour of burnt pork.' Neverbend had to admit that 'some slight flavour of the pig had been allowed to escape' but no such accidents, he was sure, would happen when the 'temple' began operating in earnest.[14]

As the time to deposit the first candidate drew near, not only the man himself and his daughter, but also Neverbend's wife and son, and indeed most of the community found the idea intolerable. The only strong support came from the young man who would inherit the property of the 'deposited' one. The reluctant candidate for the honour of being the first to 'depart in conformity with the new theory'[15] shocked Neverbend by saying that he considered it cruel of Neverbend to want to kill a man whom he called his 'brother'. But though Neverbend's inclinations and private interests tempted him to relent, he could not let himself be so cowardly and self-indulgent. Though he acknowledged that some of the details in the system might be revised, he insisted that the system itself was all it should be.

Long after he had been defeated by British intervention and was recollecting the difficulties of his experience at a distance, Neverbend saw himself as one of a distinguished company of benefactors of mankind – Socrates, Galileo, Hampden and Washington – who had been frustrated as he had by irrational prejudices: 'What great things had these men done by constancy, in opposition to the wills and prejudices of the outside world!' The Fixed Period was nothing less than 'a great world's movement', but it was 'too strong, too mighty, too divine' a truth to be accepted at once. British 'tenderness' made it useless to preach to the English, but he still hoped that the United States might be 'strong enough to stand against those hydraheaded prejudices with which the ignorance of the world at large is fortified'. So he determined to devote his life to 'long written arguments and studied logic' which would 'prove to mankind' that its salvation depended on adopting the Fixed Period.[16]

As he tells his story, and we see him dwelling with enthusiasm on the prospect of incinerating a whole townful of people, Neverbend reveals how devotion to a grand humanitarian project can blind a man to the consequences for those who walk on earth. In Neverbend, Trollope has drawn the anatomy of a utopian mind: its weird blend of meticulous attention to technical detail with indifference to reality, of devotion to making life painless for all in the future with cruelty to the living, of love for logic with a repugnance to truth. The tone of *The Fixed Period* is light – a 'jeu d'esprit', Hutton had called it. But embedded in the humorous sketch is a brutal picture of how dreams of bringing heaven to earth can reduce real men and women to dust.

* * *

Even dreaming on a smaller scale, in a more modest form, is not allowed to a gentleman. In the story of Sir Thomas Underwood, (*Ralph The Heir*) Trollope considered the kind of dreaming that is more likely to tempt ordinary men.

Sir Thomas's attempt to return to Parliament was thrust upon him by an unsolicited invitation to stand for Percycross which he accepted only after much hesitation. But as Percycross was a borough determined to be corrupt, when Sir Thomas insisted that no bribes were to be given, he was regarded by everyone there as highly annoying, if not mad. He found himself compelled to associate with men whom he found loathsome and he enjoyed nothing about the affair. He was returned, only to have the election questioned, and to be forced to endure an enquiry which quite rightly found Percycross to be rotten beyond redemption. There are many vivid scenes of the corruption, and Trollope said in his *Autobiography* that he was describing what he had witnessed and suffered when he tried to get elected for Beverly. Nevertheless Trollope's concern is not with denouncing corruption; it is more nearly the opposite.

Though Mr Griffenbottom, the long standing Tory member for Percycross, never felt the slightest scruples about bribing, Trollope takes trouble to enlist our sympathy for him by emphasizing Griffenbottom's genuine devotion to his political career. He continued to canvass tirelessly until the late hours, even when nearly overcome by the pain of his gout; he had a thorough understanding of his constituency, and we believe him when he

says: 'The House is everything to me, meat and drink; employment and recreation . . . ' Even Mr Pile, who 'feels sick' every time
Sir Thomas says something against bribery, is allowed to make an
appealing case for himself when he preaches his sermon against
purity: 'I hate the very smell of it. It stinks . . . Nobody is to trust
no one. There ain't to be nothing warm, nor friendly, nor comfortable anymore . . . ' It is not the corrupt politicians and agents,
but Sir Thomas, with all his rectitude, whom the Percycross
affairs puts in the worst light.[17]

Percycross was notorious for its corruption and Griffenbottom,
who brought him the offer, was typical of a breed with whom Sir
Thomas had become familiar during his earlier terms in Parliament. Yet he had agreed to stand. When he was disgusted by
what he found, he tried neither to change things nor to accommodate to them and he did not withdraw. He was dragged along,
protesting feebly all the way, but doing nothing effective to
enforce his objections. He paid out money recklessly because he
did not trouble to discover what, in the circumstances, had to be
paid. And after it was all over, he told himself that he had been a
fool to suppose that: 'he, a pure and scrupulous man, could go
among such impurity as he had found at Percycross, and come
out, still clean and yet triumphant?'[18]

Trollope's emphasis falls not on the villainy of the man who
had, as Sir Thomas put it, 'used him as a puppet and had compelled him to do dirty work,' but on the weakness of Sir Thomas.
He was a sad and disappointed man. He had become an esteemed
and successful Chancery barrister, had made money, and 'no
man had ever succeeded in browbeating him when panoplied in
his wig and gown; nor had words ever been wanting to him . . . '[19]
When he became a Member of Parliament and Solicitor-General,
he did his work well. But his party was turned out of office four
months later, and when they returned to power, he was passed
over without a second thought. He had found it impossible to
exchange any words in the drawing room, not even with the Lord
Chancellor; although he was returned three times for the same
town, he never managed to dine with the leading townsmen, or to
call on their wives; during all his time in Parliament he had not
learned to talk even to the Secretary of the Treasury.

The pattern was the same in all his ambitions. He intended to
write a life of Bacon, and in order to do so, secluded himself in his
chambers, where he collected a mountain of papers, spent hours

planning his book, and revelling in the 'paraphernalia of work'. But he knew, Trollope says, 'that he was not working. He went, as it were, round and round the thing, never touching it, till the labour which he longed to commence became so frightful to him that he did not dare to touch it.'[20]

In the same fashion, Sir Thomas had entertained an ambition to think through his religious faith because it seemed to him the most important of all questions and he wanted not just to believe unreflectively. But at sixty, he still 'postponed the work of enquiry'; he was 'for ever doubting, for ever intending, and for ever despising himself for his doubts and unaccomplished intentions'.[21] In the meantime, he did not go to church and so deprived himself of the comforts of religion without having discovered why he had, or indeed whether he should have, done so.

Sir Thomas was one of those men, Trollope says, who dream of doing something out of the ordinary. Of such men, some 'are contended to struggle for success and struggling fail'. Now and then one struggles and succeeds. But Sir Thomas was one of the many 'who see the beauty, who adopt the task, who promise themselves the triumph, and then never struggle at all. The dream of youth becomes the doubt of middle life, and then the despair of age.' It was not good enough for Sir Thomas 'to scrape together a few facts, to indulge in some fiction, to tell a few anecdotes, and then to call his book a biography'. He saw in Bacon's rise and fall a remarkable drama and 'had resolved that he would tell the tale as it had never yet been told,' that he would build not a mere summer-house but a great enduring castle, but at sixty 'not one line of his book was written'.[22] And it was in a vain effort to find solace for his unaccomplished intentions that he fell into the unfortunate campaign for Percycross.

Sir Thomas lacked what Trollope calls 'fibre' – he could not compel himself to do what was necessary in order to accomplish his dreams. He had 'ventured to think himself capable of something that would justify him in leaving the common circle', but had succeeded only in finding disappointment at every turn. There is no suggestion that every men who 'dares to arrange for himself' a life different from the ordinary is mistaken. Sir Thomas's error arises not from wanting to do something unconventional or grand but from failing to ask whether he was the man to do so.[23]

Why Sir Thomas is nevertheless a gentleman appears in the

contrast between him and Ontario Moggs, the bootmaker, who was the opposing candidate at Percycross. 'It was the glory of Ontario Moggs,' Trollope says, 'to be a politician; – it was his ambition to be a poet; – it was his nature to be a lover; – it was his disgrace to be a bootmaker . . .' He fought under the slogan, 'Moggs, Purity, and the Rights of Labour' and Sir Thomas felt a certain affinity with him. But Moggs had none of Sir Thomas's aversion to public performances. He loved making speeches and was good at it. He went every night to harangue the men at the Cheshire Cheese, some of whom were his father's workmen, telling them that they must engage themselves in the great battle between Labour and Capital, in which 'hecatombs of honest labourers have been crushed till the sides of the mountains are white with their bones and the rivers run foul with their blood'. And the most noble form that this battle took was the Strike, which Moggs commended as 'a sacrifice of self . . . for the sake of others who can only thus be rescued from the grasp of tyranny . . .', which would make England 'the Paradise of the labourer, an Elysium of industry, an Eden of artisans'.[24]

His audience was delighted by Moggs's speeches – they 'clattered their glasses, and broke their pipes, and swore that the words he uttered were the kind of stuff they wanted' – but not because they endorsed his opinions. His appeal was the same, Trollope says, as that of the radical earl, the free-thinking parson, and the squire who won't preserve. Moggs's audience regarded him as a capitalist, and rightly so, as his father was a master bookmaker on a large scale, and they were entranced by the spectacle of a 'rich man's position with a poor man's sympathies'. They found in the contrast and in the grandeur of Moggs's words a glimpse of 'real poetry'.[25]

But Moggs was as unaware of why he pleased his audience as of the implications of his speeches. He never for a moment considered what followed from his declaration that 'it was better that twenty real bookmakers should eat beef daily, than that one so-called bootmaker should live in a country residence . . .'. Nor did it occur to him that there was a contradiction between his fiery denunciations of the governing classes and his eagerness to become a 'gentleman' by getting a seat in Parliament. Though he could 'bite out his tongue' for calling the other Liberal candidate, 'sir', he did so because he was awed by what he mistook for the appearance of a 'gentleman'. He consoled himself by thinking that it was the man that was needed, not the outside trappings, without ever asking himself whether, if that was the case, he had any need to be ashamed of being a bootmaker and to advance himself by getting a seat.[26] Ontario Moggs was not a hypocrite – he truly believed what he said. But just as he preferred making speeches to collecting payment for the work that he did, so he cared more for the dramatic effect than the truth of his words. In everything but his love, Moggs preferred to lose himself in the world of his imagination to noticing the real one in which he moved, and without realizing that he did so or recognizing that there was anything wrong in devotion to such dreaming.

This is the great difference between Ontario Moggs and Sir Thomas. The failed politician, writer, and theologian recognized that he had an obligation to consider whether he was capable of achieving the ambitions he cherished. He had, through much of his life, failed to fulfill it but he was capable of coming to acknowledge, to understand, and to regret his fault, and therefore he was a gentleman. The moral of his story is, as Sir Thomas tells himself at the end of it, that a gentleman may not excuse himself from considering whether he is willing and able to bear the difficulties of achieving the object that he is pursuing.

*   *   *

What distinguishes the way in which a gentleman moves about in the world is a peculiarly complex understanding – a clear sense of limits and standards which does not prevent him from either seeking to change things or accommodating to what he finds unpleasant. In Trollope's account of how gentlemen conduct themselves in politics, we see this attitude writ large. The so-called political novels disclose very little about the political set-up in nineteenth century Britain, in the sense that we might expect to discover from a constitutional history. They disclose something more fundamental – the understanding of human life on which that set-up, as seen by a gentleman, rested.

In *Phineas Redux*, Trollope gives an account of an attempt at a radical innovation – disestablishing the Church of England. The episode begins with a speech to his constituents given by the Prime Minister in a Conservative government, Mr Daubeny, whose party had always been committed to defending the Established Church. The speech included the following words: 'The period of our history is one in which it becomes essential for us to renew those inquiries which have prevailed since man first woke to his destiny, as to the amount of connexion which exists and which must exist between spiritual and simply human forms of government – between our daily religion and our daily politics, between the Crown and the Mitre.' To Daubeny's immediate audience, the words carried pleasant intimations of 'good old gracious times and good old gracious things', they liked the sound of the orator's voice, and they had no idea of what the words meant.[27] But when the speech was reported in the press, the wise heads declared that something was afoot. Then came the leading articles in the newspapers which told everyone what the Prime Minister had really said. It took a few days for the 'bran to be bolted', as Trollope puts it, and by the end of the week it was known everywhere that Mr Daubeny had set his party on a course to disestablishment, although some Conservatives decided that the speech gave undeniable evidence of temporary insanity in the Prime Minister, and the squires and parsons, who were the backbone of the party, refused to believe that their leader could commit such an iniquity.

The truth about the affair, Trollope tells us, is that Daubeny had consulted no one before making the speech, that he had expected his constituents to miss the point, and had calculated that others would make the point for him within a week. When the expected clarification came, he readily explained his move to anyone who asked, but the explanations were many. Daubeny said that there was a storm approaching England and the most important thing was to save the land from being devastated by it, that he had done nothing but recognize what the current religious feeling in the country made inevitable, that it was preferable to have the Church disestablished by her friends than by her enemies. To colleagues who expressed outrage, Daubeny at once declared his willingness to resign, though he always added that such a terrible, drastic step might not, he hoped, be necessary. To some he confessed that he had known that his words would shock his followers, but that he had felt honour bound to declare his true opinion candidly to his contituents. Others were told that if they believed that the country would benefit from keeping the Conservatives in power, they had better let him satisfy the popular demand for disestablishment.

Daubeny's words were included in the Queen's Speech and in the Address to the Crown, thus becoming official policy for the government. There was a 'long and stormy' debate on the address but by then, one Conservative after another rose to argue that the measure was designed to defend the Church, that the power of the Church would be increased by disestablishment, that good Churchmen ought to have taken this step long ago. In short, the Conservatives made it clear that by disestablishing the Church they would be restoring episcopal ascendancy.

A number of Liberals decided at once that although the Liberal party had always advocated disestablishment, they were now obliged to oppose the Conservative bill. Some Liberals acquired, for the first time in their lives, a real political conviction and declared themselves ready to die in defence of the Church. Some argued that it would be best to concentrate on attacking Daubeny himself and to ignore the issue. Others muttered mysterious words about how, 'If we were all a little less in the abstract, and a little more in the concrete, it would be better for us', which still others translated as meaning 'men, not measures'.[28]

In the end, the leader of the Liberal opposition, Mr Gresham, set out to bring down the Conservative government. Gresham declared that it was the greatest of all sins to let a measure be passed by men who, in voting for it, violated their consciences, which the Conservatives would necessarily be doing. As the discussion proceeded, it was repeated often that 'the Church of England would still be the Church of England' until everyone grew weary of hearing about the Church, and moved on to quite another argument – about the wickedness of faction. Then that issue, too, melted away into a general knockabout on the relative merits of the two parties, which made everyone happy because it was a subject on which even the meekest and dimmest members of the House had something to say.

The climax came in the final debate between the two great gladiators, which held the House enraptured until ten in the evening. The next morning it was reported in some places that Mr Daubeny had been too long and turgid, and Mr Gresham too passionate, but elsewhere it was found to be an incontrovertible truth that Gresham had given his finest performance and that Daubeny had never been more lucid, and of course everyone agreed, as they always did on such occasions, that the speeches of the day were sadly inferior to the great efforts of the past. The show ended with Daubeny's losing the vote. And in his speech of resignation he assured the country that it was doomed because, though he might have saved England, Mr Gresham, backed by an unworthy House of Commons, would certainly ruin it.

It would seem reasonable to conclude that the attempt at innovation was all pretence, especially as Trollope not only tells the story throughout in an ironic tone of voice, but often likens the contest between the parties to a game. The dismay felt by the Liberals over Daubeny's sudden strike was, Trollope says, like that of a chess player mated 'by some audacious combination of two pawns and a knight, such being all the remaining forces of the victorious adversary, when the beaten man has two castles and a queen upon the board'. The Liberals believed that they owned Church reform, they considered it their legitimate property and most valuable asset, but they had not as yet used it because they were keeping it 'in the background for some future great occasion'. When Daubeny made his move, it was as if 'the adversary had appropriated to his own use the castles and the queen of the unhappy vanquished ones'.[29]

The irony and the images seem to suggest that the only reality in the proceedings is a struggle for power, that the words used were but chips in a poker game with no truth in them, that the only real question was who bullied whom into giving way, and in short that though gentlemen may wear silk gloves over their brass knuckles, they play a dirty game. Grand reasons may be given for attempting, accepting, or rejecting innovations, but as some of the Liberals said, there was 'no honesty in it'.

What went on in the country at large appears to be just as devoid of seriousness and truth as what happened in Parliament. When the pundits began saying that 'the disestablishment of the Church was only a question of time,' they spoke on little or no evidence, as such pundits generally do. Yet before long, though no one knew precisely who had said what or why, the idea became familiar to the public. The press began to teem with the assertion that 'it was only a question of time'. There was the usual set of variations on the going opinion: 'Some fervent, credulous friends predicted another century of life; – some hard-hearted logical opponents thought that twenty years would put an end to the anomaly: – a few stout enemies had sworn on the hustings with an anathema that the present session should see the deposition from her high place of this eldest daughter of the woman of Babylon.' But despite all the predictions of instant disestablishment, 'none had expected the blow so soon as this: and none certainly had expected it from this hand'.[30]

Much the same happened every time a new government was formed. While the great men were locked in consultation, it was being said outside that the difficulties in the way of forming a government would 'be found to be insuperable'. On Wednesday morning the prophets of doom wore 'their longest faces' and were 'triumphant with melancholy forebodings ... there was a deadlock. Nobody could form a government.' The newspapers carried detailed reports of wonderfully dramatic scenes – the Liberal leader had not only fallen on his knees before the Queen; he had burst into tears and begged that the Queen relieve him of his office. It was announced as an undisputed fact that in her desperation the Queen had sent to Germany for advice. But by Wednesday night, the crisis was over, not only had a government been formed, but it was precisely what everyone had always predicted, down to the last man. No one expressed any surprise; everyone behaved as if the week had passed in the same humdrum fashion as all other weeks.[31]

Where in all this can any reality or truth be found? It appears to be a frivolous game in which anyone may say anything. Why or when it comes to be played, no one knows. The future in politics, we are told, is always obscure. It is 'darker', the Duke of Omnium says, 'than any other future ... clouds arise, one knows not why or whence, and create darkness when one expected light'. The duke seems to consider it almost indecent to deliberate about what should be done. When one of his ministers proposed that the cabinet would do well to 'try and arrange among ourselves something of a policy', the duke replied: 'Things to be done offer themselves, I suppose, because they are in themselves desirable; not because it is desirable to have something to do.'[32] The duke's words suggest that an innovation is and ought to be a random event. But there appears to be a contradiction between the duke's attitude and that of Gresham and Cantrip, who are also gentleman, and who praised Daubeny's deliberate audacity in bringing in disestablishment.

The difficulty disappears, however, once we recognize the conception of politics common to all gentlemen in Trollope's world. It is politics seen as an activity without a given goal or destination. Its purpose is simply to keep things 'quiet and orderly' so as to enable everyone to go about his business in his own way, without fear of losing his liberty, his livelihood, or his property.[33] The hallmark of such a condition of things is *habeas corpus* – the 'first and greatest shibboleth of a free people' – and *habeas corpus* has this importance because it signifies that communal life is governed by stable rules and procedures, without which men cannot be secure against arbitrary power and therefore cannot live as free men. In this picture, the only substantive objects that a politician ought to pursue are to preserve the rule of law, to keep taxes low, and to secure the country against enemies from without and hooligans within. And when people are governed in this manner, 'good living' will spread through the whole of the nation, bringing 'not simply beef and pudding, though they form no inconsiderable part of it', but also education, religion without priestcraft, political freedom, the power and habit of thinking, the capacity for 'enjoying life like a man, instead of enduring life like a brute'.[34] The grandeur in politics comes from the importance and not the amount of what is done by a government – more than any other activity, politics is essential to securing the enjoyment of private life.

In order to provide such security, the politician can never sit back. He must not stand up so violently as to rock the boat, but neither dare he omit to notice that it may be filling with water in a hidden corner. Constant change is therefore intrinsic to politics. But it is not change in the sense of initiating or founding great transformations or seeking 'to rediscover the creative impulse'. It is change in the sense of a constant adjustment, carried out with an awareness that while change is inescapable, there is nothing intrinsically desirable or noble about changing things and it always carries grave risks. If an innovation removes a troublesome dissonance in the established arrangements, it may be considered useful. But there can never be any certainty about what needs to be done, and judicious men will always be full of doubts about what might or should happen, and even about the desirability of what has happened. This breed of politician does not try to bring immortality into the world, or to impose an ideal fixity on it. He is not out to capture a Holy Land or to act as a merchant of salvation. Instead of wanting to inflame the passions of men into accepting grand innovations, he strives to teach the public not to be too anxious 'to see some great effects come from our own little doings', to recognize that when 'great measures' start coming fast often 'more is broken in the rattle than is repaired by the reform'.

He recognizes, as Mr Monk put it, that politicians 'look for grievances, not because the grievances are heavy, but trusting that the
honour of abolishing them will be great'. Far from supposing that
it is the business of government always to be making new laws, he
believes that there is much to be gained from 'a lengthened
period of quiet and . . . a minimum of new laws'. To 'have carried
on the Queen's Government prosperously for three years' is for
such a politician achievement enough. Trollope was genuinely
praising Lord Brock when he described him as 'the very model of
an English statesman' because he believed in letting 'things take
their way naturally – with a slight direction hither or thither as
things might require'.[35]

But because the objects of politics are so modest, the practice
of politics is complicated and difficult to understand. Trollope's
politician lives in a world where many different people are saying
many different things and there is no voice from heaven telling
him whom he should hear. He is not at all in the situation of a
doctor who is brought a patient suffering from a distinct pain
which he asks the doctor remove. The politican is faced with a
bewildering array of candidates for the status of patient, some
genuine, others more or less bogus, with complaints in many different degrees and forms, and he has nothing even remotely re-
sembling a pharmacopoeia. He is beseiged by many different
groups, each insisting that its interest should be held paramount
or considered identical with the good of the country, and each
certain that 'the welfare of the community depends upon the
firmness with which they – especially they – hold to their own'.[36]
And yet governments are formed, questions are raised, laws are
framed, accepted, and rejected, and Englishmen go about their
affairs in an orderly fashion. How is this miracle achieved? The
answer is: by an unpredictable coming together of intentions,
motives, contrivances, and conflicts.

In this view of politics, the apocalyptic frame of mind does not
signify insight. It belongs rather to the vulgar, the cads, the
cranks, and the villains. These are men like the scurrilous journalist, Quintus Slide, the self-appointed 'people's friend' who tells
his readers that the ruling powers are the people's enemies; or
Turnbull, the Radical demagogue, who goes in 'for everything in
the way of agitation', and always carries a cause in his breaches
pocket and sherry in his carriage to 'remedy the costs of mob
popularity'; or Daubeny, the Conservative demagogue, who

assures the people of England that decay, disaster, and death are imminent. It is the toadies and the tuft hunters, the young and the thoughtless who suppose that the men on their side are 'patriotic angels' and those on the other are 'all friends or idiots', who see every defeat as a tragedy.[37] Gentlemen are more detached.

The gentlemen among the Liberals did not conclude that the behaviour of the Conservatives showed them to be 'conniving scoundrels'. Though Mr Gresham made a passionate attack on the recommendation for disestablishment in the Queen's Speech, he told Lord Cantrip privately that Daubeny was probably only feeling out the ground, trying 'to see if it is possible' to bring in disestablishment. Lord Cantrip disagreed about that but he was at one with Gresham in considering such a ploy for such a purpose permissible, even if Daubeny had been motivated by a desire to do something dramatic in order to stay in office. Both these Liberals believed also that Daubeny's party included the usual assortment of more and less honourable, patriotic, thoughtful, self-seeking men, who had a few simple ideas about their duties, not many arguments at their disposal, and no great anxiety to take on the responsibility of real work.

The truth about how the Conservatives came to accept disestablishment is neither obvious nor simple. Every one of them, Trollope tells us, did 'most certainly within his own bosom cry Ichabod when the fatal news reached his ears'. At first they could hardly believe that their leader would play Brutus to their Church, 'the very Holy of Holies', and whispered among themselves mutinously that 'their Brutus, in spite of his great qualities had ever been mysterious, unintelligible, dangerous, and given to feats of conjuring . . .'. But on the other hand, they also considered it their duty to support their party, and when the two duties seemed to clash, they were made extremely uncomfortable. Most would have preferred 'to go home', and console themselves with declaring 'morning and evening with a clear conscience that the country was going to the dogs'. To stand apart, hiding one's face beneath one's toga and dreaming of Rome in her splendour would have been easier. But they recognized that a 'party cannot afford to hide its face in its toga,' and 'has to be practical,' and that therefore Members of Parliament are obliged to stay and commit themselves one way or the other, however unpleasant they may find it to make the choice. Though disestablishment had at first seemed unthinkable, the proceedings had compelled them to think again and they came to see that perhaps disestablishment was no more at odds with long held Conservative convictions than other measures which they had endorsed in the past. After all, Catholic emancipation and the repeal of the Corn Laws, measures that had once been anathema to Conservatives, had been introduced by a Conservative government. Twenty years before household suffrage had arrived, even the most ardent reformers would not have dared to advocate it, and yet the Conservatives 'had swallowed the dose without serious disruption of their ranks'. Some did it, Trollope says, with 'face so singularly distorted' as to arouse 'true pity'; some managed it with indifference, and others with affected joy. But somehow or other they 'learned to acknowledge the folly of clinging to their own convictions . . .'.[38]

Such a change of mind is considered decent and reasonable by gentlemen like Gresham and Cantrip. Instead of being outraged by the Conservative turnabout, they recognized that they themselves might do the same. That awareness, however, also prevented them from jumping to conclusions about whether Daubeny would carry his party. Just as from the fact that 'a man rides at some outrageous fence, and by the wonderful activity and obedient zeal of his horse is carried over it in safety',[39] one must not conclude that his horse will carry him over a house, Gresham said, so there was no telling whether the Conservatives would on this occasion give up deeply held convictions.

Nor did judicious Liberals consider it to be a bad thing that the Conservatives should introduce disestablishment. The wise old Duke of St. Bungay explained that Daubeny had undertaken the job 'because he can do it, and we can't. He will get from our side much support, and we should get none from his.' When Phineas Finn objected passionately, 'There is something to me sickening in their dishonesty,' the duke told him, 'The country has the advantage; and I don't know that they are dishonest. Ought we to come to a deadlock in legislation in order that the parties might fight out their battle till one had killed the other?' The same indifference is expressed by Gresham when he says to Lord Cantrip, 'You know and I know, that the thing has to be done . . . . Would not he do it better than another if he can do it with less of animosity than we should rouse against us? If the blow would come softer from his hands than from ours, with less of a feeling of injury to those who dearly love the Church, should we not be glad that he should undertake the task?'[40] And this is a reasonable way to think, Trollope shows us, because all human affairs are mutable.

Opinions constantly change and it is no bad thing that they do in a world full of change. Men who 'ten years since regarded almost with abhorrence, and certainly with distrust, the idea of disruption between Church and State in England' advanced to enthusiasm on its behalf and learned to say 'it is only a question of time,' without even remembering how devoted they had been to the established Church a dozen years ago. In saying so, Trollope is not disparaging public opinion for being volatile, but congratulating his countrymen on having found a decent way of accommodating to the human condition. They had learned to accept without anguish so great an innovation as disestablishment, he explains, by 'reconciling themselves to it after that slow, silent, argumentative fashion in which convictions force themselves among us'.[41]

The same general attitude governs the way in which gentlemen assess the effects of accomplished innovations. The reforms designed to do away with corruption, the extension of the franchise, and the redistribution of boroughs are all acknowledged by Trollope and by his gentlemen to have been desirable. But once that was done, the millennium that the demagogues had promised was still on the horizon. All new measures, like budgets and babies, Trollope says, 'are always little loves when first born. But as their infancy passes away . . . the details are less pleasing than was the whole in the hands of the nurse.'[42] The old system had had some good points which now were lost; men who might have been especially useful in Parliament found it impossible to get in now, and some of the new people who easily gained admission were at least as bad as the worst of the old. Despite the great public outcry about reform, once it had been achieved, the electorate was not after all delighted to be enfranchised. The Duke of Omnium declared firmly that he would do nothing to influence the choice in his borough and the electors felt obliged to demonstrate their independence by choosing an outsider. But having done so once, they were relieved when the outsider resigned and they could welcome back the duke's son without being at all concerned about whether he stood as a Conservative or Liberal.

The relation between how things are and how they are moved

to what appears to be a better state of affairs, we are constantly reminded, is far from simple. Shortly after the reform, there was a trial for corruption, in which, because the prosecution was so faint-hearted, the accused was acquitted, even though everyone was certain that he had been guilty of bribery. The young Phineas Finn was outraged, but Lord Cantrip and Mr Monk saw the matter differently. Cantrip assured Phineas that 'No member of Parliament will ever be punished for bribery as for a crime. We are very far from that as yet. I should have thought a conviction to be a great misfortune . . . it would have created ill blood, and our own hands in this matter are not a bit cleaner than those of our adversaries. We can't afford to pull their houses to pieces before we have put our own in order. The thing will be done; but it must, I fear, be done slowly, as is the case with all reforms from within.' And the radical Mr Monk agreed that no disgrace was attached to the verdict even though everybody knew that the accused had been bribed because 'in political matters it is very hard for a man in office to be purer than his neighobours'. When Phineas objected 'What must we think of such a condition of things,' Monk answered, 'That it's capable of improvement. I do not know that we can think anything else.'[43]

The moral is that enacting a statute is only a small part of the story about a change in public arrangements. It takes time before the public learns to subscribe to the new conditions. While bribery in elections may not be desirable, to try to wipe it out overnight brings other evils. For one thing, it is hardly being just to make an example of one man for what is still being widely practised, and the alternative, charging half the Parliament with corruption, would hardly promote the regularity of public life which is the aim of eliminating corruption. Once the bribery had become a public issue, it was right to bring the culprit to trial and thus to give notice that a new set of standards had come into force. But as the foundation for the new standards had not yet set, it was a good thing that the prosecution had been thin and the defendant acquitted. There would come a time when that would no longer be desirable – but it had not yet arrived.

The whole is a picture in which reforms are begun and carried through in highly indirect and unpredictable ways and there is no simple explanation of how they happened. Those who tell us, that reforms are made when the powers that be yield to a demand for reform, forget to answer the hard question: what constitutes such a demand? Are speeches by the romantic bootmaker, Ontario Moggs, to his mates drinking in the Cheshire Cheese, evidence of such a demand? At times, Trollope suggests, such speeches made by such men might be, though probably in a circuitous fashion. The excitement that generates a reform may grow out of a dissatisfaction with some aspect of the existing state of affairs which is expressed 'by this mouthpiece and that' until there is 'a strong throb through the country, making men feel that safety was to be had by Reform and could not be had without Reform'. At other times, the dissatisfaction may simmer quietly for many years, and in the course of the simmering there may come, quietly and slowly, a radical alteration in men's opinions. But it may also happen that the excitement grows 'from the self-instituted leaders of popular politics down, by means of the press, to the ranks of the working men . . .'.[44]

In many cases more than one of these modes of arousing the country accounts for an innovation, and there is something to be said for all. When reform grows out of a widespread unselfconscious dissatisfaction, it is more likely that the change is desired by the country at large, and not just by a small group because it serves their interests. If there is a slow transformation of opinion, the change when it comes may be less disruptive. But it may also be the case that there exists an anomaly which ought not to be tolerated by people aspiring to be decent and just, and that men who occupy themselves with reflecting on public arrangements ought to bring such a matter to the attention of the public.

The ironic tone of voice in which Trollope relates the events leading to an innovation indicates something more profound and difficult than the falsity or unreality of the opinions and events that fashion political change. The irony points rather to the disparity between our absorption in the here and now, the importance and reality that the events of today have for us, and the evanescence of all human things. By his irony Trollope reminds us as well that even the exaggerations, nonsense, and falsehoods play a salutary part in illuminating a truth which could never have been discovered directly. The result is an intricate picture of how a variety of considerations and judgements shape events in an unforeseeable way. As Trollope and his gentlemen see things, Parliament is not what Bagehot described – 'an inquiring and discussing machine' with a constituency of 'classes' possessing given 'interests'. Instead the events in Parliament are choices made by individuals with distinct personalities, responding to one another in many different ways and creating their destination in the course of arriving. They are not troubled by a conflict between principle and expediency because there are no fixed goals which exist in isolation from contingent responses and interpretations, and no heaven-sent principles forbidding the adoption of what is expedient here and now. There are only considerations of different qualities and importance, which come to bear on events in different ways through many agencies.

But this suggests a crucial question which brings us back to the image of a game. If there are no fixed objectives and the scene is constantly shifting, what keeps chaos at bay? The answer is given in Trollope's emphasis on the resemblance of the parliamentary struggle to a game or tournament. There are adversaries, prizes to be won and defeats to be endured, and everyone takes sides. But the participants are not bent on defeating their opponents by any means whatever, with any weapons they can discover or contrive. They are undoubtedly serious about winning, but in the manner of players in a game. They are not bent on achieving victory by any stratagems at hand; they are out to win by conducting themselves in accordance with certain rules. Only some skills and tactics may be used in the battle. For underlying all the conflicts is an agreement on the obligation to subscribe to certain procedures, and this is what preserves order and gives a determinate shape to what goes on in Parliament. In this way the making of innovations is like a game.

But there is an important difference. The charm of a real game lies in its being isolated from the real world, and some of the charm is lost when players turn professional and let the concerns of the outside world intrude on the green. The peculiar virtue of the rules and rituals of politics is the opposite – that they make the outcome of the game correspond to a reality outside the playing field. What happens in Parliament reflects fairly accurately, though not always to the same degree, the opinion of the country because the parliamentary battle is neither a game nor a struggle for power. It is a set of procedures by means of which changes in the country at large are reflected in the activites of a relatively small number. How this congruence comes about is not easily discovered or explained. But we can recognize that over the years there imperceptibly grew up certain practices which have made it possible to introduce innovations in an orderly fashion without imposing a stifling simplicity.

In a sense, the whole thing is haphazard. Men may join one

party or another for no reason they could defend. As the battle proceeds, the participants may be led further and further away from the original issue, until at last a measure is opposed by one man simply because it is advocated by another, and Members of Parliament swarm into lobbies, blindly following their leaders rather than their own informed judgements. What is said in parliament does not precisely express what each or perhaps any of the speakers thinks. Nevertheless, the speakers genuinely help to expose and illuminate what many in the country believe to be true. And this happens because of the character of human judgements. For no man has only one idea or inclination but many, possibly conflicting, ones. No question has only one aspect, and there is always more than one question to consider. Therefore a new emphasis, whatever the motives or intentions that produced it, may bring some to appreciate and accept what they had before considered impossible or distasteful. The persuasion that goes on both inside and outside Parliament proceeds by enlarging the country's perception of the range of choices, though in a highly indirect and intricate fashion.

The words in a parliamentary debate bear the same relation to what is really relevant to the issue in hand as an enlarged microscopic slide of a cell does to the body from which it is taken. There is a real relation to a real thing, but it is out of proportion and many of the features which seem striking on the slide are insignificant in real life. But just as those who understand the character of a slide make such allowances without even being aware of doing it, so in the great joust between Daubeny and Gresham, those who were familiar with parliamentary practice were not misled. They were made aware, perhaps without realizing it, of aspects of the question before them that they had never before considered. An unpredictable number of variations came into play. Yet the great mass of convictions, prejudices, hopes, and fears did not fall into chaos, because at every point most people respected established procedures. Each participant was in earnest, but not always about the same matter, and yet each in his own way contributed to an outcome that was acceptable to the nation. Whether it was the best possible outcome, it was impossible to say, but it seemed to do, at least for a while.

*   *   *

But a regard for procedures is not the only thing that shapes the conduct of gentlemen in politics. Though they recognize the complexity, the uncertainity, and the mixture of honesty and falsehood that shapes events, they always distinguish sharply between what is and is not permissible for a gentleman. How steadily he can perceive the boundary even while pursuing success, without becoming either confused or intransigent, determines the quality of a gentleman's prudence.

This is evident even in his use of rhetoric. Because he takes account of how the circumstances within which words are spoken affect their meaning, he does not suppose that the ferocity displayed in the House of Commons has the same meaning that it might have elsewhere. In the United States, Trollope says, the leaders of parties 'are in earnest when they talk as though they were about to tear each other limb from limb' and their political enmity produces private hatred. But in England, political opponents strike each other 'as though each blow should carry death if it were but possible' and then dine together amicably. Though in the House, Mr Daubeny and Mr Mildmay seemed bent on destroying one another, in fact Daubeny 'almost adulated his elder rival' and would not have injured a hair of his venerable head 'even for an assurance of six continued months in office', while Mildmay 'never omitted an opportunity of taking Mr Daubeny warmly by the hand'.[45] They were so fierce on the floor of the House, Trollope explains, because there was only 'the pride of personal skill in the encounter' to provide the kind of divergence required for debate. For no one in England desired 'to put down the Queen, or to repudiate the National Debt, or to destroy religious worship, or even to disturb the ranks of society ... The men are so near to each other in all their convictions and theories of life that nothing is left to them but personal competition for the doing of the thing that is to be done.' The great parliamentary struggles were therefore like the encounters between 'two champions of the ring who knock each other about for five hundred pounds a side once in every two years'.[46]

Nevertheless there is a kind of extravagance that gentlemen shun. It is the sort regularly displayed by Daubeny, whose speeches are 'profound, prophetic, and unintelligible', and who is described by Mr Monk as a 'conjuror'.[47] That Trollope considered this a serious charge is plain from his remarks in the *Autobiography* about the novels of Disraeli, some of whose characteristics appear in the portrait of Daubeny. 'An audacious conjurer' Trollope says, has generally been Disraeli's hero – 'some youth who, by wonderful cleverness, can obtain success by every intrigue that comes to his hand . . . I can understand that Mr Disraeli should by his novels have instigated many a young man and many a young woman on their way in life, but I cannot understand that he should have instigated anyone to good.'[48]

To discover just where the rhetorician shades into the conjurer' is peculiarly difficult for gentlemen because they find earnestness and priggishness tiresome or worse. They welcome the moments of farce in parliamentary debates and do not think that they detract from the dignity of the House. When Sir Timothy Beeswax rose to explain why he was obliged to leave the ministry, Fitzgibbon said 'in a very loud whisper' something about how 'falling houses were often left by certain animals', which enraged Sir Timothy, who 'declared that words had been used with reference to himself which the honourable member did not dare to get upon his legs and repeat', but Fitzgibbon 'did not move his hat from his head or stir a limb', and all this was, Trollope says, 'a pleasant little episode in the evening's work, and afforded satisfaction to the House generally'.[49]

Gentlemen also enjoy the rituals and ceremonies and costumes that give men in certain positions a special appearance of dignity. When the occasion is solemn, it is desirable that the man performing should also be solemn. This may be assisted by 'special clothes, and wigs, and ornaments', and gentlemen can wear such disguises without affectation: 'The really clever archbishop, – the really potent chief justice, the man who, as a politician, will succeed in becoming a king of men, should know how to carry his buckram without showing it', as it was beyond the powers of Sir Timothy Beeswax to do. When he tried to put on a performance of dignity, 'You could see a little of the paint, you could hear the crumple of the starch and the padding; you could trace something of uneasiness in the would-be composed grandeur of the brow.' And yet such failings, which young men cannot easily tolerate, do not disturb 'more complaisant and more reasonable' older men: 'They, too, heard the crackle of the buckram, and were aware that the last touch of awe had come upon that brow just as its owner was emerging from the shadow of the Speaker's chair'. But they accepted such inadequacy as 'a thing of course', for they recognized that we cannot always find a real Caesar or a

Pitt 'to control our debates'. Everyone knows that it is 'all paint', but there is something to be said for the paint, for 'how would the poor girl look before the gaslights if there were no paint?'[50]

Still, 'the paint' can be overdone. In the use of rhetorical flourishes, a gross disproportion between the grandeur of the images and the smallness of the subject constitutes ungentlemanly extravagance. Mr Daubeny went too far in the debate about disfranchising seven boroughs when he likened the boroughs to 'the seven sins, and seven stars, and seven churches, and seven lamps'.[51] On the subject of churches, he roamed the world and the centuries to talk about the 'misappropriation of endowments in the time of Eli' and it was thought that he alluded to 'the order of Melchisedek'. All this could serve only to mesmerize his hearers by suggesting that 'his erudition had carried him into regions in which it was impossible to follow him,' and therefore he was a 'political Cagliostro', a conjurer. It is pleasant to have a conjurer around, Mr Monk said, 'if we know that he is a conjurer'.[52] But Mr Daubeny, by pretending to have extraordinary powers, attempted to make his audience believe that he performed his tricks without any sleight of hand, and such a man is dangerous. There is a certain decorum about the use of rhetorical devices that a gentleman observes. A politician ought to try to be persuasive but he should know when his histrionic effects are such as he should be ashamed to acknowledge. Where there is no fitness of the words to what they are meant to convey, one may suspect a lack of respect for the audience, a dangerous attempt not to persuade but to manipulate them.

Gentlemen also distinguish between a reasonable compromise and an unprincipled jockeying for power. For they believe not that virtue is incompatible with political success but that it is virtuous to recognize how different circumstances impose different obligations. When Palliser awarded the Garter to an obscure lord whom he believed to have been slighted rather than to a figure for whom the public expected such a distinction, he was being 'quixotic'. As Prime Minister he was not free to indulge his private preference, but was obliged, as the Duke of St. Bungay says, 'to follow the traditions of his country'. And if he threw over 'all the thraldom', he would, and should, 'lose the confidence which has made him what he is'.[53]

Nor was he free, as Prime Minister, to offend Sir Orlando Drought just because he considered him base. The Duke of St.

Bungay shared the Prime Minister's disgust with Sir Orlando's pretence of being in earnest about having to save the empire by building four ships. But as, at that moment, it was more important to maintain the coalition than to insist on the infamy of Sir Orlando's self-seeking, the Duke of St. Bungay urged the Prime Minister to 'hatch' a paragraph saying that 'having regard to the safety of the nation and the possible, though happily not probable chances of war,' her Majesty 'thought that the present strength of the navy should be considered'. That might soothe Sir Orlando, St. Bungay argued, by giving him 'scope for a new gunboat on an altered principle'.[54] There is no cynicism here, no sacrifice of 'principles' to 'expediency' or of 'private' to 'public' morality, only a recognition of the relative importance of the different considerations to be taken into account. In this case it was virtuous to recognize that keeping the government stable mattered more than chastising a particular member of it. That the Duke of Omnium found it so difficult to recognize this and to act accordingly was a moral defect.

When the Duke of St. Bungay said that it was a defect to lack 'instinct', to hold principles 'so high as to be out of sight . . . for everyday purposes,'[55] he described, in a rough, commonsensical way what Palliser lacked, what Trollope elsewhere describes as 'manliness'. Much as the Duke of St. Bungay believed in the Prime Minister's 'patriotism, intelligence, devotion, and honesty', Trollope says,' 'he was forced to own to himself that the strength of a man's heart was wanting'.[56] Honesty is as essential in politics as elsewhere, but it must be complemented by a capacity to adjust to unpleasant circumstances and to accept right choices that are distasteful without complain. Anyone who cannot do so would serve his country better with pen and ink in his closet. 'Manliness' means not ruthlessness nor callousness but the opposite of squeamishness. It is a quality required of gentleman (and ladies) in all activities, but in some walks of life, and above all in politics, to a higher degree. Manliness does not replace, but sustains discrimination. It is a species of courage.

*   *   *

Even in private life, no man can walk alone and a politician is expecially obliged to recognize that he depends on others as they do on him. This is insisted on even by Plantagenet Palliser. Though a gentleman was always 'enough for himself ... to restrain him from doing what he knows to be wrong', he said, a Prime Minister could no more ignore his colleagues than a shipbuilder could produce his ship single-handed. Of course there were some jobs of a different kind, even in politics, and when he had been employed in such work, he could say whether he 'would or would not undertake the work that was proposed' because he had 'only a bit of the ship to build'.[57] But as head of Her Majesty's government, he could do nothing without the co-operation of others and had to conduct himself accordingly.

Another reason why gentlemen remain loyal to their party is that they consider it arrogant for individual members, especially young and untried ones, to suppose that they know better than the wiser older heads who decide the party's policies. When in his early days in London, Phineas declared to Barrington Erle that if he went into Parliament it would be 'not to support a party, but to do the best I can for the country', Erle began to fear that he might be one of those 'parliamentary hermits' or 'dwellers in political caves' who were either 'knavish or impractical'.[58] And the same opinion was expressed by Mr Monk when he criticized Phineas for wanting to vote against his party in support of Turnbull's proposal for disfanchising certain boroughs. Mr Monk told Phineas, with some asperity, that though they all knew that some boroughs were inexcusable, 'There must be compromises, and you should trust to others who have studied the matter more thoroughly than you, to say how far the compromise should go at the present moment ... Believe me, Finn, if you want to be useful, you must submit yourself in such matters to those with whom you act.' Of course there are contemptible ways of submitting to others. The model is not Sir Timothy Beeswax who discovered what he thought by ascertaining the opinions of Lord Drummond, and asserting the contrary. But to attempt to decide everything for oneself is neither 'useful nor manly'.[49] A House full of such men would be incapable of governing.

What appears as loyalty to party in the circumstances of English parliamentary life is an instance of the larger principle, that the bonds among men who have for some time lived and worked together should be respected. Casting one's lot with those who have long been your associates makes it more likely that you and they think alike and that in working with them, you will be acting in accordance with your own convictions.

Nevertheless, a gentleman may also be obliged to change his allegiance. But when he does so, there should have been 'a hard contest in the man's breast between loyalty to his party and strong personal convictions, the result of which has been an inability on the part of the struggler to give even a silent support to a measure which he has disapproved'.[60] To dissent with good reason, a man must have thought long and earnestly. Otherwise he is not justified in saying that his opinions are the results of his own thoughts. And the dissenter must be ready to bear the penalty rightly attached to disloyalty.

As in all other things, the moral quality of a gentleman's disloyalty or loyalty to party depends on his motives. This is the lesson that the Duke of Omnium tried to teach his son both when he deserted the family affiliation to stand as a Conservative, and when he returned to the Liberals. When Silverbridge announced that he meant to leave the Conservatives because he so heartily disliked 'the skipper', the duke condemned his action for being 'unstatesmanlike, unpatriotic, almost dishonest'. Silverbridge was moved merely by his 'personal liking for an individual', and that ought not to determine a gentleman's conduct in politics. He himself had thought it beneath him to eulogize Mr Mildmay in the House even though he almost worshipped him, and 'the same policy in reverse' required Silverbridge to keep silent about Sir Timothy. Whether Silverbridge was a Conservative or a Liberal, what mattered to the duke was how well he performed his duties. When Silverbridge became a Conservative, the duke had said to him that though they could not act together, though he would at times try to disprove all his assertions, he would take pride in seeing Silverbridge on the other side of the House if he did his work 'as gracefully and as fitly as I am sure you may if you will give yourself the trouble'.[61] He disapproved of Silverbridge's leaving the Conservatives when he doubted the rightness of the motives, but when Silverbridge made it clear that something better than a personal antipathy moved him, the duke was ready to welcome his decision.

*   *   *

That only certain motives are acceptable for gentleman does not mean, however, that they expect everyone in politics to be alike. The notion that Parliament should have 'the best possible men', Monk teaches Phineas, is a 'most repulsive idea if it were not that by its very vagueness it becomes inoperative'. And taken in any precise sense it is even worse. Unlike the historical Radical, John Stuart Mill, who believed precisely what Monk denies, here the Radical holds the view of gentlemen who do not want to be managed into perfection but expected their government rather to adjust and maintain the laws of their country in a sensible manner. Mr Monk assumes that his countrymen are not 'half-barbarous' but 'thoughtful, educated, and industrious', and wants legislators to be representative of the people not in the sense of speaking for the 'interests' of their constituents, but by voicing in the deliberations about national concerns, the different considerations that might be relevant.[62] His tolerance for a variety of characters in politics is a consequence of taking politicians to be engaged not in a battle between good and evil, or a technical enterprise, but in deliberating about national concerns which may be understood and dealt with in a variety of ways and from many different standpoints, none of which can be demonstrated to be absolutely right.

Another reason why it takes different sorts of men to make up a good committee of the nation is that no one is exactly what one would like him to be, and no man can be useful in all ways. Plantagenet Palliser was best suited to a 'regular office' such as that of Chancellor of the Exchequer. He had not the 'gift of the gab' nor a thick enough skin to make a good prime minister. Yet just because he was notorious for being 'above politics', a variety of men with no particular loyalty to him, were ready to trust him, and that made him the ideal head of a coalition government. After a while, that same purity made him offensive to both sides of the House and it was time for him to go. Though Palliser is a perfect gentleman he has his shortcomings as a politician and must be complemented by others, even by those of lesser virtue.[63]

Barrington Erle, who never pretended to be hard-working, was 'ordinarily honest' and did his bit as one who understood how things worked in parliament and was staunchly loyal to his party. Lawrence Fitzgibbon was nonchalent and idle to a fault, and disgraced himself by his laziness at the Colonial Office. But he was an effective speaker, honest about his indolence, and good 'at the outside skirmishing'. Phineas Finn, for all his rawness and irregularity, could 'stick to a desk from twelve to seven, and wish to come back after dinner . . .'.[64] And when we see him at the end of the story, earnestly and carefully trying to solve the riddle of Ireland, it is clear that Barrington Erle had been right in promoting his career.

Even Sir Orlando Drought has his points: 'He could speak volubly – and yet slowly – so that reporters and others could hear him. He was patient, both in the House and in his office, and he had the great gift of doing what he was told by men who understood things better than he did himself. He never went far astray in his official business, because he always obeyed the clerks and followed precedents.'[65] But he is typical of a set of men who have the outward marks without the substance of a gentleman. Such men allowed themselves to be thrust into any open hole in a government, professing that the good of the country was their only consideration. But though this made them useful when governments were being formed, resentment rankled in their bosoms, their judgements of their colleagues bore the colour of their grudges and when the opportunity came, they tried to get back their own without any care for country or even party.

The most ignoble of the politicians whom we meet in Trollope's novels are Bonteen, Ratler, and Roby, men who rise by making themselves detested and feared, who succeed because of their audacity and insensitivity. No head of a party wants them, but he may nevertheless send for them because otherwise they will 'sting' and 'goad' him to distraction. They make it plain to everyone that they are indispensable, that the country's survival rests on their shoulders, and that they alone know what everyone in the House feels about everything. They always announce that they had been offered the highest jobs but declined them, and they report conversations which, if they took place at all, hardly resemble the report. And they never forgive anyone who dissents from their own opinions. Whereas Lord Cantrip told Phineas, when he voted against his party – 'Do not suppose that I blame you. I have known the same done by . . . the best and noblest of our modern statesmen', Bonteen felt that Phineas had 'scuttled the ship and should never be forgiven'.[66] To men of this kind, politics is a matter of gang warfare and the only question to ask about a man is whether he is 'for' or 'against' you. Nevertheless there is work in which the peculiar talents even of such men might be useful. They could smell the temper of the House; they knew when Sir

Orlando's little jokes began to irritate rather than amuse; and they had a real talent for discovering which way the wind of success was blowing: 'When Mr Ratler won't come to the Prime Minister's house,' Lady Glencora said, 'you may depend that something is going to happen. It is like pigs carrying straws in their mouths. Mr Ratler is my pig.'[67]

The model politicians in Trollope's gallery are two men of very dissimilar origins and temperaments, Joshua Monk and the Duke of St. Bungay. They were the men whom Plantagenet Palliser trusted and admired without qualification, and consulted whenever he wanted an absolutely honest, just, and judicious opinion, whether on a matter of party policy or of constitutional propriety or of personal conduct.

In his early years, Mr Monk had 'inveighed against one minister after another as though they all deserved impeachment. He had advocated political doctrines which at that time seemed to be altogether at variance with any possibility of governing according to English rules of government. He had been regarded as a pestilent thorn in the sides of all ministers.' But he had outgrown all that and become a Cabinet Minister without anyone's suggesting that he had done so for gain or power even though he came from a family in trade and was not wealthy. Monk is an example of how men can grow in politics. It is with men as with horses, Trollope says: 'There are but few horses which you cannot put in harness, and those of the highest spirit will generally do your work the best.'[68]

But even Monk was better at some things than others. His talents as a speaker were most in evidence in opposition and he enjoyed it more than being in office: 'it is freedom against slavery, fire against clay, movement against stagnation ... Give me the full swing of the benches below the gangway, where I needed to care for no one, and could always enjoy myself on my legs as long as I felt that I was true to those who sent me there.' But though he hesitated to accept office, he felt that it would have been self-indulgent to stay out. He knew that the delights of opposition could easily corrupt a man and that, 'A man who is combating one ministry after another, and striving to imbue those ministers with his convictions, can hardly decline to become a minister himself when he finds that those convictions of his own are ... at least for some time to come, – to be the ministerial convictions of the day.'[69]

Monk is remarkable above all because he possesses what is so unusual, both a theoretical and practical understanding of politics. He was as judicious as the Duke of St. Bungay, but could also articulate a coherent view of political issues at a more abstract level. And yet, he kept a good sense of the unimportance of what any man did. When Phineas was downhearted after his first attempt to speak in the House, Monk told him that it was quite a good speech for a first effort, though not a great speech; 'Do not suppose that you have made an ass of yourself, – that is, in any special degree.'[70]

The old Duke of St. Bungay was not at all given to general or abstract reflection and he never spoke in Parliament because he had no talent for it. His genius was for arranging cabinets. He could see, as no one else could, how men of assorted virtues, temperaments, and convictions could be brought to work together, and when it was imperative to remain firm and when to give way. But though he was invaluable to a Prime Minister, he himself, he knew, was not fit to be one and would have been the first to say that if all men in politics were like him, things would be quite as bad as if all Members of Parliament were like Plantagenet Palliser.

Although his personal life was not very satisfactory – his wife was so silly that he was ashamed to appear with her in public, his interest in politics did not consume his life. He had willingly accepted office when it came, but always left it without regret: 'As a man cuts in and out at a whist table, and enjoys both the game and the rest from the game, so had the Duke of St. Bungay been well pleased in either position.' If he or his party were defeated on some point, 'it never occurred to him to be unhappy'. While he was President of the Council, he did his duty and enjoyed life in London, and when he was out of office, he took pleasure in his freedom to linger in Italy until May and to attend 'to his trees and his bullocks'. Though he was patriotic, 'his patriotism did not disturb his digestion'. He had been ambitious, but only moderately so, and he felt that 'his ambition had been gratified'.[71] There is nothing saintly about the Duke of St. Bungay. His perfection is that of an 'essentially . . . practical man who never raised unnecessary trouble'.[72]

His outstanding virtue is his ability to keep a sense of proportion about everything, even the crisis of the moment. When the Duke of Omnium declared that the iniquity of Sir Orlando made him feel that an honest man should have nothing to do with politics, the old duke replied: 'According to that the honest men are to desert their country in order that the dishonest men may have everything their own way.' When the young duke was shocked by the unblushing pretensions to office of the Robys and Ralters, the Duke of St. Bungay assured him that there was nothing especially new in that: 'We've heard of that before to-day ... perhaps the present world is less reticent in its eagerness than it was ... I doubt, however, whether it is more dishonest ...'.[73] Though he had modest expectations of his fellow men, the old duke was never cynical. He believed in loyalty to party (though he did not, as Erle did, confuse it with patriotism) and he believed also that there were men who were truly patriotic and scrupulous. But he knew as well that 'loyalty in politics' was in many cases simply devotion to the side which a man conceives to be one that he cannot leave without danger to himself.[74] For ordinary men, 'self-advantage' was perhaps the chief ingredient of loyalty and this was probably just as well, as a parliament full of Plantagenet Pallisers would hardly get much work done. There were no Catilines or Caesars to fear in England, but there was a good assortment of fools and rogues who would always be there in one form or another. When the scurrilous newspaper editor, Quintus Slide, tried to blackmail the Prime Minister into inviting him to Gatherum Castle, the Duke of Omnium saw in it 'a terribly bad sign of the times'. But the old duke replied; 'Well, hardly that, I think. The man is both a fool and a blackguard; but I don't think that we are therefore to suppose that there are many fools and blackguards like him.'[75] Of course such men might do harm, but they are part of the way of the world, at all times and in all places and it is neither prudent nor honourable to waste time on lamenting it.

The patriotism that motivates men like Mr Monk and the two dukes cannot be defined. It can only be roughly described as a concern to do what is good for the country as a whole without adopting blueprints for perfection, or enlisting in crusades for national glory, or descending to paternalism. And it renders them incapable of thinking of governing as an activity of serving 'classes', or balancing 'interests', or excluding 'outsiders'. Only those who are not gentlemen, the Bonteens and the Ratlers are intent on excluding 'outsiders' and insist that the Liberals are the 'rightful kings' and their opponents, 'usurpers'. Though Mr Monk is a Radical and hardly an aristocrat, he does not think of

'outsiders' as contenders for a share of the good things that power
can bring. The Duke of St. Bungay believed that the state of the
country was satisfactory – 'Workmen were getting full wages.
Farmers were paying their rent, capitalists by the dozen were
creating capitalists by the hundreds.'[76] But still, as a Liberal, he
felt obliged to assist, 'year after year', in pulling down institutions
which he regarded 'as the safeguards of the nation'. Trollope says
that there must have been 'a shade of melancholy' in the old
duke's mind as he contemplated the wreckage, and perhaps it
occurred to him that it would be well to have departed before
'everything was gone'.[77] But there is no suggestion that the duke
valued those institutions for serving the special interests of his
order. The young Silverbridge speaks a language foreign to his
father when he declares himself to be a Conservative because
'we've got to protect our position as well as we can against the
Radicals and Communists . . . The people will look after themselves and we must look after ourselves.' He had learned such talk
from his friend Tregear, who was not born an aristocrat but
hoped to join the aristocracy through marriage, and had learned
his politics from books. And when Silverbridge acquired some
experience of politics, he lost his enthusiasm for defending his
'class': 'I believe I have some vague idea as to supporting property
and land and all that kind of thing. I don't know that anybody
wants to attack anything.'[78]

When the brewers sent to Mr Monk, as they had to many other
Chancellors of the Exchequer, many extremely 'respectable' and
'imperative' deputations who threatened to cease supporting his
government if they did not get what they wanted, Mr Monk was
not moved, nor were his colleagues. Of course the brewers were
influential, 'both by general wealth and by the presence of many
members of the House' – it was likely that the 'average wealth of a
deputation of brewers could buy up half London'. The Press
cried that the brewers were being treated infamously. But as Mr
Monk, the Duke of St Bungay, the Duke of Omnium believed
that satisfying the brewers' claim was not for the good of the
country, they remained firm even though their policy was declared to be 'a disgrace to the fiscal sagacity of the country'.[79]

The conduct of the Duke of St. Bungay and Mr Monk makes it
clear that a gentleman walks a knife edge between crass indifference and a nice sense of proportion, between cynicism and
detachment. He takes seriously the responsibility of using well

whatever power he wields, but he also appreciates the truth in the
duchess's remark that 'The country goes on its own way, either for
better or for worse, whichever of them are in.' The kind of detachment required is illustrated in an exchange between the old
Duke of St. Bungay and the younger Duke of Omnium, who is
Prime Minister. They are arranging the new cabinet and the
Prime Minister says, 'The thing itself is so momentous that one
ought to have aid from heaven.' St. Bungay replies, 'Aid from
heaven you may have by saying your prayers . . . But an angel
won't come to tell you who ought to be Chancellor of the Exchequer.' As this fails to soothe the Prime Minister, the old duke
tries to produce better comfort by reminding him of what 'dear
old Lord Brock' used to say – that 'it was much easier to find a
good Sec'y of State than a good coachman'. But the young duke
regarded a joke on 'so solemn a subject' as blasphemy.[80]
Omnium's earnestness was a shortcoming. It prevented him from
being robust enough to weather the fortunes of politics. The old
duke was better at recognizing both the gravity and triviality of
everything they did. That awareness did not distract him from
taking seriously and acting decisively on what he perceived to be
his duty here and now, but it enabled him to shrug off both the
fear and reality of failure.

As they are mortal, even such men are not altogether immune
to the attractions of power. Despite his deep reluctance to become
Prime Minister, the Duke of Omnium succumbed to 'the gradual
love of power created by the exercise of power'. He felt useless and
yet, just because there was no task that absorbed him, he could
not let go. But Trollope's stress falls on showing that the lust for
power was an abberration in him and not at all present in Mr
Monk and St. Bungay. Though the coalition still had a good
working majority and the Duke of St. Bungay was subtle enough
to contrive ways of keeping the Government going for many years,
he now believed that it had served its term. Earlier, when the old
duke had thought the Coalition essential, he had patiently nursed
the younger duke to keep him from resigning. But now he could
see that 'the Coalition which he had created had done its work'.
Mr Monk said the same: 'We have served our turn and we ought
to go.' St. Bungay found as much to divert him in managing the
art of resigning as in his earlier task of preserving the Coalition.
And the Prime Minister, restored to himself, came to agree that
'The play has been played.'[81]

The story of these men, who had satisfied what they and others believed to be the highest ambition of all and had stepped down, ends with a quiet, amiable conversation between the former Prime Minister and Mr Monk, who had been once his colleague and was now serving under Mr Gresham. Monk says bluntly that he considered the present 'legitimate division of parties' preferable to the coalition, but that nevertheless the coalition had not been a mistake: 'There was a difficulty at the time, and that difficulty was overcome.' They had not reduced everything to 'divine order', but they had performed their unexciting task fairly well.[82]

His only regret, Mr Monk said, was that the Duke of Omnium had retired from official life. Palliser had yet to master the difficult lesson that Caesar might learn to serve under Pompey, but he succeeded in learning it. His reconciliation to returning to public life in a more obscure post points to another quality of gentlemen in politics – a readiness to take pride even in performing unnoticed, tedious tasks. This quality is emphasized in the scene where the House and the galleries empty leaving Mr Monk 'to explain his proposed alteration in the dog tax to a thin House of seventy or eighty members'.[83] But we feel sure that though Monk had risen to be Chancellor of the Exchequer, he did not find this either odd or irksome.

What explains the attitude of Mr Monk and the Duke of Omnium is not so much a readiness to be self-effacing as an accurate appreciation of the object of their ambition. They recognized the glory of being associated with a long line of the most illustrious men of England in perpetuating and perhaps improving the greatest civilization on earth. Every imaginative Englishman, from the country vicar to the barman in Cheapside, Trollope says, must have dreamt of walking up 'that more than royal staircase' and felt that to die without doing that is 'not to have done that which it most becomes an Englishman to have achieved'.[84] But on the other hand, the reality of what goes on in Parliament is far from glorious. Mrs Finn was not exaggerating when she said, 'It isn't in human nature to listen hour after hour to such platitudes ... I look upon the Treasury Bench in July as a sort of casual-ward which we know to be necessary, but is almost too horrid to be contemplated.'[85] Many a politician has had to suffer the fate of Lord Middlesex, who had worked earnestly for months on his proposals for Church Reform, only to watch the Members 'swarming away thru the doors like a flock of sheep' as he struggled to go on speaking to the Speaker and the two remaining reporters who 'used their pens very listlessly'. Even when Palliser spoke, and everyone approved of his words, 'more than half the House had been asleep more than half the time that he was on his legs'.[86] But for all their black moments, neither Palliser nor any of the other gentlemen in politics regretted his vocation. They accepted its tedium as part of its glory. Like all good craftsmen, they were dedicated to completing a job that they considered worthwhile, in accordance with a true estimation of their own capacities, and with a full appreciation of the intractability of the material with which they had to work.

In his stories of gentlemen seeking success in the world, Trollope portrays an ambition that is nothing like the 'honour' that Falstaff ridiculed and that destroyed Richard of Gloucester, Coriolanus, or Macbeth. It is not an ambition that despises loyalty to persons and principles as a sign of weakness because it is not an abstract, uncontrollable, aimless drive for power that overrides morality and law. The gentleman's ambition is shaped not only by 'dreams of something better' but also by 'fears of something worse'. It readily acknowledges both the mortality of men and the civilized shaping of human life. It can therefore possess and enjoy its achievements, and come to a rest satisfied.

11 Religion

It might seem that a man who is committed to pursuing the pleasures of life on earth cannot be seriously affected by believing in God. Yet Trollope not only takes it for granted but frequently emphasizes that being a gentleman is connected with being a Christian. And he speaks of belief in a life after death as if it were central to a gentleman's faith. Even a pagan like Cicero might be called a gentleman, Trollope said, because he believed 'in eternity, in the immortality of the soul, in virtue for the sake of its reward in the hereafter'.[1] But on the other hand, Trollope shows us characters whose preoccupation with eternal bliss disqualifies them from being gentlemen. There he makes it clear how easily the part is played by religion in the life of a gentleman can be misunderstood.

The most common misconception identifies a gentleman's religion with a stern devotion to duty. That undoubtedly has been the view of some Christians, as well as of some doubters, such as George Eliot, for whom God became 'inconceivable', Immortality 'unbelievable', and only Duty remained 'peremptory and absolute'. But how far that is from a gentleman's view is evident in Trollope's treatment of those two ardent Christians, Mrs Prime (*Rachel Ray*) and Mrs Bolton (*John Caldigate*).

The symptom of what is wrong with their religion is their abhorrence of anything pleasant. Mrs Prime not only wore widow's weeds but wore them as if she had vowed to make herself look repulsive and always looked fit to bury someone. Small comforts like buttered toast, tea, and gossip were shunned by her; she preferred having stringy, bitter tea at Miss Pucker's, with other ladies of her persuasion who sewed for the poor in virtuous silence. Mrs Bolton rejoiced in the misery of getting up early on a nasty, dark morning to dress without heat or light so that she was always stubbing her toes on the furniture. And because she prayed with her knees on hard boards, she knew that her prayers were more effective. For both these women, it was a duty to be miserable.

Their own devotion to cheerlessness was not enough; they felt
obliged to wage war also on the pleasures of others. The readiness
of her sister, Rachel, to chat with a young man in a churchyard
was for Mrs Prime a sure sign that the girl was on the road to
damnation, and when Rachel went to a ball wearing a pretty
frock, the stench of sin in her mother's house became so strong in
Mrs Prime's nostrils that she felt obliged to move out. The same
purity is displayed by Mrs Bolton in her battle first to prevent her
daughter's marriage to John Caldigate, and then to end it. Just as
Mrs Prime, without knowing her sister's suitor, never doubted the
rumour that he had stolen property and left town without paying
his debts, so Mrs Bolton knew at once, when John Caldigate was
accused of bigamy, that it was her duty to imprison her daughter
so as to rescue her from living in sin. Even the danger that the
imprisonment might cause her daughter's death did not make the
mother hesitate, so intent was she on saving the girl's soul. All
persecutions were justified by the motto, 'Those whom you love
you must chastise.'[2] Both women lived for 'a cause', confident
that they were securing a brighter future by making the present
painful.

The most obvious defect of such Christianity is its inconsistency. Trollope points out that though the good ladies acknowledged that human beings ought to reproduce themselves
and expected such reproducing to be the fruit of marriage, they
saw nothing odd in their efforts to prevent young men and women
from finding mates. When they declared that every young man
was a 'wicked wild beast',[3] they never noticed that they were condemning a considerable portion of the human race. Though Mrs
Bolton hated Papists for their superstitious beliefs in celibacy,
flagellation, and fasting, she confidently tried to achieve the same
deprivation and pain by different means.

The refusal to cherish life as a gift from God was in itself bad
enough. But Trollope saw in it a symptom of a deeper vice, an
un-Christian and ungentlemanly pride. Mrs Prime and Mrs Bolton never doubted that they possessed an insight into God's
thoughts which others lacked and which allowed them to exercise
special powers. Mrs Prime ruled her mother and sister by claiming the right to identify and punish their wrong-doings and dismissing any attempt to differ with her as evidence of sin. But her
belief in human frailty was never turned on herself. Though overwhelmed by the iniquity of her sister's meeting with a young man

in the churchyard, when she herself was closeted with Mr Prong in a small back parlour, Mrs Prime did not hear the steps of the Evil One. Her assurance that she belonged to the company of saints allowed her to behave as she chose. When she and Mr Prong became engaged, they congratulated themselves on their freedom from the 'poor creature longings of the heart' which afflicted other mortals.

The same self-righteous certainty enabled Mrs Bolton to terrify her husband into yielding to her will: 'when she spoke to him of his own soul . . . or even of souls in general, he was frightened and paralysed'. The charge that her daughter had been deceived by the husband she loved and had borne a bastard enabled Mrs Bolton to rejoice in her own infallibility: 'She had been right, – right from first to last, right in everything . . .' Far from hoping that the husband would be proved innocent or worrying about her daughter's suffering, Mrs Bolton was happy when the evidence seemed to tell against him. It enabled her to hope that she would realize her dearest wish – that she and her daughter might be shut up forever in her house, to 'pray together, struggle together, together wear their sackcloth and ashes, and together console themselves with their hopes of eternal joys, while they shuddered, not altogether uncomfortably, at the torments prepared for others'.[4] Of course Mrs Bolton often repeated the Christian injunction, 'judge not', but she had no doubt about how God would judge. When she prayed, she knew that God would give the right answers, and that those who received answers different from hers had prayed wrongly.

By emphasizing that there was no hypocrisy in either of these women, Trollope makes it plain that the fault lies in their genuine belief that the human world consists of worthless sinners. They longed for a crisis that would expose the damned and confirm the ascendancy of the saints. About everyone, they asked only one question: Is he one of us, or one of them? Their self-denial was really a form of self-indulgence, and the 'self-indulgence of saints in this respect', Trollope assures us, 'often exceeds anything that is done by sinners'.[5] They were not troubled by fear of sins such as 'evil thoughts, hardness of heart, suspicion, unforgivingness, hatred', sins which are 'too impalpable for denunciation in the Decalogue' but are more tempting for ordinary people. Indeed they dismissed pity and love as 'emanations from the Evil One' which might tempt them into being tender with sinners.[6]

How a gentleman regards such religion is summed up by the non-churchgoing Mr Caldigate when he denounces the clergyman, who declares that the young Mrs Caldigate is a lost soul because she stayed with her husband, for being 'impertinent, unmanly, inhuman, and blasphemous'.[7] 'Saints' possess a self-confidence that gentlemen find repugnant. The Mrs Boltons of this world know nothing of the difficulty to which a gentleman is never immune – of doubting how much he should allow to the convictions of others and how far he is justified in condemning those who reject his own. Because 'saints' equate virtue with performances rather than motives, they are obsessed with securing uniformity in outward actions. Any deviation is equally a transgression, and therefore courting and promiscuity, indolence about church going and absence of faith are all the same to them. Worst of all, their indifference to motives keeps the saintly from noticing that their own preoccupation with eternal bliss springs from an ambition to be as gods among men and dictate the conduct of others. In short, what is wrong with Mrs Bolton and Mrs Prime is their 'love of power',[8] which they disguise from themselves by clothing it in religious fervour.

The very different way in which thoughts of eternal bliss affect the conduct of a gentleman is illustrated in *The Vicar of Bullhampton*. In his preface to the novel, Trollope explained that he hoped to persuade his readers that the misery of Carry Brattle, who was seduced into a life of sin was as 'worthy of alleviation as is every misery to which humanity is subject'. But in fact Trollope did much more than make a plea for showing compassion to fallen women. He explored a gentleman's attitude to sin and mercy.

At the centre of the story is the attitude of the vicar, Frank Fenwick, to the fallen girl. He was a clergyman who often wondered about the nature of his duties. Though he believed that there was nothing so hateful as the constant interference of a self-constituted adviser, that seemed to be what a clergyman had to do. Worse still was his consciousness of inconsistency when on the one hand he warned his parishioners of the everlasting fires that awaited sinners, while on the other hand he told them to believe in God's mercy.

Both these difficulties, in their severest form, confronted him in the family of the miller, Brattle. Not only had two of the children gone astray; the miller himself was a stubborn old heathen who refused to step inside a church. The pious Mrs Brat-

tle had expected that her husband's habits would be 'as worm-
wood and gall' to her vicar, that he would try to frighten her
husband with stories of the punishment that awaited him in the
next world. Was it not the duty of a minister of God to 'pronounce God's threats to erring human beings?' Instead the vicar
talked more of 'life with its sorrows, and vices, and chances of
happiness and possibilities of goodness' than of God's vengeance
on sinners; he treated the heathen miller with sympathy; and he
spoke warmly of the fallen daughter without denouncing her as a
'castaway', indeed as if she might 'be worthy of happiness here
and of all joy hereafter'. Mrs Brattle was surprised and even al-
armed that 'God's messenger should . . . never say a word of his
message to that hard lord . . . who was . . . too stubborn to receive
it,' though she was also comforted in a way that she herself could
hardly understand. But the vicar himself suffered from mis-
givings worse than Mrs Brattle's. How could he tell Mrs Brattle
that her faith could bring her eternal happiness, but that nevertheless her husband, bereft as he was of faith, might escape that
everlasting fire?[9]

The vicar's leniency with the Brattles is especially remarkable
because he is a pugnacious man, one of Trollope's fighting parsons, inclined to enjoy rather than to fear a contest, and not at all
disposed to advocate turning the other cheek. To give in so as to
avoid a fight, Fenwick said firmly, is not virtuous: 'If a man be
quite certain that he is really actuated by a Christian desire to forgive, it may be all very well; but if there be any admixture of base
alloy in his gold, if he allows himself to think that he may avoid
the evils of pugnacity, and have things go smooth for him here,
and become a good Christian by the same process, why then I
think he is likely to fall to the ground between two stools.'[10] Fenwick needed to be pugnacious for his project of restoring Carry to
a respectable life. His neighbours did not support him and the
fact that Carry was a pretty girl made his efforts to find her an
easy subject for unpleasant rumours.

But though the vicar worked relentlessly for Carry, he never
denied that she had sinned. He saw her as a 'fallen woman', and
even believed that there was a visible mark of her wickedness. As
he talked to her, he noticed, Trollope says, that 'there had come
across her mouth that look of boldness which the use of bad,
sharp words, half-wicked, half witty will always give'. Far from
telling Carry that she was blameless, Fenwick endeavoured to

teach her that 'she could have no escape from that dirt and vileness and depth of misery into which she had fallen, without the penalty of a hard, laborious life, in which she must submit to be regarded as one whose place in the world was very low ...'.[11] Trollope does not present this as an unjust penalty imposed by society on a victim, but as the consequence of the choices that Carry had made for herself, which she was obliged to accept. That there is sin, and that it should be recognized as such, and atoned for, is a truth that gentlemen do not question.

But believing that all men are sinners does not mean that there is an evil spirit or a dark, irrational force within human beings thwarting their better spiritual selves, or that all pleasure is wicked and that whenever a man enjoys being alive he has succumbed to sin. It means that the virtuous are not justified in regarding themselves as so superior to sinners that they need show them no sympathy, and that however well some men may avoid sinful acts, by comparison with the perfection of God, the differences among men are as nothing. However good a man is, he is imperfect.

All men are sinners because all men are mortals. They live in a world of constant change and they can never know all that they would need to know in order to discern perfectly what they ought to do. This is because, for one thing, every human action is a response to other human responses which cannot be predicted or perfectly understood and may in turn evoke responses that take an unexpected shape. Therefore men cannot foresee all the consequences of their choices or be certain even about which outcome would have been best. Besides, mortals cannot do all things at once and must choose this or that. As every good necessarily excludes another, nothing can be more than partially desirable. And in addition, men can be distracted from a distant, less strongly felt good by a more immediate, though less important discomfort. Or their judgement may be clouded by a failure to think coherently and see the true proportions of things. All this obliges men to recognize that however well they may have tried to judge, though they have precepts and examples to guide them, they can never be sure that they have made the one and only right choice because even if it is the best possible one, it will necessarily have some defect.

But it is important to notice also that, in this picture, what keeps human beings from perfection is their mortal rationality, their capacity to interpret and respond from different standpoints without being able to see or do everything at once. Such imperfection was absent in the Garden of Eden because that was not a human world, not a life among other men interpreting and responding to one another. In short, a gentleman understands the Christian belief that 'we are all sinners' to be a doctrine not about inborn evil but about the conditions attached to a human condition. It obliges men to recognize that in the best of all possible worlds there will still be much amiss, and to remember that dissatisfaction is inseparable from being a rational mortal. It does not mean that men are rubbish or that there is a duty to abhor what is pleasant on earth. It is rather a warning against presumption, a ground for resignation, an injunction to keep our expectations modest.

But it is not only because they are all as distant from the perfection of God as any sinner that mortals are obliged to show compassion to the fallen. It is also because human beings should not arrogate to themselves the office, which belongs to God, of condemning their fellows to unending punishment. That is the meaning of the Christian injunction, 'Do not judge'. It reminds men both that God will judge them and that they cannot know how God will judge. Men need not and should not refrain from judging, but they should not presume to identify their mortal judgements with those of God.

Carry's neighbours had no right to be certain that there was nothing good in her, that she could not saved, that they had no obligation to help her to escape from sin. On the contrary, they were obliged to let her hope that she might in time restore herself. When the vicar rebuked the dissenting clergyman, Mr Puddleham, for describing Carry Brattle as 'a lost soul', it was not for considering her a sinner but for refusing to ask whether she had not repented, or could not be brought to repent:

How do you know she has not married, and become an honest woman . . . as did Mary Magdalene, for instance? If she believes and repents, all her sins will be white as snow . . . Then speak of her as you would of any other sister or brother – not as a thing that must be always vile because she has fallen once. Women will so speak, – and other men. One sees something of a reason for it. But you and I, as Christian ministers should never allow ourselves to speak so thoughtlessly of sinners.[12]

Puddleham's talk of Carry as 'a lost soul' implied that he could survey the whole of the things to the end of time, as God did; it was the judgement of a superior upon an inferior being, not that of a human being upon his equal. A similar presumption is displayed by Mrs Fenwick when she felt 'almost tempted to ask why such misery should have fallen upon parents who have been honest, sober, and industrious'. Her question implied, her husband told her, that she 'was measuring the Almighty God with a footrule'. The insistence of Carry's sister-in-law, Mrs Brattle, that she was 'a vile thing' for whom 'there ain't nothing too bad' and that it was sinful to help her because 'If such as them is to be made all's one as others as have always been decent, I'm sure I don't know who it is as isn't to be saved' makes Mrs Brattle 'an abominable case of the Pharisee thanking the Lord that he was not such a one as the Publican', who, in fact, 'was in a fair way to heaven'.[13]

At no point does Trollope suggest that it is wrong to make rules and judgements, to venerate or reward some men more than others, or to impose pain or even death to enforce human decisions. He insists rather that in taking such action, a gentleman does not pretend, as self-appointed saints do, to possess more than human insight or to know the destiny of men, to claim a right to manipulate or use others as if they were masters and the others, slaves.

There is a profound difference between the vicar's efforts to save Carry and the exertions of Mrs Prime or Mrs Bolton because he is giving help where it is requested, not imposing his will. It is crucial for the vicar that Carry had expressed a desire to abandon her sinful life, and that he believed her to be sincere in doing so. Had there been pretence or falsehood in her penitence, Trollope makes it clear, the vicar would have been, and should have been, unforgiving. The help that he offers is not to the sinner but to the sinner who repents.

How faith contributes to the ability to forgive, Trollope shows us in Carry's father who, though his daughter had been the light of his life, felt obliged to banish her utterly from his heart. Her sin had violated the proper order of things; he meant to restore the balance by punishing the sinner, and his determination to punish one sinner grew into a desire to punish the world at large for his own sufferings. Thus he 'brooded over injuries done to him, – injuries real or fancied,' till he taught himself to wish that 'all who hurt him might be crucified for the hurt they did to him'. To let himself be comforted when he had been visited by disasters which he had done nothing to deserve would, he felt, be dishonest and he considered it a duty neither to forgive the trespasses of others nor to forget his own wrongs. This conviction made it impossible for the vicar either to move or to comfort him: 'Of what use could it be to preach of repentance to one who believed nothing . . .?' But when the physical presence of his daughter brought the miller to relent, his words suggest that in some way, unknown to himself, he had grasped the truth of Christianity – 'them as falls may right themselves . . .', and with that truth, had discovered the kind of resignation that faith can bring.[14]

But forgiving a sinner may not be enough. Indeed Trollope insists that something more than a readiness to say kind words or give help constitutes real charity. In encouraging a sinner to hope, one must recognize that a sin repented is only the first step on the way to learning to live in another fashion, and that new habits are not learned in a day. When Carry lamented, 'Nobody loves me now . . .', the vicar was inclined to tell her that God loved her, but he saw that someone who felt so forlorn, and found it so difficult to think beyond her immediate misery, needed rather to be reminded of a love 'that was more easily intelligible' and could be 'more palpably felt' than the abstract love of God.[15] Nor would it do to expect someone with her past to live a lonely life without human support.

Trollope makes a point of condemning those who, when they find 'that a young man is neglecting his duties, doing nothing, spending his nights in billiard rooms and worse places, and getting up at two o'clock in the day,' recommend 'that he should lock himself up in his own dingy room, drink tea, and spend his hours in reading good books'.[16] A change from billiards to good books requires a strength of character which, if he possessed them, would probably have kept the young men from falling into bad habits. Such expectations reflect not charity but unChristian pride, a refusal to come to terms with the reality of another person and an overweening confidence in one's own powers. Here as elsewhere, Trollope is insisting on the strenuousness of genuine compassion and distinguishing it from the destructive arrogance of complacent reformers.

Ultimately the belief both that all men will have to answer for their sins before God and that sinners can repent means that human beings are what they learn to be and are responsible for what they become. One way of expressing this belief is to say that each has an immortal soul to make and save. It commits men to recognizing that individuality is of the essence of being human, and not a fixed identity given at birth but made by men over the course of their lives. Far from encouraging an aspiration to lose one's selfhood by merging with an immortal whole, it condemns such aspirations as an attempt to escape from mortality, a refusal to acknowledge the unbridgeable chasm between a mortal and his omnipotent Creator. Of course, there can be communion with God through love and grace, but that must be sharply distinguished from claiming to be one with God, or to have certain knowledge of God's will. Such claims are tantamount to denying that God is a creator who made man out of nothing, that he is the Judaeo-Christian God whose only name is He Who Is and who is incomprehensible because between a creator and his creatures there is nothing in common. For if men have nothing in common with God, they cannot hope to understand him or to read his thoughts. A man may receive direct personal communication from God, but his claim to have received such a communication does not give him a right to impose it on others because others have no way of knowing that he is correctly or genuinely reporting God's instructions. They might choose to believe him and accept him as a true prophet, but their faith in God does not oblige them to do so. And a man's refusal to believe those who say that they have spoken to God casts no doubt on his faith. The relation between man and God is a mystery mitigated solely by the will to believe.

* * *

Whereas in the *Vicar of Bullhampton* no one denies that Carry Brattle had sinned, in *Rachel Ray* and *John Caldigate* there is sharp disagreement about whether a sin had been committed. And this raises the questions: How are men to know what constitutes sin? Is it ever right to resist the opinion of the recognized pastors? Can sin be avoided by obeying rules or can there be disagreement about how to interpret rules? These questions are explored in *Dr Wortle's School*.

Dr Wortle, a clergyman who owns and runs a highly successful

preparatory school, had found in Mr Peacocke a paragon of a
teacher – a clergyman, a schoolmaster and scholar of distinction,
with a wife who fulfilled the duties of a matron just as admirably.
But there was a flaw of which the doctor was unaware – that the
Peacockes were not in fact husband and wife. They had married
after being told that Mrs Peacocke's husband was dead; when he
turned up afterwards, though only to disappear again, they decided to go on living together as husband and wife.

Trollope makes it plain that according to custom, law, and the
Church, marriages could not be dissolved and that therefore the
Peacockes were living in sin and should have separated. But that
there is more to be said on the matter, Trollope also makes it
plain by revealing the truth about the Peacockes at the beginning
of the story in order that, he says, the reader's interest would be
'simply in the conduct of my persons, during this disclosure, to
others'.[17]

The Peacockes' own attitude to themselves was far from simple.
Although Mrs Peacocke felt 'at liberty to proclaim to herself a
gospel of her own for the guidance of her own soul', she understood that Mr Peacocke was not equally free from 'the bonds
which religion had imposed upon him'.[18] But when she offered to
leave, he took the view that, as their lives had been welded together, on no account should they separate. He did not feel
ashamed of living with her; they were not injuring anyone; they
had clung together 'as a man and woman should who have loved
each other'. And therefore he regarded their relationship as 'fixed
by fate'. The trouble might have to be discussed from time to
time but 'the necessity of enduring it may be taken for granted'.[19]

That according to the rules by which men lived they were committing a sin, Peacocke acknowledged and in some way felt. But
he was reconciled to the fact that they were pretending to be that
which they were not: 'there are circumstances in which a lie can
hardly be a sin'. He did not, however, expect others to take the
same view. He had not sought the post with Dr Wortle, but had
been invited to take it. He imposed certain conditions on himself
and his wife: They had never broken bread with the doctor nor
accepted any other invitation and Peacocke had refused to act as
curate despite Dr Wortle's repeated requests that he should do so.
When he agreed reluctantly to preach occasionally on Sundays,
he refused pay. Still, Peacocke had come to think that he must
tell the truth to Wortle. The doctor had relied on him as on no

other man. Had they been regarded 'as people simply obscure, to whom no mystery attached itself', nothing perhaps need ever have been said. But people had begun talking, and such talk endangered the school: 'We must cling to each other,' he told his wife, 'let the world call us what names it may. But there may come a time in which one is called on to do a special act of justice to others.'[20]

The rumours about the Peacockes had earlier moved the bishop to persuade the doctor to question them. Since so much that we believe and do depends on the characters that we attribute to others, the bishop argued, we have to pay attention to reports of bad character, and especially about a clergyman because the force of his sermons 'depends much on the idea that the audience has of the piety of the man who preaches it'. Although the words of God do not get their value from the man who utters them, they are bound to lose some of their effectiveness if he is known to be or even only suspected of being 'a breaker of the Commandments'.[21] The doubts about Mr Peacocke were not unreasonable – there was no other clergyman in the parish about whose life, for five years, no one knew anything. When questions about the character of a man in such a position became widespread, one was bound to notice them.

Dr Wortle's convictions and temperament should have disposed him to agree with the bishop, indeed to be severe with Mr Peacocke. He had fought and triumphed over a number of bishops and parents to build up a very distinguished and successful preparatory school, and though he looked after the bodies and souls of his pupils with great care, he insisted on being paid well for his pains, just as he expected to be charged the going price for meat by his butcher. He was not given to overlooking infringements on his rights, or to yielding rather than fighting for what he believed to be his due. And he had good reason to be offended by a man who had, it would seem, taken advantage of his confidence and who might cause him considerable trouble. Yet after he had heard Peacocke's account, the doctor's immediate response was: 'I would have clung to her, let the law say what it might . . . and I think that I could have reconciled it to my God.'[22]

There is no suggestion that the doctor was condoning bigamy or adultery, or that he in any way denied, questioned, or rebelled against the established laws of God and man. He did not construe the dilemma of the Peacockes as a clash between 'morality and circumstances', 'orthodoxy and sensibility', 'the dictates of a rigid code and human sympathy'. The question that concerned him was rather: What, according to the morality by which I live, ought I to do? He judged the moral quality of Peacocke's answer according to Peacocke's motives, and what prevailed with the doctor was his conviction that Peacocke had genuinely striven to live as a Christian should. Nevertheless though the doctor was prepared to say that he would have done the same, it did not follow that Peacocke's behaviour had been right: 'I might have been wrong . . . Both might have been wrong.'[23]

But to the doctor's wife it seemed obvious that the Peacockes could not be excused because she clung to a simple certainty – that 'a woman should not live with a man unless she be his wife'. Trollope emphasizes that 'there was no softer-hearted woman than Mrs Wortle anywhere in the diocese, or one less likely to be severe upon a neighbour'.[24] What is at issue between the doctor and his wife is how moral rules are to be understood. For Mrs Wortle, they were simply commands, ordering what ought to be done. No one in her community had ever doubted that the rules by which they lived forbade taking a second husband while the first still lived; the Peacockes themselves did not deny that Mrs Peacocke had done just that; therefore the Peacockes had to be condemned as unrepentant sinners and were certainly not fit to teach the young. The doctor, however, saw moral rules as a short-hand for all that a good Christian should consider in deciding his conduct, which implied that a sensitive moral judgement might not coincide with the simple conclusions drawn from ordinary interpretations of rules.

The Peacockes' circumstances were extraordinary and therefore required to be judged in an unusual fashion: 'it is not often that one comes across events like these, so altogether out of the ordinary course that the common rules of life seem insufficient for guidance. To most of us it never happens; and it is better for us that it should not happen. But when it does, one is forced to go beyond the common rules.' His concern to preserve the moral understanding rather than the rules had always made the doctor hostile to clerics with 'signs of a special pietistic bearing', and led him to 'despise the fear of sin which makes us think that its contact will soil us'.[25] The notion that by obeying a set of rules men and women could avoid being sinners was not Dr Wortle's conception of Christianity.

He did, however, acknowledge another consideration about the 'laws of God and man' which tipped the scales in the other direction. If men and women were to live together, they had to live by common rules and not claim special exemptions. Unless certain expectations were respected, there could be no trust among men. When Peacocke said, 'I was wrong . . . in supposing that the nature of my marriage need be of no concern to others, but to herself and to me,' the doctor agreed: 'Yes, – Mr Peacocke; yes. We are, all of us, joined together too closely to admit of isolation such as that.' He had therefore to consider more than Peacocke's character and his own feeling for the man; he had to take into account also what his parishioners and the parents of his public expected of him, and what he owed to them. His difficulty came from the fact that he could not reconcile his two quite different judgements:

> He could not bring his conscience and his inclination to come square together. And even when he counselled himself to yield to his conscience, his very conscience, – a second conscience, as it were, – revolted against the first. His first conscience told him that he owed a primary duty to his parish, a second duty to his school, and a third to his wife and daughter. In the performance of all these duties he would be bound to rid himself of Mr Peacocke. But then there came that other conscience, telling him that the man had been more 'sinned against than sinning' . . .[26]

Peacocke had no such doubts. He was certain that the doctor could not keep him on: 'Would it do, do you think,' Peacocke said to his wife, 'for a priest to preach against drunkenness, whilst he himself was a noted drunkard? . . . It is not what the drunken priest might think of himself, but what others might think of him. It would not be with us the position which we know that we hold together, but that which others would think it to be . . . We shall have to go, and I shall be forced to approve of our dismissal.'[27] A school was supposed to teach its pupils to respect certain ideas of right and wrong. If its teachers appeared to disregard those ideas, even if it was only an appearance, the school could not fulfil the expectations of the parents who entrusted their children there.

But as the doctor could not see his way so easily, he consulted Mr Puddicombe, who was a simpler and less clever man and therefore less liable to be confused by subtleties. Puddicombe insisted that the telling question was: 'Would you have taken him into your establishment had you known it all before?' And since the doctor could not answer, Yes, Peacocke ought to be sent away. Even though Mr Peacocke was a good man, it could not undo the fact that, by keeping Peacocke, Dr Wortle seemed to condone sin. This was not what the doctor wanted to hear and he told himself that Puddicombe was a 'fanatical, hard-hearted bigot'. But he felt obliged to 'acknowledge that all the man had said was true'. He therefore broke with his established practice and refunded the fees to parents who withdraw their children, while making his position perfectly clear:

> A circumstance has happened which, though it cannot impair the utility of my school and ought not to injure its character, may still be held as giving offence to certain persons. I will not be driven to alter my conduct by what I believe to be a foolish misconception on their part. But they have a right to their own opinions, and I will not mulct them because of their conscientious convictions.[28]

But though Mr Puddicombe was right and the doctor was obliged to respect conventional opinion, Trollope also makes it plain that this opinion should not be confused with the judgement of God. This was acknowledged by both wives in different ways. When after telling the tale of her husband's kindness, Mrs Peacocke asked Mrs Wortle: 'Will God condemn him?', Mrs Wortle replied: 'We must leave that to Him,' but she never again spoke of Mrs Peacocke's 'sin'. On the other hand, though Mrs Peacocke insisted that when her husband was called to his account, 'he would stand there pure and bright, in glorious garments, – one fit for heaven', she could not be persuaded that she was fit for the society of Mrs Wortle. Her personal belief in her husband's goodness did not, Mrs Peacocke felt, absolve her of an obligation to respect the conventions of the community in which she lived.[28]

The same nuances in respect for 'the laws of God and man' are expressed in still another way by Mr Puddicombe in his last interview with the doctor. The doctor had written a letter justifying his conduct to the bishop and the disaffected parents. But the letter would not do, Puddicombe argued, because the doctor had not said that 'They did live together though they were not married; –

and under all the circumstances, I did not think that they were on that account unfit to be left in charge of my boys.' That was the truth of the matter and that had to be stated if the doctor insisted on explaining himself. But it was impossible to say that in a letter without causing even greater misunderstanding, and therefore the doctor had better 'live it down in silence'. Nevertheless Puddicombe added: 'There will be those, like myself, who though they could not dare to say that in morals you were strictly correct, will love you the better for what you did . . . '[30]

Dr Wortle's dilemma is unusual, but it is only an exaggerated version of a universal difficulty about the relation between moral rules and moral choices of which a gentleman never loses sight. On the one hand, he cannot absolve himself from respecting the rules recommended by his pastors and accepted by his community. Not only do they offer a kind of guidance that no mortal should disdain. They also help to order his relations with others and to sustain the stable expectations without which civilized life is impossible. But on the other hand, the rules by which men have to live are an abridgement of a complicated moral understanding. Just what rules are relevant and what they require in particular circumstances is never indisputable. The conventional interpretations may not be the most sensitive ones. Breaking the rules made by God-fearing and judicious men may not offend God. Not all choices of which good men disapprove are necessarily evil, and may even be praiseworthy. Nevertheless, that does not absolve anyone from taking the established rules seriously. They may not be broken lightly. And no one is justified in feeling aggrieved when his violation subjects him to disapproval. A gentleman should have the strength to go his own way when he has persuaded himself that he should, while recognizing that he must suffer certain penalities for doing so. For otherwise mortals cannot stave off barbarism.

*   *   *

The fact that the Church is not an armoury from which thunderbolts issue forth to strike down sinners makes it tempting to conclude that the Church is merely an embellishment in the life of a gentleman. And that impression is strengthened by the readiness of Trollope and even his most pious gentlemen to mock earnestness about religious practices.

Mrs Proudie's insistence on three services and three sermons on Sundays gets no more sympathy than her conviction that services on saints' days are rank papacy or that a letter dated 'St. John's Eve' is sure evidence of idolatry. The purest of Trollope's clergymen, the Warden, Mr Harding, seems hardly to care what Christians do in the way of religious observances. When Mrs Proudie denounces Sabbath travelling and demands action 'to control so grievous a sin', the most that Mr Harding can bring himself to say is that 'all porters and stokers, guards, breaksmen, and pointsmen ought to have an opportunity of going to church' and that he hoped they did.[31] Mr Harding concentrated on making good music in the church. And when he recalls wistfully how in the good old days, before the austere reign of Bishop Proudie, the clergymen of Barchester used to play cards after dinner and joined in the dancing, we are encouraged to agree with the archdeacon's rejoinder: 'I believe the work was done a great deal better than it is now ... There wasn't so much fuss, but there was more reality. And men were men, and clergymen were gentlemen.'[32]

The archdeacon's animosity to Mrs Proudie is ridiculed quite as much as Mrs Proudie's belief that the archdeacon 'was an actual emanation from Satan' sent to devour souls which she had been sent to save from his depradations.[33] And Trollope does not suggest that there is any more piety in the contentment of the archdeacon's wife with her husband's ordinary black cloth waistcoat, than in the pleasure taken by the dean's wife in her husband's high, silken one. Indeed all the controversies, whether between the High and the High and Dry Church, or between High and Low churchmen, whether about chanted services and intoned prayers, genuflection and the length of sermons, lecterns and credence tables, candles and embroidered altar cloths, are treated as something of a joke. At the end of *Barchester Towers*, Trollope declares: 'If it be essentially and absolutely necessary to choose between the two, we are inclined to agree with Mrs Grantly that the bell, book, and candle are the lesser evil of the two. Let it however be understood that no such necessity is admitted in these pages.'[34]

Even the quarrel between Mr Fenwick and the dissenting clergyman, Mr Puddleham (*Vicar of Bullhampton*) is not taken seriously. Fenwick did not want to destroy Puddleham's following. Pugnacious though he was, Fenwick recognized that as a clergyman of the Established Church had great advantages over a Dissenter, there was some reason for Puddleham's envy. The vicar's refusal to engage in warfare with Puddleham may have had an element of guile, but it was in aid of what Fenwick truly believed – that the same truth might and could be better taught to different men by different teachers: 'Of this he was quite sure, that Mr Puddleham's religious teaching was better than none at all; and he was by no means convinced, – so he said, – that, for some of his parishioners, Mr Puddleham was not a better teacher than he himself.' Of course the vicar did not enjoy the psalm singing of Puddleham's followers almost at his doorstep, but he felt obliged to restrain his irritation: 'Was it not his special duty to foster love and goodwill among his people?' He 'always shook hands with Mr Puddleham, even though Mr Puddleham would never look him in the face'. Though Trollope clearly disapproves of Puddleham, it is not because of his religious convictions but because of his disposition to equate religion with a competition for the saving of souls: 'It had been his glory to be a poacher on another man's manor, to filch souls, as it were, out of the keeping of a pastor of a higher grade than himself'. And when Fenwick refused to fight, Puddleham felt cheated 'out of that appropriate acerbity of religion, without which a proselytizing sect can hardly maintain its ground beneath the shadow of an endowed and domineering Church'.[35] Puddleham's fault lies in turning religion into war, not in being a Dissenter. Far from suggesting that Dissenters suffer from faults absent in Anglicans, Trollope points out that Mr Puddleham's sentiments were probably not shared by many of his followers and that people join different churches, as they do everything else, for a variety of reasons. A man may become a Dissenter because 'he can be somebody in the management of his chapel and would be nobody in regard to the parish church'. Or he may remain with the Established Church only because he thinks it is the 'most respectable'. And on the whole, 'not one in fifty really believes that this or that form of worship is more likely to send him to heaven than any other', with which a gentleman would agree.[36]

The distinction between Anglicanism and the Roman Church is no more important. Although Phineas Finn is a Roman Catholic, that fact is drawn to our attention only when Lady Baldock thoughtlessly lamented that 'some nasty, low lying, wheedling priest got hold' of her daughter. When she noticed her mistake – 'I beg your pardon, Mr Finn, but you're one of them', Phineas replied as a gentleman should by saying: 'Not a nun, Lady Baldock'.[37] The virtues and follies of Roman Catholic priests are pointed out and accepted in the same spirit as those of Anglicans. The very conservative squire, Sir Roger Carbury (*The Way We Live Now*) liked the frankness of Father Barnham and invited him to dine. But he objected to the fact that the priest was always trying to prove that his Church was the only true one, and when the priest tried to convert him, Carbury replied, 'I have the most thorough respect for your religion, but it would not suit me.' It was only because the priest persisted that Carbury began to feel that he preferred to dine with the bishop who had never uttered 'a single word of religious thinking'.[38]

In more direct ways, too, Trollope seems to belittle organized religion. No thoughtful man, he says, could 'swallow his parson whole'. Though the parson claims to be a man of God, such men 'have oppressed us, and burned us, and tortured us' and have come to 'love palaces, and fine linens, and purple'. The extreme wealth along with the burning has disappeared, but injustices within the Church remain. There are clergymen who live in great luxury and do hardly anything but advance their worldly interests, while others, honest and hardworking, suffer in great poverty.[39]

This might seem to indicate that organized religion is at best of no importance to a gentleman and that its pretence to unworldly concerns is distasteful to him. But any such conclusion is decisively repudiated in Trollope's portrait of the Rev. Josiah Crawley (*Barchester Towers; The Last Chronicle of Barset*) whose career is a striking example of ecclesiastical injustice. Despite his misery and resentment, no man could be more certain than Crawley of man's need for the Church. He walked all the way from Hogglestock to Framley Parsonage to tell Mark Robarts that his mode of life was not one 'befitting a soldier in Christ's army', that he could hardly serve as 'a lamp to guide' his parishioners if he consorted 'with horse-jockeys and hunters'.[40] Though we can be sure that Trollope did not consider hunting wicked, it is equally clear that he means us to take seriously, as Robarts did, Crawley's lesson – that the task of a clergyman is distinctive and essential to the life of his parishioners. Although Crawley's victory over the lady bishop in *Barchester Towers* is one of Trollope's greatest scenes, its forcefulness is well matched by Crawley's declaration of respect for the authority of his bishop. Throughout there is a flavour to the life of the gentleman that is associated with the Church. But it is easy to overlook or mistake the part that the Church plays because it is not doing what is now expected of religion. A gentleman does not look to the Church for moral certainties, hair shirts, or a social gospel. It provides something more subtle and profound.

What the Church means in the life of a gentleman is explored in the development of Dr Arabin, who became the dean in Barchester. At Oxford, he had become inflamed by an ambition to demonstrate his faith in indifference to worldly things, perhaps even in some great sacrifice. He was strongly tempted to follow Newman into a Church that offered 'ceremonies and pomps', 'august feasts and solemn fasts', and laws so certain that they could not 'be broken without loud, palpable, unmistakable sin'.[41] For the ordinary country parson, Arabin had something close to contempt and he longed to teach the English clergy a higher view of religion that would redeem and rectify their inferiority. But far from commending this attitude, Trollope says that Arabin suffered from the 'modern stoicism' that afflicts many Christians and that is just as mistaken as the ancient stoicism. For human beings are not and should not be indifferent to joy and sorrow and it is vain to pretend that they are: 'Is not modern stoicism, built though it be on Christianity, as great an outrage on human nature as was the stoicism of the ancients? The philosophy of Zeno was built on true laws, but on true laws misunderstood and therefore misapplied. It is the same with our Stoics here, who would teach us that wealth and worldly comfort and happiness on earth are not worth the search. Alas, for a doctrine which can find no believing pupils and no true teachers.'[42] In being seduced by stoicism, in repudiating the pleasures of human life, in his religious enthusiasm, Arabin was displaying an ungentlemanly arrogance and self-deception.

He learned better from a poor curate in a small bleak parish in Cornwall, from just such a clergyman as he had despised. It was the tortured Mr Crawley 'who gradually calmed his mind, quietened his imagination, and taught him something of a Christian's duty,' leaving him content to do his work in the church to which he was born. Arabin learned to recognize that he was seeking a kind of certainty that no Church can provide, that 'no man can become a serviceable servant solely by obedience to written edicts', that there was no escape from doubt and dissension.[43]

The story of Dr Arabin makes it clear that to a gentleman, religion comes 'as a thing to believe in'. It is something that is 'there', with all its written laws, ceremonies and pastors. But this does not mean that the Church is merely a worldly convenience. On the contrary, the Church is dedicated to reminding men that there is something other than the pleasures or pains here and now, that they have something to guide them other than fear of the law or the displeasure of other men. The Church reminds men that they are creatures of an omnipotent God whom they are obliged to obey and love. Religious observances and the guidance of pastors help to keep that awareness alive and show men how to give shape to that awareness in daily life. In doing this, the Church stands against the world. It is a refuge from the business of this world. The concern of the Church is with the Kingdom of God, and its clergymen are therefore truly men of God. But nevertheless the Church is a human institution; its functions are defined and performed by human beings. And because a gentlemen insists that the Church is opposed to the human world and yet is a human artefact, his attitude to the Church is easy to misunderstand.

The implications of this attitude for ecclesiastical practice are neither simple nor certain. It means that no Church should be identified with Christianity but that in practice the two cannot be separated. To try to think through for oneself all the dogmas of Christianity and what they require in the way of ecclesiastical practice is an ambition that a man might reasonably and creditably entertain. But even for a man not so indolent as Sir Thomas Underwood and as reflective and energetic as Dean Arabin, it is close to impossible. This does not mean that men should never ask questions about their religion and their religious practices. The agitation begun by the followers of Newman, Trollope says, was on the whole salutary even though the master of Arabin's college might have had a point in seeing a touch of madness in Newman's concern with ecclesiastical practices. And therefore schism is not wholly a bad thing: 'Moderate schism, if there may be such a thing at any rate calls attention to the subject . . . and teaches men to think upon religion.'[44] But the majority of the clergy are bound to be, and should be, men who feel that the battle has been fought and won and that their job is to defend the fortress that they hold.

Such men are likely, however, to enjoy the 'temporalities' of the Church perhaps more than they should, and a little ridicule, even criticism, of them does no harm. Of course John Bold (*The Warden*) was being a presumptuous troublemaker when he began enquiring into the terms on which the pensioners' hospital had been founded and it was nonsense to suppose that the warden, who was the least grasping of men, was embezzling money. Nor was the lot of the pensioners bettered by having the warden removed and part of his salary distributed among them. Nevertheless, it is useful to have such enquiries from time to time because injustices accumulate in the Church as in any other institution. When questions are raised, parties will be formed, and entrenched interests will defend themselves. And gentlemen are apt to be found on both sides. What distinguishes a gentleman is not his allegiance to this or that party, nor an unwillingness to fight, but his readiness to acknowledge, even while he is striving to win the battle, that his opponent may also be contributing something to maintaining a worthwhile institution.

Disagreements over doctrines and ceremonies are as inescapable as other differences. Preference for the sombre austerities of the Dissenters or the red lettering and high silk waistcoats of the High Church may be due to accident or to temperament. There is no need either to eliminate the variety or to insist on the universal superiority of any set of observances. If one were compelled to choose, the less austere High Church might be preferable, but only because High churchmen take their addiction to their robes and ceremonies less seriously than their opponents pursue their antipathy to such practices, which suggests that they are more inclined to remember the human character of the institution to which they are wedded. To some men, the Roman Church is irresistible because it appears to provide a clear set of injunctions for a Christian life, such as cannot be found in the Anglican Church. But as Arabin came to see, the appearance of agreement and certainty is an illusion. There are dissensions within the Roman Church just as within the Anglican Church. And it may be because they are also obvious that the dissensions in the Roman Church have been more scandalous.

Anyone who is troubled by ecclesiastical quarrels makes the mistake of supposing that because clergymen are men of God they can work with godlike perfection. Clergymen will engage in 'ungodly quarrels,' struggle over 'scandalous differences', and generally display the same acerbity and the same enjoyment of victory as other men because 'peace on earth and good will among men are, like heaven, promises for the future'. When that promise will have been fulfilled, 'there will no longer be any need for clergymen'.[45]

Until then, a good working rule is to honour God according to the established practices of one's community. For a man should not disdain the support that he can get from intercourse with those among whom he familiarly lives and who can keep him 'staunch to the principles of that system of the Church to which he had always belonged'. Whether the church roof is pitched to a greater or lesser degree, whether or not there is chanting and intoning or more or less of tedious sermons does not affect the truthfulness of what the fallible human teachers are trying to convey. Pastors would do well not to impose on their captive audiences long sermons full of platitudes and truisms and 'false conclusions from misunderstood texts'.[46] But such shortcomings are matter for ridicule, not for earnest crusades.

Only the vulgar, like Mr Slope and Mrs Proudie, will presume to intrude on long established practices and insist that their way of teaching Christianity must replace all others. They would do better to notice the purity of Mr Harding than to condemn his love of music in church because it does not accord with their certainty that the 'meretricious charms of melody' prevent the ministers' invaluable words from falling 'intelligibly into the listener's head'.[47] Of course ecclesiastical practices are bound to change over time. But sensible men will agree with Mr Harding who, though he regretted the changes, believed that if the old bishop came back, 'he would not disapprove because the new ways are changed from his ways,' as he 'never thought himself infallible'. For all that one knew, odd though the new ways seemed, it might all be 'for the best'.[48]

This way of seeing the Church may appear to be full of inconsistencies. A gentleman may criticize or even ridicule the established forms of worship, and yet strongly resist attempts to overthrow them. He may declare that the truths mouthed by clergymen are no more plausible than other truths, and yet expect a clergyman to discharge his priestly duties with earnestness. He may point out difficulties in the dogma of his Church, and yet preach and practise utter submission to its creed. He may be fierce against infidels and yet insist that no man can know the truth. But there is no real contradiction. What reconciles these attitudes is summed up by Trollope when he says: 'I may question the infallibility of the teachers, but I hope that I shall not therefore be accused of doubt as to the thing to be taught.'[49]

Those who think in terms of a simple dichotomy between certainty and nihilism may take this to be nonsense or irony, but in the gentleman's world it is neither. Acceptance of Scripture as a revelation of God's will signifies a willingness to believe that certain men are true prophets. But the possession of Scripture does not eliminate the difficulty of deciding what the words mean, for that difficulty attends any human utterance. Though Scripture is taken to be God's Word, it does not give men access to non-human guarantees of human conclusions. There is no way to destroy the gap between the revealed Word of God and human interpretations of it. And therefore men may will to obey God but disagree about the manner of doing so. They can resolve their disputes by agreeing to regard a communal interpretation of God's will as authoritative. But nothing follows about the character of a man's faith from the Church that he attends.

The Church is a human institution which gives men a mode of living and a mode of dying. When a gentleman abides by the dogma and practices of his Church he accepts its right to determine for him how to interpret God's Word and obey his commands. But in recognizing the authority of the Church, even if he accepts its claim to 'infallibility', a gentleman does not take the Church to be infallible in the strict sense of possessing indisputable knowledge of God's will. That explains why a gentleman is never too particular about his religion, though he is wholly serious about it.

A gentleman may even refuse to accept so concrete a formulation of his belief as Christianity provides. He may just be resigned to seeing himself as a being who can wonder about why and how he has come to be, who can feel sure that he, as every other man, has a unique destiny for which he must accept responsibility, but who cannot expect to understand why he or anything else ever came to be or what purpose his existence serves. Trollope suggests that it is possible to hold such an outlook in a wholly abstract form. But he also makes it clear that to maintain it without the aid of formal religion is exceedingly difficult and, for most men, probably impossible.

*   *   *

In religion, as in politics, different sorts of men may make different yet equally valuable contributions. Therefore it is not a reflection on a church to show, as Trollope does, that it contains a great variety of clergymen.

Archdeacon Grantly was an ambitious, managing, pompous, noticeable man who fully enjoyed wealth and power. He believed that 'the hard uphill work of ascertaining what the duty of a clergyman should be had been already accomplished in full; and that what remained for an active militant parson to do, was to hold his own against all comers'.[50] He was sure besides that for the work of the Church, a 'very fine razor is not an appropriate instrument', and therefore he distrusted clergymen who had scruples or refused to drink wine. But for the rough work that he believed needed doing, he exerted himself and he did it well. He relentlessly fought that 'vulgar, interfering, brazen-faced virago', Mrs Proudie, and when she died, would have none of that 'namby-pamby' insistence that one was obliged to express regret when no 'regret could be felt'.[51] Neither the sort of doubt that nearly led Arabin to leave his church nor the weakness that made Mr Harding ready to yield to criticism ever afflicted the archdeacon. He accepted the Church as it came; he had a clear conception of his duties; and in his belligerent grand fashion he served the Church conscientiously.

But the Church was served just as well, though in quite another way, by Mr Harding in whom there was not a grain of 'militancy'. He was not a hero or saint, not a man to be admired or talked of or toasted at dinner, but simply 'a good man', who believed humbly in the religion and its precepts that he tried to teach. When he thought it right to do so, he gave up, without effort, the house and garden which he had enjoyed as warden of Hiram's Hospital, for rooms in the high street where he lived on contentedly, coveting nothing but 'a new case for his violoncello and somebody to listen to him when he played it'. Though Mrs Proudie 'had wounded him in every part that was most sensitive', though she had despised and ridiculed him and driven him to the 'only personal rebuke which he had ever uttered in Barchester', when Mrs Proudie died, Mr Harding thought of her 'simply as an active pious woman who had been taken away from her work before her time'.[52]

No one was more aware than the archdeacon of how different he was from Mr Harding. Yet he could fully appreicate the other man's virtues and when Harding died, the archdeacon sincerely praised him without qualification: 'The fact is, he never was wrong. He couldn't go wrong. He lacked guile, and he feared God, – and a man who does both will never go far astray.'[53] The words that he spoke about Harding prompted the archdeacon to confess to himself that he certainly had coveted many things, and had not been short of guile, and he was not even sure that he had feared God.

Yet the archdeacon was unmistakably a Christian. The reason why is evident in the contrast to his worldliness provided by the Stanhopes. They help to define the religious quality of Barchester because they are heathens in a Christian world.

The father, Dr Vesey Stanhope, is a model of a corrupt clergyman who, though he had lived away from England for some twelve years, had the care of three parishes, held a prebendal stall in the diocese, one of the best residences in the close, and two large rectories. His wife occupied herself entirely with questions of fashion. His beautiful, crippled daughter, the Signora Neroni, devoted herself to reducing men to a stupor of admiration. His son was incapable of doing anything that might be construed as a duty. It was left to his other daughter to manage the various members of the family through one crisis after another.

The Stanhopes were not out to do harm, and preferred to see the people around them contented. The Signora Neroni's exercises in charm did not seriously damage anyone, and the son could not bring himself to deceive the widow whom he courted for her money. The great weakness of the Stanhopes was heedlessness. But it was accompanied by so great a readiness to oblige their neighbours as to hide their real indifference. They would visit the sick, though not if there were any danger to them, and they heard of the patient's death or recovery with equal composure. They behaved no differently with one another. In their careless, pleasant, good-natured way, Trollope says, 'it is astonishing how much each of the family was able to do and how much each did to prevent the well-being of the other four'.[54]

Their irresponsibility and waywardness make the Stanhopes heathen. They lack a sense that something more is required of a man than surviving as effortlessly and pleasantly as he can manage. They lived as if they were permanently on the move, without wanting to be anywhere or do anything. It never occured to them to consider the consequences of their actions or the quality of their lives. Their ruling concern was to evade all questions. This is what Trollope describes as a lack of 'conscience', the possession of which marks a Christian and a gentleman.

A 'man of conscience' has what might be described as a voice within him' which he feels obliged to heed. It reminds him that there is something more for him to do in this world than to satisfy his wants. Such an awareness might be described as a fear of eternal agony, or a hope of eternal bliss, or a belief that every man 'has a soul to make and save', or a recognition that there is in each a 'divine spark' or bit of 'godliness'. But when used by a gentleman, these are all metaphors indicating that he feels obliged to think of something other than what seems advantageous or pleasant here and now, that he is aware of being responsible for what he makes of himself. Without that awareness a man can but drift or rush from one satisfaction to the next. Such a life is empty of substance and shape. And it is from this kind of emptiness that his religious faith saves a gentleman.

*   *   *

What makes such faith both difficult to maintain, and yet a sure support for resignation, is shown in the story of the Rev. Josiah Crawley, the most profound of Trollope's clergymen.

Crawley had only one ambition – to bring the word of God to his fellow men. He had married a lady who was well educated and softly nurtured but without wealth, and they had gone forth determined to look only to God and to each other for comfort. He was tireless, and as effective as he was conscientious, both in his preaching and his pastoral work. Regardless of the weather and his health, he taught in his school and went from cottage to cottage among the poor brickmakers. At the same time, he managed to remain something of a scholar. Though he demurred when the bishop flagrantly violated his authority, otherwise he submitted entirely to the authority of his Church.

But while others, far less deserving, had become successful and rich, Crawley had been passed over repeatedly and was poorer than his humblest parishioners. He lived in a barely furnished hovel and did not have a decent coat to his back; some of his children had died and those who had survived, he could not feed;

his parishioners had watched his furniture being carried out by the bailiffs and he was in debt to the butcher and the baker. Then on top of all these misfortunes, he was accused of having stolen a cheque.

The very real wrongs suffered by Crawley are, however, only a part of the story. There was a serious flaw in him. His 'deep angry, remonstrant eyes' and his habitual frown told of repressed indignation. He wore his threadbare old coat with an ostentatious bitterness. He refused help that might have lightened his burdens. When he went to see the bishop, he turned down offers of transportation, did not trouble to pick his way through the mud, and revelled in the thought that whereas the bishop would be 'sleek and clean, and well-fed', his being hot, mud-stained, and hungry after his walk would make him 'an object to be wondered at by all who should see him, because of the misfortunes which had been unworthily heaped upon his head'.[55]

There is a strong resemblance between Crawley's self-pity and Louis Trevelyan's. But the interest of Crawley's story lies in the difference. Despite his being so muddled on practical questions that even his wife acknowledged him to be unreliable, unlike Trevelyan, Crawley remained able to doubt himself and to take account of the opinions of others. He could see that Dan, the bricklayer, believed him to have been driven by his terrible poverty to steal the cheque, and he took the bricklayer's opinion as reason to suppose that the world might be right in thinking him mad. Even while he took comfort in his triumph over the bishop, he continued to consider whether after all he should obey the bishop and resign his office. To the lawyer's direct question about where he had got the cheque, Crawley replied: 'I know myself as no one else can know me in spite of the wise man's motto. Had I picked up a cheque in my house, or on the road, I should not have slept until I have taken steps to restore it to the seeming owner. So much I can say. But otherwise, I am in such matters so shandy-pated, that I can trust myself to be sure of nothing.' To his wife, Crawley confessed, 'that there are times when I am not – sane. I am not a thief, – not before God; but I am – mad at times.'[56] In fact Crawley had been right in thinking that he had received the cheque from the dean. But when the dean had denied giving it to him, because Crawley knew himself to be capable of making bad mistakes in such matters, he did not trust his own memory even though 'all the little circumstances' of the envelope in which he believed that he had found the cheque came back to him repeatedly 'with an exactness that has appeared to me to be almost marvellous'. Crawley possessed the humility that Trevelyan lacked. His troubles over the cheque came about because he could not bring himself to contradict the dean, and his humility on that score was, as the lawyer said, saintly: 'To find a man who was going to let everything in the world go against him, because he believed another fellow better than himself! There's many a chap thinks another man is wool-gathering; but this man has thought he was wool-gathering himself! It's not natural; and the world wouldn't go on if there were many like that.'[57]

Nevertheless, Trollope does not present Crawley as a martyr in a corrupt world. On the contrary, he emphasizes that Crawley's humility was not all that it should have been. Whereas his wife bore the full burden of their poverty without feeling disgraced or becoming bitter, he considered himself to have been degraded. And he thought so because he never allowed himself to lose his awareness of his wrongs. Rehearsing the disproportion between his virtues and his reward had become a habit with him. He would sit speechless for hours, telling himself that of all God's creatures he was the most heavily afflicted, reviewing his education and learning, his determination to devote himself to the service of the Saviour and his diligent work for his parishioners, and comparing his failure with the success of other men who were in all ways his inferiors. His constant prayer was: 'My God, what have I done against thee, that my lines should be cast in such terrible places?' Though he had a good measure of noble pride, he also possessed a false, crushing pride which rendered him unable to resist the dangerous luxury of self-pity. And so he 'pitied himself with a commiseration that was sickly in spite of its truth . . . He could keep up his courage in positions which would wash all the courage out of most men. He could tell the truth though truth should ruin him. He could sacrifice all that he had to duty. He could do justice though the heavens should fall. But he could not forget to pay a tribute to himself for the greatness of his own actions; nor, when accepting with an effort of meekness the small payment made by the world to him, in return for his great works, could he forget the great payments made to others for small work.'[58]

The agony of Crawley displays in its severest form the danger involved in a gentleman's obligation to recognize how things

really are. For such clarity can also undo him. A man like Crawley, whose profundity makes him better able than more ordinary
men to reflect on the reality that he encounters, is most vulnerable to this danger. It was the fault of Crawley, Trollope says,
'that he was imbued too strongly with self-consciousness'.[59] His
superior intellect exposed him to the temptation of driving his
understanding beyond all limits in an effort to penetrate the in-
congruities of a human life.

If it becomes too searching, awareness of the human condition
can destroy the balance of a mortal mind. And the ability to sus-
pend awareness and refrain from rushing into the abyss of despair
and dread is the blessing conferred by religious faith. Though
Crawley was sorely tempted, he did not go so far as self-destruction because his faith obliged and enabled him to 'bear what He
sends us'. Though his prayers were mixed with protests against
'all things around him' and almost 'all things above him', still he
did strive 'to reconcile himself to his Creator'. When his wife told
him 'Be a man and bear it. Ask God for strength, instead of
seeking it in an over-indulgence of your own sorrow', he felt
bound to acknowledge the justice of her rebuke. When she told
him bluntly that she feared he would stand out in the cold until
he lost all will to live, he found the strength to reply, 'And even
then I will bear my burden till the Lord in His mercy shall see fit
to relieve me. Even then I will endure, though a bare bodkin or a
leaf of hemlock would put an end to it.'[60] Instead of committing
suicide, he devoted himself to losing his grief in work. From
morning to night, he went among the poor at Hoggle End, 'reading to the brickmakers, or turning the mangles of their wives, or
teaching them theology, or politics, or history, after his fashion,'
and he kept repeating to himself the words of the old brickmaker
who had dared to preach a sermon to his pastor – 'It's dogged as
does it. It ain't thinking about it.' He had learned from the brickmaker 'that a man should force himself to endure anything that
might be sent upon him, not only without outward grumbling,
but also without grumbling inwardly'.[61]

Religion, in the gentleman's sense, enables men to recognize
that they are obliged to cultivate and cherish their capacity to
understand themselves and their world, and at the same time to
acknowledge that the reason of things can never become trans-
parent to them. The religious attitude may be described in the
words of Keats, as a 'negative capability' of living with 'uncer-

tainties, mysteries, doubts, without any irritable reaching after fact and reason'. Or it may be formulated as a belief that the undeserved sufferings and rewards in this world will receive their just recompense in the next. Or it may appear as confidence that there is 'a moral order' in the universe or as a simple readiness to trust in God. But however he expresses his attitude, a gentleman does not presume to assign the blame for every wrong, nor to hold himself responsible for setting the world right. And though it may seem surprising, such resignation brings him hope. For his consciousness of inescapable ignorance and uncertainty becomes a ground for believing that there is always 'a fresh running stream of water for him who would care to drink from a fresh stream'.[62] In short, a gentleman feels obliged to reconcile himself to 'the unavoidable dissonances of a human condition'[63] and his ability to achieve such a reconciliation makes him gentle.

12 The Danger of Being a Gentleman

One might be pardoned for concluding that a man who feels bound to resign himself to what he finds distasteful in the world could easily fall victim to knaves, rogues, and scoundrels. And it is not the only thing that makes a gentleman vulnerable. His charity and diffidence, his aversion to suspecting others make him amiable and pleasant to have around. But how can a gentleman survive among those who feel no qualms about imposing on others?

Questions of this sort began to be asked during Trollope's lifetime, and by the end of the century doubts about the practical possibility of being a gentleman had become commonplace. When the *National Review* considered the question in 1886, the passing of the gentleman had become an accepted fact but was still being deplored. 'In that new Democracy, with which Mr Labouchère and others threaten us,' the writer lamented, 'the English gentleman will be allowed no place, and would not claim it if he could ... The House of Commons used to be called the first assembly of gentlemen in Europe. But their number in the present House of Commons has been estimated at eighty.' The reasons given for the gentleman's decline were different from those given nowadays. He was said to have 'a deep-seated contempt for politics' and to be 'hardly likely to bestir himself much even to defend his order; for much as he loved fighting, it must be fighting which is fair'. Even so, the gentleman was expected to survive because 'he is not likely to let himself be improved off the face of the earth. He is quite capable of taking care of himself and will simply betake himself to fresh pursuits and fresh scenes ...'[1]

By 1932 when Harold Laski held forth jauntily on 'The Danger of Being a Gentleman',[2] he left his readers in no doubt that a gentleman was as incongruous in the modern world as a dinosaur. His charm had been irresistible, Laski explained, when England had had no rivals and no need to take long views or to consider serious questions, when working-men were docile and masters were too powerful to be resisted. Now, however, the gilded age was over, and the world refused to adjust to adjust itself to the tastes of gentlemen; working-men no longer believed that only gentlemen were fit to govern; modern industry required men capable of doing hard work, making large plans, acquiring real technical knowledge and meeting new challenges in a world full of science and changes. Therefore the gentleman had become a dangerous luxury whose dominion, because it had lasted too long, had brought England to her knees.

Although Laski was wrong in his diagnosis of why it had happened because he mistook the character of a gentleman, there is no disputing his conclusion that the gentleman seems less at home in our world than in Trollope's. Moreover Trollope himself has given us intimations of such a world. They appear, not as many have supposed in *The Way We Live Now,* but in *The Prime Minister.* It consists, as do many of Trollope's novels, of a set of variations on a theme, which in this case is the danger of being a gentleman in a world of cads. The theme is illustrated as much in the relations between Phineas Finn and the scurrilous journalist, Quintus Slide, as in the attempt by Ferdinand Lopez to blackmail the Prime Minister and Lady Glencora, but the story of Mr Wharton's vulnerability before Lopez is the most revealing.

Like Madame Goesler, Lopez was a foreigner and suspected of being a Jew. But unlike her he did not have to pick his way carefully. He no sooner appeared in London than he was accepted in the highest circles. Though no one supposed that he was well born, no one doubted that he was a gentleman. His immediate success was all the more remarkable because he was not thought to have an occupation that gave a 'warrant of position'. He was believed to employ himself on the Stock Exchange and elsewhere in the City, though no one knew just how, and that, added to the complete ignorance about the state of his affairs or even about where he lived, should have made everyone suspicious of him. But Lopez was one of the those exceptions, Trollope says, allowed for even by those who profess to adhere to Johnson's dictum that 'any other derivation' of gentleman 'than that which causes it to signify "a man of ancestry" is whimsical'. Lopez slipped into the world of gentlemen without provoking any of the questions that were asked about Madame Goesler. Of course his manner was charming and unfailingly courteous. But besides he was reserved without any sign of constraint – he never 'hesitated, blushed, or palpably laboured at concealment'. Indeed, a duke might have envied his self-possession. He even passed that most delicate test – his horse was 'not a prancing, restless, giggling, sideway-going, useless garran, but an animal well made, well bitted, with perfect paces, on whom a rider if it pleased him could be as quiet as a statue on a monument. It often did please Ferdinand Lopez to be quiet on horseback; and yet he did not look like a statue . . .' In short, Lopez's gentility had every appearance of being deep-seated and offered strong reasons for agreeing with Emily Wharton's argument against her father: 'And why should not a foreigner be as good as an Englishman? His name is foreign, but he talks English and lives as an Englishman.'[3]

But Wharton was right and Emily wrong. Lopez was bogus. At home with his wife or servants, in his office with his partner, he was a very different man. His perfection before the world was a thin veneer which hid worse than coarse words, brutal behaviour, and a ruthless desire to climb higher. Lopez was not merely an adventurer seeking Emily's fortune with no qualms about deceiving anyone; his utterances were always acts of manipulation, and necessarily so, because he recognized himself only by his power to manage someone into doing his will. But he wanted not just to get the better of others. He wanted to be esteemed as a gentleman while doing so. Once he had failed, he refused to go on living because his ruling passion was to destroy all limits and yet be honoured within a world whose defining quality was a sense of limits. Because he so skilfully used the outward marks of a gentleman to violate what they promised, the story of Lopez illustrates the most insidious threat to gentlemen.

That he had won over a young girl was not surprising. But his success in conquering Mr Wharton, who had made a fortune as a lawyer and become a judge and was both discerning and courageous, is another matter. Of course Lopez had planned his campaign carefully. He had extracted from Emily's brother the information that established the financial soundness of marrying her, and then exploited his friendship with her brother, along with her aunt's silliness, to gain access to Emily without Mr Wharton's knowledge. Once he had persuaded Emily to love him, he did not delay in presenting himself to the father as a formal suitor. And it is here, in his conversation with Mr Wharton, that

Lopez displays his most dangerous quality.

His manner and tone were faultless, and nothing that he said was a lie. Whereas Wharton became impatient and nearly lost his temper, Lopez remained calm and courteous. His replies to Wharton's questions were clear, direct, and firm. And yet Wharton learned nothing. When Wharton asked whether Emily knew of his intention to ask for her hand, Lopez replied: It is hardly possible that I should have learned to love her as I do without some consciousness on her part that it is so.' When Wharton asked him more pointedly whether he had been making love to Emily, Lopez answered: 'Who is to say in what making love consists . . .?' Wharton did not accept that easily: 'D____ it, sir, a gentleman knows whether he has been playing on a girl's feelings, and a gentleman when he is asked as I have asked you will at any rate tell the truth. I don't want any definitions.' But Lopez rejected Wharton's criticism staunchly: 'I think, Mr Wharton, that I have behaved like a gentleman; and that you will acknowledge at least so much when you come to know exactly what I have done and what I have not done. I have endeavoured to commend myself to your daughter, but I have never spoken a word of love to her.' He admitted candidly that he had discussed his desire to marry Emily with her brother and he made a point of defending the brother's conduct: 'I spoke to him yesterday on the matter very plainly, and he told me that I ought certainly to see you first. I quite agreed with him, and therefore I am here. There has certainly been nothing in his conduct to make you angry, and I do not think that there has been anything in mine.' Mr Wharton was impressed by the 'dignity of demeanour' and 'quiet assured courage' of Lopez and became ashamed of his outburst. After all, Wharton told himself, he had done nothing but 'storm and talk in ambiguous language of what a "gentleman" would or would not do', and he could not point to any impropriety in Lopez's conduct: 'How were lovers to approach the ladies of their love in any manner more respectful than this?'[4]

Nevertheless, Mr Wharton persisted: 'you must forgive me if I say, that you are comparatively a stranger to us . . . I don't know who your father was, – whether he was an Englishman, whether he was a Christian, whether he was a Protestant, – not even whether he was a gentleman . . . And I know nothing of your means; – nothing whatever.' Lopez agreed most civilly that Mr Wharton had every right to ask such questions and offered to set the record straight. With seeming directness, he told Wharton that his father had been Portuguese. But Lopez made this admission because that way, 'he thought he might avoid present discussion on matters which might, perhaps, be more disagreeable, but to which he need not allude if the accident of his birth were to be taken . . . as settling the question'. Lopez even volunteered that he had become an orphan 'before I understood what it was to have a parent'. It was undeniably a piece of additional information, but one certain to close off further questioning from a man like Wharton. Of course Wharton felt that it would be indelicate to go on. And he also became afraid of doing so. Perhaps the Portuguese father had been a nobleman 'and therefore one whom he would be driven to admit to have been in some sort a gentleman'. Or perhaps Lopez would tell him 'that his ancestors had been noted as Christians since St. James first preached in the Peninsula'.[5]

In several different ways, Wharton was hampered by his own decency. He found it difficult to suspect that a man who came to his house, and moreover as the guest of his son, was not a gentleman. As he was aware of his prejudice against foreigners, he was fearful of being unjust. Although he described Lopez as an adventurer and insisted that a father had a right to use even his prejudices as bulwarks against attacks on his daughter, he also believed that a gentleman might be discovered in the most unlikely circumstances. When he told his son that Lopez was 'a man fallen out of the moon' and that a mystery about a man's antecedents 'should be held to be utterly antagonistic to any such alliance', his words did not sound convincing to himself. His fair-mindedness led Wharton to admit that he had no hard evidence against Lopez, and he continued to ask himself: 'Was the man necessarily unworthy because his name was Lopez, and because he had not come of English blood?'[6] And so at last he yielded to his daughter's view that there was nothing against Lopez other than his being a foreigner.

Wharton's defeat by Lopez is all the more impressive because Lopez was as ignorant of Wharton's way of thinking as Wharton of his. Lopez did not recognize that he might have been more successful in getting money from Wharton if he had asked him directly rather than tried to bully him through his daughter. But his misconception of Wharton's character did not keep him from pursuing his project because the more he was hindered, the more he was disposed to insist. The opposite was true of Wharton. His ignorance was fatal because it reinforced his disposition to doubt his own certainties, and left him helpless before Lopez's manipulation.

The story of Wharton and Lopez encapsulates the vulnerability of a gentleman. When, in a quite different context, Trollope considered a more elaborate example of the same difficulty, the conclusion is even gloomier.

He saw the dilemmas of Mr Wharton writ large in the controversies which continue to this day – about whether Cicero was weak and vacillating or a hero valiantly fighting a hopeless battle. The discouraging conclusion is all the more impressive because Trollope's *Life of Cicero* is a brief for the defence. Cicero possessed, Trollope insists, that 'superiority of inward being'[7] that distinguishes a gentleman. Those who criticize him, Trollope argues, fail to appreciate his difficulties. In circumstances like Cicero's, even the most discerning are bound to find it hard to decide on the right thing to do. The Roman Republic in its true form was dead by the time that he came on the scene; it was not easy to see what could be salvaged or how; anyone who wished to do something useful had to be willing to 'touch pitch'. But while Cato sulked in his tent, Cicero remained on the battlefield, and in order to accomplish anything there, he was obliged to dirty his hands.

It was reasonable for him to dine with Caesar before the crossing of the Rubicon because he still hoped that he might be able to influence Caesar so as to save something of the Roman Constitution. Caesar was, after all, a remarkable man from whom it was reasonable to expect something better than a ruthless indifference to the greatness of Rome. When it became clear that Caesar had won and intended 'to be lord of all', Cicero was not obliged to commit suicide, and should not be blamed for accepting Caesar's conditions, as they could be endured with honour. Cicero's early support of Pompey was due to a mistaken but honourable belief in an old friend, and later his reluctance to abandon Pompey sprang from his habit of loyalty, which is also a virtue. Though Cicero lied sometimes, it should be remembered that he lived among people who had 'forgotten what honesty was' and had never had a punctilious notion of speaking the truth. And finally, any doubts about whether Cicero's heart was in the right place are settled for Trollope by his behaviour to Anthony.

Cicero recognized him at once for the thug that he was and made no efforts to placate as he had done with Caesar. Against Anthony, Cicero spoke out boldly, and submitted readily to the death that he expected.[8]

Nevertheless, Trollope acknowledged that Cicero had not always behaved nobly, that he had been indecisive and wavering when he might have been sure and strong. But the reason lay in his being too delicate for such rough work as he had to do. 'It may be,' Trollope says, 'that an instrument shall be too fine for our daily uses.' For ordinary purposes, for 'the work of the world, the coarse work', it may be better to have a clock that does not strike the minutes and is less 'liable to sudden impressions'. There are conditions in which a highly scrupulous man may lack the toughness needed to do what is necessary. And that was Cicero's fatal flaw. His awareness of how unpleasant were the choices that he had to make both reduced him to a tortured man and weakened his effectiveness for fighting ruffians. At the same time, having gone into the arena and 'fought the beasts', he had had to adopt rough weapons and to become the friend of men whom he knew to be 'bad', which, by the end of his life, showed in a 'tarnished character' and 'blunted' feelings.[9]

The story of Cicero as Trollope tells it, is a tragedy. It seems to prove that in a struggle against thugs, a gentleman is bound not only to be defeated but also to lose the quality of a gentleman.

Yet in another story, the moral is very different. In *Is He Popenjoy?*, the Dean of Brotherton proves a marquis to be a liar. The dean's story is all the more telling because there is reason to doubt whether he is a gentleman. Though Lady Sarah had accepted him because 'holy orders are supposed to make a gentleman, for she would acknowledge a bishop to be as grand a nobleman as any, though he might be born the son of a butcher,' in the privacy of their drawing room, she and Lord George told one another that the dean 'isn't quite . . .', though they hesitated 'to pronounce the word which was understood by both of them'. There was an obvious explanation for the flaw in the dean – his father had kept livery stables at Bath and his father-in-law had been a candlemaker. Though he had become the Dean of Brotherton, acquired a fortune, and married his daughter to the brother of a marquis, the result bore just the slightest porcine taint: 'With great care and cunning workmanship one may almost make a silk purse out of a sow's ear, but not quite. The care which Dean Lovelace had bestowed upon the operation in regard to himself had been very great, and the cunning workmanship was to be seen in every plait and every stitch. But still there was something left of the coarseness of the original material.' The taint appeared in the dean's attitude to his origins. Instead of being proud of 'the fact that, having been humbly born, he had made himself what he was', he had never ceased 'to be ashamed of the stable-yard,' and was convinced that 'the only white-wash against such dirt was to be found in the aggrandisement of his daughter and the nobility of her children'.[10] Besides there was about the dean a self-assertiveness which suggested the absence of a gentleman's diffidence.

But what these traits really signify emerges in the dean's response to the sudden reappearance of the Marquis of Brotherton, with a mysterious woman whom he declared to be his wife and a child whom he presented as Lord Popenjoy, the marquis to be. The marriage and the child were a complete surprise to the marquis's family, and there was no evidence to prove that the child was the legitimate heir. And if he were not, then the title would go to the dean's grandchild. The dean suspected fraud and was determined to discover the truth.

His son-in-law shared the dean's doubts. Lord George admitted that there was some impropriety about the affair; he knew that his brother was mendacious, vindictive, and beastly. Yet he preferred to do nothing. He ascribed his reluctance to take action to a disdain for worldly ambition, and comforted himself with the observation that although his father-in-law looked like a gentleman, 'still there was a smell of the stable'.[11] But in fact he resented what he recognized to be the dean's superior strength. Lord George had always submitted to his mother and sisters because he had not dared to stand up to them. He was very nearly manipulated into ruining his marriage by a woman who chose to play with him. And the same weakness kept Lord George from acting against the marquis. He found it unpleasant to think that his brother had perpetrated a fraud, he was generally disposed not to exert himself, and he had no idea of how to proceed. In short, what seems to be, and what Lord George represented to himself as being, the fastidiousness and charity of a gentleman was in reality weakness and lack of intellect.

In the dean, the relationship between appearance and reality was reversed. Despite the 'porcine taint', in his efforts to lead

Lord George into action, the dean passed the subtlest tests of a gentleman. That there were liars in the world, the dean said, was a fact that had to be recognized, and there were good reasons for thinking that the marquis was lying. What the marquis demanded was not reasonable – 'When a man marries before all the world, in his own house, and a child is born to him as I may say openly, the proofs are there of themselves ... The thing is simple, and there is no suspicion and no inquiry. But he has done the reverse of this, and now flatters himself that he can cow those who are concerned by a domineering manner.'[12] What establishes the dean's moral quality is the fact that his reasons for suspecting the marquis were sensible and not sordid, and that he made his case with complete directness and never descended to flattery, even though he well knew how easily Lord George would have succumbed to such management.

Besides, his attitude to the marquis shows that despite his ambition to make an alliance with the aristocracy, the dean was not in the least blinded by the grandeur of a title. When the bishop declared that the marquis must be a cruel man, the dean assured him that the marquis was much worse: 'No, my lord; he is no man at all. He is a degraded animal, unfortunately placed almost above penalties by his wealth and rank.'[13] Although in spite of his doubts, the dean began by being generous with the marquis, after the marquis received him in an insolent manner, the dean made no more attempts at polite enquiry, but told the marquis staunchly, 'When I have anything which I conceive it to be my duty to fight for, I think I do.' And so he did, to the point of physical assault. When they met at Scumber's hotel, the marquis deliberately provoked the dean by describing his daughter with an unmentionable word. The marquis had counted on the dean's taking the insult without retaliation because deans were normally 'sleek, bookish', not fighting men, and besides the dean was at least ten years his senior. Nevertheless, 'speedy violence' followed the marquis's utterance 'of the abominable word'. The dean was at the lord's throat at once – he 'had got him by his cravat and shirt-collar before he had begun to expect such usage as this ... Fire flashed from the clergyman's eyes, and his teeth were set fast, and his very nostrils were almost ablaze ...' And when the marquis lay in a heap, the dean rang the bell and announced clearly to the servant: 'His Lordship has been much hurt. I knocked him down.'[14] The marquis let it be known that if he still lived, it was not clear for how long. And it seemed likely that the dean would be charged and found guilty of manslaughter.

Even so, when the dean spoke to the bishop, he insisted that his attack had been justified and expressed no regret for his violence. If he hadn't killed the marquis, it was not for want of trying: 'I should have been neither more nor less to blame than I am now, for I certainly endeavoured to do my worst to him,' and if the fall had killed him, 'he would have deserved it'. The marquis had deliberately set out to 'wound a father in his tenderest part,' and had hoped to get away with it because that father was a clergyman. The bishop, who was a severe, ascetic, urbane man and hardly disposed to condone rowdiness, let alone in a clergyman, not only thought that the dean had been right to assault the marquis, but liked and admired the man all the more for it. The affair showed that 'the Dean could take a blow and give a blow'.[15]

The dean's straightforward confession and defence of his attack on the marquis was typical of the man and executed in the same spirit as his brushes with his clerical enemies. His colleagues in the church resented his rise from the stable-yard, and his being a hunting clergyman gave them many openings. Though he himself saw no evil in hunting, the dean recognized that 'thinking as the world around us does about hunting – a clergyman in my position would be wrong to hunt often'. But he saw no reason to give up hunting altogether. When attacked directly, he explained his views without equivocating. Anyone who was horrified by the thought of a clergyman riding to hounds was a 'prig in religion', but more likely, a hypocrite who only affected horror. The hostility to him did not worry him: 'I am not going to be frightened out of my own manner of life, or my own manner of thinking by fear of a quarrel.'[16]

It was not just because he was unafraid and ready to exert himself that the dean was able to take a strong stand and to persist in it. He chose his occasions well and knew when to give way. When Lord George became unjust to his wife, the dean recognized that his son-in-law had merely made a mistake in judgement and had learned better, and let the episode be forgotten. But on other matters he took a firm stand with his aristocratic connexions. He insisted that his daughter should have a house of her own in London because he thought that she needed it to protect her independence from her sisters-in-law, and he saw no good objections to such an arrangement. He neither denied the fact that her fortune had played a part in the marriage nor exploited it, and he freely offered Lord George money when he needed it. But when the dean felt that he was not welcome to his son-in-law, he refrained from staying in the house for which he had paid.

There is a suggestion that the dean's origins may help to explain his readiness and ability to fight. But Trollope makes it plain that the dean's clarity about when he was being ill treated, and his readiness to take effective action is not only compatible with being a gentleman, but essential, and that the inability to recognize this is an error typical of those who are not gentlemen. Whereas the vulgar considered the dean a pugnacious 'reprobate, who was born in a stable', the wisest of his aristocratic relations came to think that she had not 'read the man's character aright' and declared him to be a true gentleman.[17]

Any doubts about whether a readiness to take a stand and to fight is characteristic of a gentleman are definitively settled by the fact that the best fighters in Trollope's novels are parsons. Not only Mr Fenwick and Dr Wortle, but even Crawley enjoys a tough battle. When Crawley quoted, '"Vengeance is mine. I will repay", saith the Lord', or admonished his wife for hoping that Mrs Proudie would be punished for calling him a thief, he meant that the power to condemn for eternity belongs to God and that it is wrong to harbour resentment. And he also said that in the mortal world, which men inhabit, it is right to hit back then and there, 'while the smart remains'.[18]

Even defiance of authorized officials might be obligatory. Although Crawley was the first to insist on respect for the authority of the Church, when he felt that he had a duty to oppose the bishop, he spoke up firmly. And he declared that if the bishop ordered him to abandon the freehold rights in his perpetual curacy, or if the judge of the assizes commanded him to go to prison without a verdict from the jury, he would disobey because 'in no case, in this land, is he that is subject bound to obey, further than where the law gives authority and exacts obedience . . .'. Just because respect for the law is an imperative which a gentleman understands better than ordinarily honest men might, he is obliged to be peculiarly adamant in refusing to tolerate violations of the law. The same clarity and courage that led Crawley to defy the bishop also enabled him to tell the bishop's indomitable lady to be quiet when she spoke out of turn: 'Madam' he said to Mrs Proudie, 'You should not interfere in these matters. You simply debase your husband's high office. The distaff were more fitting for you.'[18] This memorable scene clearly establishes the superiority of Crawley over the poor bishop who is incapable of saying, No. The lesson taught by Trollope's fighting parsons, and even by more placid ones, is that there are times when it is wrong to turn the other cheek and a positive duty to strike hard enough to win.

The belief that a gentleman is defenceless against attack is a misconception born of confusing a gentleman's sense of proportion and his care to take proper notice of others, which leads him to distinguish nicely between more and less important, with the impostor virtue of tolerance. The fact that he feels obliged to endure much that he finds distasteful does not mean that a gentleman will or should endure everything. He does not shut his eyes to the possibility of evil or refuse always to suspect others. He takes care to discriminate between justifiable and vulgar suspicion, and does not confuse charity with a cowardly unwillingness to think ill of any man. His adaptability and freedom from dogmatism springs, not from a so-called 'neutrality' or indifference to moral judgements, but from the opposite – from a firm hold on an abundance of considerations to be taken into account when judging and courage to stand by his judgements. It is not an easy assignment. But to remain aware of evil and ready to fight it without descending into vulgar suspicion and aggressiveness is the burden of discretion that a gentleman should have the strength to bear.

The inability of Cicero or Plantagenet Palliser to take the hard decisions demanded by their circumstances is not a virtue. That it arises from too great a sensitivity to the complexities involved explains why it does not keep them from being gentleman. But it is nevertheless a serious flaw in their characters.

Trollope has nothing but contempt for the notion that squeamishness about recognizing and dealing with evil is a gentleman's way. What he really condemns throughout *The Way We Live Now* is neither 'modern industrial society' nor 'the rise of new men', but the disposition to equate gentility with an unwillingness to recognize and fight evil.

The corruption in the literary world is shown to be no more inevitable or excusable than the corruption in the financial world. Lady Carbury's disposition to blame her shoddy work on her circumstances is treated as a moral fault. Trollope condemns her indifference to doing her work well: 'she had no ambition to write a good book, but was painfully anxious to write a book that the critics should say was good'. He lets us see that writing well was within her powers, and that she was not ignorant of what it means to be a genuine writer. But even the possibility of writing books that deserved the good reviews, that she so painstakingly cajoled editors into giving her, never occurred to Lady Carbury because she was so much in the habit of thinking that 'shams and pretences might do the work of true service, that a strong house might be built upon the sand'.[20] The same failing disfigures Mr Booker. Because he had received a helpful review from Lady Carbury, he felt obliged to return the favour even though he knew that in saying all those 'valuable' things about him she had in fact bedaubed his book in a 'very thoughtless fashion', and knew also, that in order to repay her compliments, he would write similar rubbish. He lamented his corruption but comforted himself with the thought, 'If I didn't, somebody else would . . .' By blaming his action on the injustices of the world, he absolved himself of responsibility for what he did. But he gets no sympathy from Trollope: 'It did not occur to him to reflect', Trollope says as he often does elsewhere about other such men, that he was quite at liberty 'to break stones, or to starve honestly, if no other honest mode of carrying on his career was open to him'.[21]

In his account of the financial world, Trollope makes it just as plain that the corruption was made possible by the compliance of those who should have resisted it. The 'gentlemen' who assist Melmotte's progress are not victims of 'new methods of finance' but are guilty of indolence and cowardice as well as folly. A vignette of what is wrong with them appears in the incidents at the Beargarden club, which are dovetailed with futile discussions about Melmotte's strange powers by his victims.

The foursome who regularly played cards at the Beargarden knew that one of their company never paid his debts, and they suspected that he cheated. But they let the matter pass until a newcomer to the group, Sir Felix Carbury, began urging them to take action against Grendall. Lord Nidderdale's response was to take refuge in charity, humility, and the sinfulness of all men: 'What's the use of being beastly ill-natured? . . . Of course cheating isn't very nice: and it isn't very nice for a fellow to play when he knows he can't pay; but I don't know that it's worse than getting drunk . . . or quarrelling . . . or trying to marry some poor devil of a girl merely because she's got money . . . Live and let

live; – that's my motto.'[22] Dolly Longestaffe declared that he saw
no reason why he should agitate himself over a man who slipped
aces out of his sleeve. A gentleman, he tried to teach Carbury,
would refuse to believe his own eyes and would take care not to
look at him. And anyway it was a nuisance to think about such
things – 'it'd be such a bore breaking up'. When Carbury insisted
that he had actually seen Grendall cheating, Dolly turned on
him: 'Why did you pick me out to tell me? Why didn't you tell
Nidderdale. If I'd known that you were going to tell me such a
story as this I wouldn't have come with you.' The truth was that
they 'would infinitely rather be cheated than suspect anyone of
their own set of cheating them'.[23]

But what prevented the gentlemen of the Beargarden from
taking any action was not loyalty to an old friend. They were just
as reluctant to be disturbed about the losses that they had all suffered at the hands of Herr Vossner, the purveyor of the club, who
had regularly robbed each man individually and the Beargarden
as a whole, and which they all knew from the beginning. Nevertheless when he went off with everything, they felt only regret for
the loss of the services that he had provided: 'As a thief he had
been so comfortable that his absence was regretted with a tenderness almost amounting to love even by those who had suffered
most severely from his rapacity.'[24]

The conclusion that Carbury drew from the behaviour of Dolly
Longestaffe and Lord Nidderdale indicates how such indifference spreads corruption. Although Carbury had never before
dared to cheat deliberately, now he saw a new career open before
him: 'If such a man as Miles Grendall could cheat at cards and be
brought to no punishment, why should not he try it?' Indeed why
should he not manage a good deal more along that line without
being detected?[25]

The Way We Live Now contains many variations on what
happened in the Beargarden. Although Lord Alfred thought
sometimes that 'he would kick Melmotte and have done with it',
he suffered Melmotte's bullying without saying a word. His excuse
was that he had boys to support and that Melmotte held his bills.
But Trollope makes it clear that if Dolly had stopped to think
about it, he might have recognized that Melomotte was also dependent on him. How easily Melomotte might have been stopped
is illustrated by Paul Montague's encounters with him. Montague
failed on a number of occasions to make Melmotte answer ques-

tions about the fate of his investment, but when at last Montague refused to let Melmotte bully him into silence and declared: 'In reference to what I may or may not say to any friend, or how far I should be restricted by the scruples of a gentleman, I do not want advice from you,' Melmotte had no defence against him. The weakness that kept Montague from being firm with Melmotte earlier is displayed also in his inability to extricate himself from a carelessly acquired entanglement and to tell the true story to the girl whom he wanted to marry. The moral is made clear by the tale of the simple farmer, Joe Crumb, who suffered from no such irresolution, who pursued his love to London and, in the admirable spirit of the Dean of Brotherton, beat up the fine 'gentleman' who was seducing her.[26]

Far from demonstrating that new developments had made gentlemen obsolete or defenceless, *The Way We Live Now* shows that the flabbiness and self-deception, that disqualified the leaders of London society from being gentlemen, made it unnecessary for Melmotte to exert himself in order to dupe them. 'Keeping up with the times' is shown to be an excuse employed by men who are indolent and servile. That such people may be found in any walk of life and are not produced by the worldliness of the City, is evident from the conduct of two clergymen, the Bishop of Elmham and Father Barham. When Sir Roger insisted that Melmotte's contributions to charity did not alter the fact that his character left something to be desired, the bishop argued that even if Melmotte was 'not the sort of gentleman whom you have been accustomed to regard as a fitting member of a Conservative constituency', considerations of that kind had become irrelevant because 'the country was changing' and the changes were 'largely to the good', even if there happened to be less of religion. The Roman Catholic priest was no better. He managed to deceive himself into believing that Melmotte was 'a great man . . . perhaps one of the greatest known on the face of the globe' because he had become a Roman and so demonstrated that at last 'the Truth is prevailing'. When the disturbing rumours that Melmotte was, after all, a Protestant moved Father Barham to go to see the great man himself, the priest was treated to outrageous rudeness. Nevertheless, Father Barham managed to persuade himself – 'with a simplicity that was singularly mingled with his religious cunning' – that no offence was meant and that Melmotte 'was certainly a Roman Catholic'.[27]

What a true gentleman thinks of such cheerful responses is expressed by Sir Roger Carbury. He declared Melmotte to be 'a hollow vulgar fraud from beginning to end', no better than 'dirt in the gutter', and that he should have climbed so high was a reflection on all those who had allowed themselves to associate with him. Anyone who wished to do so could keep his house free from Melmotte, and such fastidiousness was an obligation for those who were supposed to set the standards of good society. When they were seen to dine with a swindler, it became easier for others to 'reconcile themselves to swindling'. The fact that Melmotte was a businessman and a foreigner, rather than a squire, had nothing to do with Sir Roger's disapproval. He would not have let Melmotte come 'even to the kitchens' because he had made his money by unknown tricks – as does a card-sharper – 'instead of by honest trade'. To treat Melmotte with 'charity' and 'tolerance', as did Dolly Longestaffe, Lord Nidderdale, the bishop and the priest, was inexcusable. Sir Roger was a pious Christian and 'anxious to conform to the spirit of Christianity', but he did not believe that 'an injury should be forgiven unless the man who did the injury repented of his own injustice'. If good Christians were obliged to be kind to thieves, 'honest industry would go naked in order that vice and idleness might be comfortably clothed'. He would not for a moment, Sir Roger said, hesitate to put any one who stole his cloak into prison and 'as soon as possible and not commence his lenience till the thief should at any rate affect to be sorry for his fault'.[28] Sir Roger, Trollope says, voiced the opinion of the sound gent indolence of Dolly Longestaffe is only a milder manifestation of the deeper corruption in his father. Mr Longestaffe thought of himself as someone who was bound to be recognized at once, by discerning observers, as 'a gentleman of the first water' because sharply ridiculed by Trollope when he shows how the self-indulgent indolence of Dolly Longestaff is only a milder manifestation of the deeper corruption in his father. Mr Longestaffe thought of himself as somone who was bound to be recognized at once, by discerning observers, as 'a gentleman of the first water', because he possessed everything that defined a perfect gentleman: 'land, and family title-deeds, and family portraits, and family embarrassments, and a family absence of any usual employment'. He knew himself to be far superior to anyone who earned his living, and after having failed to get elected to the House three or four times, he acquired also the opinion 'that a seat in the House was rather a mark of bad breeding'. His understanding of his position amounted to believing that there was much that it forbade him and hardly anything that it obliged him to do. Though he felt no uneasiness about leaving trademen's bills unpaid, he would not lower himself to question their accounts. He bullied his servants but was above checking on whether they were stealing his wine. Nor could he bring himself to insist that his family give up the house in London that he could not afford. When he became overwhelmed by debt, he could think only of selling the family property to a man suspected of being a swindler. And when Melmotte failed to pay, instead of taking action to collect the money owed to him, Mr Longestaffe comforted himself with feeling 'the absurdity of pressing such a man as Mr Melmotte', assured himself that there was a new era in money matters, and concluded his reflections on the subject with the fatuous reasoning that usually distinguished him: 'As for many years past we have exchanged paper instead of actual money for our commodities so now it seemed that, under the new Melmotte regime, an exchange of words was to suffice.'[29]

The same sort of folly kept Mr Longestaffe devoted to the old family solicitors, Slow and Bideawhile. There is no mercy for genteel incompetence in Trollope's description of Slow and Bideawhile: 'It had grown to be a rule in the house that anything done quickly must be done badly. They never were in a hurry for money, and they expected their clients never to be in a hurry for work.' Their rival, Squercum, worked from the depths of Fetter Lane, instead of Lincoln's Inn; some said that he did not work on Saturdays because he was a Jew; and, of course, his name was 'odious' to the fastidious ears of Mr Longestaffe. But Trollope's description of Squercum's energy and effectiveness could hardly be more sympathetic: 'He had established himself, without predecessors and without a partner, and we may add without capital, at a little office in Fetter Lane, and had there made a character for getting things done after a marvellous and new fashion. And it was said of him that he was fairly honest, though . . . among the Bideawhiles of the profession this was not the character which he bore.' Squercum was accused of having done, 'sharp things', we are told, because he dared to compute 'for a young heir the exact value of his share in a property as compared to that of his father . . .'. Any doubt that Trollope thought well of Squercum is settled by the fact that the real reason why Squercum did not work on Saturday was that he went hunting.[30]

There is just as much emphasis on a gentleman's obligation to speak plainly and act effectively to defend himself in Trollope's portrait of Brehgert, a Jew, a man of the City, and an associate of Melmotte. Georgina Longestaffe had managed to overcome her horror of marrying a Jew by dwelling on Brehgert's great wealth and the fact that he would provide her with a residence in London. But her father could not reconcile himself to such a son-in-law, though he had thought nothing of letting his daughter stay with the Melmottes, where even she was overcome by the vulgarity of their 'gold and grandeur, pomatum, powder and pride'. Brehgert's rebuttal of Mr Longestaffe's arguments against the marriage was so 'plain-spoken and truth-telling' – which is Trollope's regular description for a gentleman's manner – that its honesty was apparent even to Georgina Longestaffe. Brehgert not only denied flatly that he had behaved badly because he had not first consulted Mr Longestaffe but pointed out the father's negligence: 'Your father, no doubt with propriety, had left you to be the guardian of yourself, and I cannot submit to be accused of improper conduct because, finding you in that condition, I availed myself of it.'[31]

The objection to his being 'in trade', Brehgert said, had no force: 'I can hardly conceive it to be possible that any gentleman in England should object to his daughter marrying a banker, simply because the man is a banker. There would be a blindness of arrogance in such a proposition of which I think your father to be incapable.' The objection to his religion was more serious: 'I acknowledge the force of what your father says, – though I think that a gentleman brought up with fewer prejudices would have expressed himself in language less likely to give offence. However . . . I am ready to take what he has said in good part . . .' Then Brehgert went on to call a spade a spade: 'But no doubt your father objects to me specially because I am a Jew. . . . On this matter as well as on others it seems to me that your father has hardly kept pace with the movements of the age . . . Your father does not admit the change; but I think he is blind to it, because he does not wish to see.'[31]

This odd love letter from a Jew in trade displays a gentleman's objectivity about what is due to others and to himself, and a gentleman's courage to defend himself. That Brehgert's firmness had no taint of ruthlessness and was entirely compatible with the highest magnanimity is underscored by the fact that when Brehgert had in his possession the documents with Melmotte's forgeries, he refused to use them to revenge the losses that Melmotte had inflicted upon him. There can be no doubt that Trollope agreed with Brehgert when he told Longestaffe: 'I think that throughout I behaved like a gentleman.'[33]

The people who made Melmotte a success were indeed helpless against crooks. But they are not gentlemen. They are people who confound their fantasies, their self-indulgence, and their incompetence with gentility.

Should we then conclude that there was no excuse for Mr Wharton's defeat by Lopez, and that men such as Lopez are no real threat to gentlemen? It was not impossible to recognize Lopez for what he was. The signs of his true character were there, Trollope says, even in his love-making. He had been too giving a lover, too anxious to please, too self-conscious in his devotion, which indicated 'that something was expected where so much was given'. The signs were there also in Lopez's charitable acts. When he gave a penny to a woman at a crossing, he did so with 'a look which argued at full length her injustice in making her demand and his freedom from all liability let him walk the crossing as often as he might'. Indeed at all times, he carried 'his empire in his eye', making it clear that he considered it to be his 'neighbour's duty to submit and his to exact'. And his 'unflinching, combative eyes', 'the pugnacity of his steady glance' gave Lopez a hardness of expression.[34]

It seems likely that Wharton, who was an experienced and judicious man had unwittingly noticed these signs. But he was unable to put his observations into words, just as he was unable to defend his belief that he ought not to trust his daughter to a man of whose family nothing was known. Wharton gave in to his daughter because that belief seemed to contradict his other convictions – that a man might be a gentleman even though he was a foreigner. In fact both beliefs were entirely justified and compatible with one another. But lawyer though he was, because Wharton had been bred among gentlemen, his knowledge of how a gentleman behaved was instinctive and he lacked a self-conscious clarity about what he considered to be decent conduct. He could not therefore explain what reconciled his beliefs, or what made him feel that Lopez was not what he called a gentleman, and this made it easy for Lopez to disarm Wharton by making him uncertain of what be observed and how he ought to respond.

Wharton's defeat by Lopez illustrates the only real danger of being a gentleman. Swindlers like Melmotte are a threat to sham gentlemen like Longestaffe, to the weak, the silly, the indolent and the cowardly, but not to gentlemen like Sir Roger Carbury. Lopez is a very different kind of threat. He disarmed gentlemen by confusion, and even Sir Roger might have been misled in the same fashion as Wharton. What made Wharton vulnerable to Lopez was not his being a gentleman, but his lack of self-consciousness about what he believed.

Wharton's story shows that the instinctive certainties that belong to an inherited practice are not enough when one is compelled to produce public justifications for one's beliefs and conduct by wily opponents who know how to misuse words to their advantage. To deal with such opponents, one has to have struggled to imagine the arguments that they might bring and the ruses they might use and how to deal with them. To resist subtle deceivers like Lopez, gentlemen have to be able to make explicit what they believe and to present that understanding effectively to others who may not be so clear-headed.

But that raises another question. Can an inherited moral practice maintain its character once it is reflected upon self-consciously? Is not the disposition to engage in self-conscious reflection a sign that the practice has been lost, that it has been replaced by nostalgia, and become a dream which we will try in vain to recapture?

It cannot be denied that there is a tension between maintaining the quality of an unselfconscious practice and being able to make it explicit. It may not only be difficult to articulate what one is doing. Self-consciousness may make it impossible to perform effortlessly and gracefully. Besides, the self-conscious articulation of a practice may prevent some people from learning it, as often the most gifted pupils are paralyzed by explicit instruction and can learn only by receiving intimations from examples. Even for those who can benefit from explicit instructions, there is another danger – that they may become addicted to formulas and lack an appreciation of the nuances that constitute the perfection of a practice.

All this suggests that the kind of self-consciousness needed to defend the gentleman's world against its worst enemies might destroy its life from within. Efforts to articulate the instinctive knowledge of a gentleman may not only fail to convey what matters most but confuse the seasoned practitioners along with the acolytes. As the confusion spreads, and as the gentleman's en-

emies and corrupters grow more numerous and powerful, it becomes increasingly difficult to transmit the understanding that
makes a gentleman. And that may be why a gentleman has come
to be thought of as a piece of parchment, a bundle of gestures, an
effete dandy, a man of straw, an anachronism, an illusion, a
dream.

But that is not the whole story. There have been teachers with
the courage to resist the demands of mediocrities for vulgar formulas and the clamour of hacks to be recognized as true practitioners, who have also possessed the delicacy to refrain from
saying too much to pupils able to learn from intimations. There
have been teachers who have also been great performers. What is
a parent but such a teacher?

To manage both the grace of unselfconscious practice and the
rigour required for a self-conscious understanding of it is inconceivable only for those who refuse to recognize that a mastery of
many voices is the essence of a high culture. As a gentleman is
supposed to have a talent for making and living with fine discriminations, he should be better able to endure the tension between
spontaneity and self-consciousness. Of course the job of un-
masking a Lopez may be too much for some. It may be beyond
the gifts of a Plantagenet Palliser or a Mr Wharton. But Madame
Goesler, Mr Monk, Dr Wortle, the Dean of Brotherton, the Vicar
of Bullhampton, Luke Rowan or Will Belton could certainly
manage it.

If the gentleman has become a rarity, it must be because few
wish, or know how, to be gentlemen. How such a state came
about is for the historian to explain. But there is nothing in the
nature of a gentleman that makes him dependent on circumstances. For he is not an ideal, a model, or a pattern, not, that is
to say, a rigid mould which will fail to make an impression on material that is too tough. What defines a gentleman is a way of
being in any circumstances. Even alone on his island, Robinson
Crusoe is a gentleman. He reveals a gentleman's attitude to his
plight in his unfailing respect for the humanity of himself and all
men; his ability to appreciate the treasures of civilization; his efforts to refashion them for new circumstances; his readiness to
build new skills on old; his learning to recognize and repent for
his sins; his determination to give his days an orderly shape, to reconcile himself to his misfortune and endow his life with what
grace and contentment he can manage.

Not any doctrine about what to do makes a gentleman's morality a distinctive idiom of moral conduct, but its interpretation of what men are. Fidelity to this interpretation gives the world of gentlemen its characteristic atmosphere of serenity. What may be mistaken for passivity or lack of energy is really a refusal to think in terms of the brutal dichotomies that govern the world of the self-divided man. The gentleman's world does not require a choice between rebellion and submission, violence and reason, alienation and unity, struggle and apathy, certainty and nihilism. It is a world full of nuances. Everything depends on fine distinctions – between wilfulness and originality, rigidity and discipline, distortion and disagreement. Nothing stands still but there is no sign of chaos. Order rests on proportion, harmony and continuity, not uniformity or changelessness. Men are not bound together by domination or submission but by affections, habits, duties and aspirations, as well as friendship, love, loyalty, obedience, respect, and admiration. They can alter and remain consistent. They can be amiable without being dishonest. Deference is no bar to independence nor respectability to originality. Firmness does not exclude sensitivity and moral clarity is one with compassion.

In a world of people who think only of getting and spending, who are trying to wipe the slate clean or tie up everything in large, neat, sharp-cornered parcels, who feel obliged to rebel in order to go their own way, or think of peace as the achievement of repression, who confuse authority with power and deference with slavishness, who shudder at the dappled diversity of the human world, the gentleman will not feel at home. He may respond by trying to persuade his fellows to think differently, by taking action to stop their projects, or by finding a corner in which he can quietly keep to his own. But whatever he does, he will remain self-balanced in the midst of turmoil, always attentive to what is before him and especially to the pride of others however misplaced, never exacting more than a reciprocal respect, nor preening himself on being engaged in great crises and struggles, a search for the key to the universe, or even a progress to perfection. And he will not try to escape responsibility by pretending to be a pool of genes of a blob of putty, or by seeking to immerse himself in a cosmic enterprise. He may be a statesman, a farmer, a brewer, a doctor, or a parson, but still he will work in the spirit of a potter, shaping and moulding as best he can, resigned to the defects of his material, grateful for what he has learned from his teachers, without trying to discover patterns in the sky or feeling debased by the lack of them. He has firm convictions about what is good and true, for which he will fight, without forgetting that nothing in nature prevents other men from questioning his verities and that he himself cannot keep hold of them without support from others to keep him aware of what he has overlooked or distorted. But whatever disagreement he encounters, however uncongenial he may find his neighbours or his fortune, he will always be thoroughly at home in the human world because he can enjoy its absurdities and has no ambition to overleap mortality.

Notes and References

This list includes only those of Trollope's books which are referred to repeatedly in the endnotes (dates of original publication in brackets).

Endnote numbers refer to all unnumbered preceding quotations in the paragraph.

The American Senator, Oxford, 1951 (1877)
Lady Anna, 2 vols, London, 1874 (1874)
An Autobiography, Oxford, 1961 (1883)
Barchester Towers, Oxford, 1966 (1857)
The Belton Estate, Oxford, 1951 (1866)
Can You Forgive Her?, Oxord, 1963 (1864)
The Claverings, Oxford, 1946 (1867)
Doctor Thorne, Oxford, 1951 (1858)
The Duke's Children, Oxford, 1951 (1880)
The Eustace Diamonds, Oxford, 1960 (1873)
The Fixed Period, 2 vols, Edinburgh and London, 1882 (1882)
Four Lectures, London, 1938 (1861–70)
Framley Parsonage, Oxford, 1949 (1861)
Sir Harry Hotspur of Humblethwaite, Oxford, 1950 (1871)
He Knew He Was Right, Oxford, 1963 (1869)
Is He Popenjoy?, Oxford, 1948 (1878)
John Caldigate, Oxford, 1946 (1879)
The Last Chronicle of Barset, Oxford, 1967 (1867)
The Life of Cicero, 2 vols, London, 1880 (1880)
An Old Man's Love, Oxford, 1939 (1884)
Orley Farm, Oxford, 1950 (1862)
Phineas Finn, 2 vols, Oxford, 1944 (1869)
Phineas Redux, Oxford, 1952 (1874)
The Prime Minister, Oxford, 1951 (1876)
Rachel Ray, Oxford, 1951 (1863)
Ralph the Heir, 3 vols, London, 1871 (1871)
Mr Scarborough's Family, Oxford, 1946 (1883)
The Small House at Allington, Oxford, 1950 (1864)
The Vicar of Bullhampton, Oxford, 1963 (1870)
The Warden, New York, 1936 (1855)
The Way We Live Now, Oxford, 1968 (1875)
Dr Wortle's School, Oxford, 1960 (1881)

CHAPTER 1

1. D. Sutherland, *The English Gentleman* (Debretts Peerage Ltd., 1978) p. xi.
2. D. Defoe, *The Compleat English Gentleman,* ed. Bulbridge (London, 1729) p. 5.
3. *Certaine Precepts* (London, 1617) p. 8, quoted in R. Kelso, *The Doctrine of the English Gentleman in the Sixteenth Century* (Illinois, 1929) p. 28. See for further examples of this view, along with an emphasis on ancestry, although Kelso also says: 'The assumption throughout, however . . . was that some distinction existed in the individual which raised him above his fellows', p. 27.
4. *Topica,* 6, 29.
5. R. T. Hampson, *Origines Patriciae* (London, 1846) pp. 348–50, maintains that 'it nowhere appears that the subjugators of Britannia adopted the distinction' and that therefore 'gentleman must be regarded as an exotic title, and its precise signification is to be found, not in the circumstances of its origin, but in its subsequent history . . .'.
6. Sir T. Elyot, *The Gouvernour,* ed. Croft (London, 1880) II, 29.
7. G. Sitwell, 'The English Gentleman', *The Ancestor,* no. 1 (London, 1902) pp. 58–103.
8. A. Wagner, *Heralds and Heraldry in the Middle Ages* (London, 1939); *English Genealogy* (Oxford, 1960); *English Ancestry* (Oxford, 1961). Whether 'gentleman' designates a status is part of a much broader historical question which is not my concern here. I have summarized in the text the historical conclusions on which I have relied. In addition to other works cited, see M. Bloch, *Land and Work in Medieval Europe,* tr. J. E. Anderson (London, 1967); G. C. Brodbrick, *English Land and English Landlords* (London, 1881); A. Macfarlane, *The Origins of English Individualism* (Oxford, 1978); H. Maine, *Lectures on the Early History of Institutions* (London, 1875); *Dissertations on Early Law and Custom* (London, 1883); F. Pollock and F. W. Maitland, *History of English Law before the Time of Edward I* (Cambridge, 1968) 2 vols; J. H. Round, *Feudal England* (London, 1895); *Studies in Peerage and Family History* (London, 1901); *The King's Serjeants and Officers of State* (London, 1911); P. Vinogradoff, *Villainage in England* (Oxford, 1892); *The Growth of the Manor* (London, 1920). For later developments, see H. R. Trevor-Roper, 'The Gentry 1540–1640', *Economic History Review,* (supplements) no. 1 (1953). The literature in the controversy that followed is summarized in J. H. Hexter, 'Storm Over the Gentry', *Encounter* (May 1958), reprinted in Hexter, *Reappraisals in History* (London, 1961).
9. This was acknowledged even by William Harrison, *Description of England,* in *Holinshed's Chronicles* (1577), bk. III, ch. 1. Though he held that arms make a gentleman, he went on to say, not very consistently, that 'citizens often change estate with gentlemen, as gentlemen do with them, by a mutual conversion of the one with the other' and that yeomen, too, by buying the lands 'of unthrifty gentlemen, and setting their sons to the schools, the universities, and to the Inns of the Court, or otherwise leaving them sufficient lands whereupon they may live without labour, do make

them by those means to become gentlemen'.

10. Cf. T. Fuller, *The Worthies of England* (1662).
11. A. L. G. de Staël-Holstein, *Letters on England* (London, 1830) p. 133.
12. G. Della Casa, *The Rich Cabinet* (London, 1616) p. 51.
13. Defoe, *The Compleat English Gentleman*, p. 25.
14. *Notes and Queries* (London, 1891) 7th St., xi, 76, in A. Smythe Palmer, *The Perfect Gentleman* (London, 1892) p. 97.
15. Cf. P. Vinogradoff, 'Agricultural Services', *Collected Papers* (Oxford, 1928) I, 112–28.
16. Cf. Chaucer's Franklin in *Canterbury Tales*.
17. Cf. A. L. Poole, *Obligations of Society in the XII and XIII Centuries* (Oxford, 1949); also A. Wagner, *English Ancestry*, pp. 53—60.
18. Wagner, *English Ancestry*, pp. 71, 73, 64–5, 90–91.
19. For all that he says about the mixed ancestry of anyone in England, Sir Anthony Wagner also points out that what made it possible to rise quickly to 'great estate from lowly beginnings' was 'not an absence of class distinctions but a lofty structure with many shallow steps by which the skilful and persistent might climb, while some others slipped down and many more kept the framework solid by standing still. Even those who stood still might find that the ground had moved under them.' *English Genealogy*, p. 9.
20. Cf. C. L. de Secondat de Montesquieu, *The Spirit of the Laws*.
21. A. de Tocqueville, *On the State of Society in France before the Revolution of 1789* (London, 1856) pp. 151–3; 179–81.
22. Staël-Holstein, *Letters on England*, pp. 130–1; 124–5; 136; 131–2; 137.
23. D. M. Mullock (Mrs Craik) *John Halifax, Gentleman* (London, 1961) p. 301. First published in 1856 and republished regularly throughout the century.
24. Allen, Grant *Philistia* (London, 1884) I, pp 296–7; 299–300 (1858).
25. Elyot, *The Gouverneur*, II, 28–30.
26. Quoted in A. Smythe Palmer, *The Ideal of a Gentleman, or a Mirror for Gentlefolk: A Portrayal in Literature from the Earliest Times* (London, 1908) p. 75.
27. Ferne, *Blazon of Gentrie* (London, 1586) p. 4.
28. J. Selden, *Titles of Honour* (London, 1631) p. 854.
29. *The Gentleman's Calling* (London, 1673) p. 127.
30. *Tatler*, no. 207 (1710).
31. S. Smiles, *Life and Labour* (London, 1887) p. 35.
32. A comprehensive, though haphazard anthology of such references can be found in A. Smythe Palmer's *The Ideal of a Gentleman* (see above) which is an enlarged version of *The Perfect Gentleman* (London, 1892). Palmer did not try to explain 'the central idea' that defines a gentleman but he says firmly that his work is 'designed to instruct a gentleman not as to what he should *do*,' but as to 'what he is *to be*, always and under all circumstances', and that this has nothing to do with the 'cut-and-dry rules' of manuals which pretend 'to turn out "gentlemen" according to pattern'. (*Perfect Gentleman*, p. vii). For a much smaller anthology, see Thomas Ballantyne, *Essays in Mosaic* (London, 1870).
33. J. Ruskin, *Modern Painters* (New York, 1888) V, 261, 262 fn.

34. J. S. Mill, *System of Logic* (London, 1851) II, 227. The same view appears also in the *Cornhill Magazine* (1862) V, 330.
35. D. Defoe, *The Compleat English Gentleman*, p. 5.
36. *Quarterly Review* (London, 1858), vol. 103, p. 39.
37. *Romaunt of the Rose*, 2197. But see also *Wife of Bath's Tale*, 1.6, 692 seq.
38. T. Malory, *Historie of King Arthur*, ed. Wright (London, 1634) II, 6.
39. Cf. *Henry V*, IV, 1, 42; *Winter's Tale*, V, 3, 164; *Pericles*, II, 3, 27.
40. W. Harrison, *Description of England*, ed. G. Edelen (Ithaca, 1968).
41. J. Selden, *Table Talk* (published posthumously 1689) s.v. 'Gentleman'.
42. C. Lamb. *Essays*, ed. Kent (London, 1827) p. 446.
43. *Institucion of a Gentleman*, quoted in D. Defoe, *The Compleat English Gentleman*, pp. xxxvi–vii.
44. H. Brooke, *A Fool of Quality* (London, 1906) p. 138.
45. W. M. Thackeray, *The Book of Snobs* (London, 1911) p. 260.
46. A. and J. Hare, *Guesses at Truth* (London, 1889) p. 158.
47. S. Raven, *The English Gentleman* (London, 1961) pp. 15, 59, 63.
48. W. Hazlitt, 'The Look of a Gentleman', *Essays* (Camelot ed., London, 1889) p. 184.
49. N. Breton, *The Good and the Bad* (London, 1616) p. 12.
50. L. Sterne, *Tristram Shandy* (1760), bk IX, chap. 2.
51. Breton, *The Good and the Bad*, p. 12.
52. Brooke, *A Fool of Quality*, p. 137.
53. R. Brathwaite, *The English Gentleman* (London, 1641) 3rd ed., pp. 255–6.
54. *Essays*, pp. 184, 182.
55. P. D. Chesterfield, *The Gentleman's Library* (London, 1813) pp. 8–9.
56. *Essays*, p. 195.
57. W. J. Browne, 'The English Gentleman', *The National Review*, Apr. 1886, pp. 263–5.
58. R. Steele, *The Guardian*, no. 34 (1713).
59. R. Allestree (?), *The Gentleman's Calling* by the author of *The Whole Duty of Man* (London, 1673) p. 24.
60. W. Davies, A Fine Old English Gentleman (1871) pp. 229–31, quoted in Palmer, *The Ideal of a Gentleman*, p. 444.
61. S. J. Coleridge, *Biographia Literaria* (London, 1817) II, pp. 208–9.
62. *Essays*, 192.
63. J. H. Newman, *On the Scope and Nature of a University Education* (London, 1956) p. 181.
64. *Guesses at Truth*, p. 158.
65. *Life and Labour*, pp. 35–6.
66. Breton, *The Good and the Bad*, pp. 11–12.
67. *Gentleman's Companion* by a Person of Quality (London, 1676) p. 6.
68. W. Davies, *A Fine Old English Gentleman*, pp. 251–3, in Palmer, p. 446.
69. *Guardian*, no. 34.
70. F. Lieber, *Character of the Gentleman* (Charleston, S.C., 1847) pp. 14–15.
71. *Compleat Gentleman*, pp. 240–1.
72. R. C. Trench, *Letters and Memorials* (London, 1888) II, 36.
73. *Saturday Review*, 1892, LXXIII, 318.
74. Brathwaite, *The English Gentleman*, pp. 255–6.

75. Ibid.
76. Ibid., Preface, para. 2.
77. Ibid., p. 148.
78. Ibid., p. 261.
79. R. L. Stevenson, 'Gentlemen' *Scribner* (1888) III, 637.
80. G. P. Marsh, *Lectures on the English Language* (London, 1862) p. 437.
81. A. L. G. de Staël-Holstein, *Letters on England*, p. 132.
82. H. Taine, *Notes on England* (London, 1957). p. 144.
83. V. A. Huber, *The English Universities*, ed. F. W. Newman (London, 1843) II, 320.
84. W. Dibelius, *England* (London, 1930) p. 165.
85. Cf. Taine, *Notes on England*, pp. 144 ff.
86. Coleridge, *Biographia Literaria*, p. 20.
87. E. Barker, *Traditions of Civility* (Cambridge, 1948) p. 125.
88. Taine, *Notes on England*, p. 144.
89. Huber, *English Universities*, II, 347–8.
90. J. Harrington, *The Commonwealth of Oceana*, 1659–60 (Cambridge, 1977) p. 183.
91. E. P. Day, *Collacon* (London, 1883) p. 320.
92. (1848) quoted in Palmer, *Ideal of a Gentleman*, pp. 49–50.
93. R. W. Church, *Spenser* (London, 1880) pp. 157–9. Cf. also Marsh, *Lectures on the English Language*, p. 437.

CHAPTER 2

1. A. Trollope, *An Autobiography*, p. 12.
2. Ibid., p. 8.
3. Ibid., p. 14.
4. Ibid., p. 11.
5. Ibid., p. 24.
6. Ibid., p. 51.
7. Ibid., p. 54.
8. 'A Walk in a Wood', *Good Words*, Sept. 1879, p. 8.
9. *An Autobiography*, pp. 315; 14, 51.
10. Ibid., p. 61.
11. Ibid., p. 314.
12. M. Sadleir, *Trollope* (London: Oxford, 1961) pp. 339–40.
13. Review of *Framley Parsonage, London Review,* 11 May 1861, 544.
14. Review of *Orley Farm, Athenaeum* no. 1741, 9 Mar. 1861, 319.
15. Review of *Framley Parsonage, Saturday Review,* XI, 4 May, 1861, 451–2.
16. D. Skilton, *Anthony Trollope and His Contemporaries* (Longman, 1976) p. 20. I am very much indebted in this chapter to Mr Skilton's eminently thorough and illuminating account of the responses to Trollope, even though I disagree with some of his conclusions.
17. Ibid., p. 26.
18. *An Autobiography*, pp. 80, 200.
19. Rebecca West, *The Court and the Castle* (London, 1958) p. 127.
20. Cf. Erving Goffman, *The Presentation of Self in Everyday Life* (London, 1971).

21. Review of *Framley Parsonage, London Review*, 11 May 1861.
22. Review of *Doctor Thorne, The Leader*, 29 May 1858.
23. Review of *The Warden, Examiner*, 6 Jan. 1855.
24. *An Autobiography*, pp. 126; 188; 126; 189.
25. Ibid., p. 191.
26. *Spectator*, 22 July 1876, 922–3.
27. *British Quarterly Review*, 1 July 1869.
28. *Spectator*, 26 June 1875, 825–6.
29. *Athenaeum*, no. 2348, 26 Oct. 1872, 527–8.
30. *National Review*, Jan. 1863, 29.
31. *Spectator*, 22 July 1876, 922–3.
32. *Academy*, 7 Feb. 1874, 141–3.
33. Sadleir, *Trollope*, p. 369.
34. Cf. especially R. ap Roberts, *Trollope: Artist and Moralist*, (London, 1971). A directly contrary view is taken by James R. Kincaid, *The Novels of Anthony Trollope* (Oxford, 1977) who finds in Trollope a highly rigid, abstract 'code', which 'situations can diversify, even break', but 'the codes derive always from a civilized base independent of situations'. Kincaid concludes therefore that 'Trollope's method and morality are no less, but no more modern than Cervantes" pp. 15–16.
35. *An Autobiography*, p. 196.
36. Cf. reference to 'Mr Sentiment', *The Warden*, p. 144.
37. The essays collected in R. Paulson (ed.) *Fielding, A Collection of Critical Essays* (Twentieth Century View Series: Englewood Cliffs, N.Y., 1962) are a good illustration of the conflicting interpretations of Fielding.
38. For examples of the range of opinions about Jane Austen, see: *North British Review*, LXXII, Apr. 1870, 129–152; Kinkead-Weakes, 'This Old Maid: Jane Austen', *Nineteenth Century Fiction*, Dec. 1975, University of California; Lionel Trilling, 'Mansfield Park', in *The Opposing Self* (New York 1955) and 'Emma and the Legend of Jane Austen', in *Beyond Culture* (London, 1966); Brian Southam, ed., *Critical Essays on Jane Austen* (London, 1968); Brian Southam, ed., *Jane Austen: Critical Heritage* (London, 1968); J. Halperin, *Jane Austen: Bicentenary Essays* (Cambridge, 1968); S. Tave, *Some Words of Jane Austen* (Chicago, 1973).

CHAPTER 3

1. *Nation* (New York) 13 July 1865, in H. James, *Notes and Reviews* (Cambridge, 1921) pp. 68–76.
2. Ibid., 4 Jan. 1866, in *Notes and Reviews*, pp. 124–32.
3. H. James, *Partial Portraits* (London, 1888) pp. 104, 110, 105, 106, 104.
4. Ibid., p. 109.
5. Ibid., pp. 103, 104, 124.
6. Cf. S. R. Letwin, *The Pursuit of Certainty* (Cambridge, 1965) and R. Ashton, *The German Idea* (Cambridge, 1980) for a study of some aspects of this change.
7. See unsigned essay on Trollope's death, *Spectator*, 9 Dec. 1882, 1v, 1573–4; 'Rachel Ray' *Spectator* xxxvi, 24 Oct. 1863; R. H. Hutton, *Essays Theological and Literary* (London, 1871) 2 vols.; *Aspects of Religious and Scien-*

8. Cf. F. A. Hayek, *The Counter-revolution in Science* (Allen and Unwin, 1952).
9. Cf. David Cecil, *Early Victorian Novelists* (London, 1964) and B. A. Booth, *Anthony Trollope. Aspects of his Life and Art* (Indiana, 1958) for similar, more recent judgements of Trollope's lack of profundity and spiritual insight.

CHAPTER 4

1. The first attempt to formulate this morality is Michael Oakeshott's *On Human Conduct* (Oxford, 1975)

CHAPTER 5

1. *Phineas Finn*, II, 270.
2. Ibid., II, 272–3.
3. Ibid., II, 263, 261, 259.
4. Ibid., II, 387–8.
5. Ibid., II, 167, 211–12.
6. Ibid., II, 213.
7. *The Duke's Children*, I, 17.
8. *Phineas Finn*, II, 43.
9. *Doctor Thorne*, pp. 186–7.
10. *Phineas Finn*, II, 270.
11. *The Duke's Children*, I, 119.
12. Ibid., I, 140–2.
13. *An Autobiography*, p. 310.
14. *The Prime Minister*, I, 116.
15. Ibid., I, 211.
16. Ibid., I, 211–15.
17. Ibid., I, 199: 309.
18. Ibid., I, 311–12; 316.
19. *The Duke's Children*, I, 48.
20. *Can You Forgive Her?*, II, 231.
21. *The Prime Minister*, I, 70; 84–5; 70.
22. *Phineas Finn*, II, 266.
23. *The Duke's Children*, I, 215. Cf. also II, 21.
24. Ibid., II, 95–6. Cf. also II, 16–17.
25. Ibid., II, 85–6; 239.
26. Ibid., I, 212.
27. Ibid., I, 230; 109.
28. Ibid., I, 52, 81; II, 379.
29. Ibid., II, 301.
30. *The Prime Minister*, II, 318.
31. *The Duke's Children*, I, 236–41.
32. Ibid., I, 171–2; 251.
33. *Mr Scarborough's Family*, pp. 526, 196, 373.

34. Ibid., pp. 472; 368.
35. Ibid., pp. 614; 188.
36. Ibid., pp. 193–5.
37. Ibid., pp. 201–2; 390.
38. Ibid., pp. 567; 514.
39. *Doctor Thorne*, p. 270.
40. Ibid., pp. 127–8.
41. *The Eustace Diamonds*, p. 18.
42. Ibid., p. 38.
43. Ibid., pp. 45, 55.
44. Ibid., pp. 50; 185.
45. Ibid., p. 410
46. Ibid., pp. 654; 672; 656.
47. Ibid., p. 459.
48. Ibid., pp. 286–7.
49. Ibid., p. 557.
50. Ibid., pp. 174–5.
51. Ibid., p. 726.
52. Ibid., p. 194.
53. Ibid., p. 195.
54. Ibid., pp. 196; 197–8. Cf. also p. 13.
55. Ibid., p. 576.
56. Ibid., pp. 175; 719; 667–8.
57. Ibid., p. 714.
58. Ibid., p. 576.

CHAPTER 6

1. *Doctor Thorne*, p. 293.
2. *He Knew He Was Right*, p. 864.
3. *The Last Chronicle of Barset*, p. 173.
4. *Rachel Ray*, p. 77.
5. *Life of Cicero*, II, 387, n.
6. *Doctor Thorne*, p. 30.
7. *The Belton Estate*, p. 71.
8. Ibid., pp. 95; 134.
9. Ibid., pp. 323–4.
10. Ibid., p. 35.
11. Ibid., p. 46.
12. Ibid., pp. 199; 40.
13. *He Knew He Was Right*, p. 713.
14. *John Caldigate*, pp. 361; 255.

CHAPTER 7

1. *Rachel Ray*, pp. 27; 207.
2. Ibid., pp. 213, 240.
3. Ibid., pp. 139; 340–1.

4. *Doctor Thorne*, p. 12.
5. *Phineas Redux*, II, 250.
6. *Orley Farm*, II, 218.
7. Ibid., II, 359.
8. *The Eustace Diamonds*, pp. 223–4.
9. *Mr Scarborough's Family*, p. 153.

CHAPTER 8

1. *The Duke's Children*, II, 95–6, 207.
2. *He Knew He Was Right*, p. 714.
3. *Lady Anna*, II, 17.
4. *Doctor Thorne*, p. 26.
5. *He Knew He Was Right*, pp. 763–4.
6. *Lady Anna*, I, 225.
7. Ibid., I, 289; II, 94–5.
8. Ibid., I, 48; 308; 153.
9. Ibid., II, 60; 297; 298–9. Cf. also *The Prime Minister*, II, 320–4: 363.
10. *Doctor Thorne*, pp. 26; 33.
11. Ibid., pp. 41; 97–8; 357–8.
12. In *The New Zealander*, Trollope uses 'aristocrat' in the sense of 'custodian' in a broader sense. He argues that it is important that labourers learn to love their work and respect themselves and that only in a country where this spirit is widely spread, will people both work well and be 'manly'. But 'no Government, no Cabinet, no Minister', he says, 'can produce the change that is needful in this matter. No Houses of Parliament can pass a law that shall be efficient to make labour respected and respectable. Laws they may pass by dozens with their assumed omnipotence, but they will be wholly inoperative. People cannot suddenly be made great and good by the wisdom of a Jew.' [This is an obvious reference to Disraeli's *penchant* for paternalist government.] But 'every aristocrat may do much in his own sphere, be he an aristocrat over thousands of acres, or an aristocrat over hundreds of factory children, or simply the humblest of aristocrats guiding some score of men in a founder's yard. The task of each is the same. To each it has been given to rule the work of others. From each will be demanded not only that he has well done his own duty in his own state, but also that those under him have been encouraged so to do. No farmer that employs a ploughman and a carter can divest himself of this responsibility; no small grocer to whom is entrusted the care of a single shopboy can be exempt from the necessity of answering as to his amount of governance. No father of a household under whose roof two red armed maidens earn their humble bread, but has on his shoulders as much of the burden of an aristocrat.' (Oxford, 1972) pp. 27–8.
13. *Lady Anna*, I, 171.
14. *The Duke's Children*, II, 255.
15. *An Autobiography*, pp. 145–6.
16. *Phineas Redux*, I, 216.
17. *Doctor Thorne*, p. 191.

18. *Framley Parsonage*, pp. 308–9.
19. *Doctor Thorne*, pp. 221–2; 245.
20. Ibid., pp. 226–7.
21. *Framley Parsonage*, pp. 426–7.

CHAPTER 9

1. C. S. Lewis, *The Allegory of Love* (New York, 1958) p. 17.
2. Socrates says in the *Phaedo*, 'in this life, we come closest to knowledge when we have the least possible intercourse or communion with bodily nature' (65).
3. See D. de Rougemont, *Passion and Society* (London, 1940) for a very different view of the relation between the modern and ancient ideas of love.
4. T. Hobbes, *Leviathan* (Oxford, 1947) p. 75.
5. Aristotle's account of *philia* might appear to be an ancient idea of love that genuinely respects individuality because Aristotle's friends do not in any way use or possess one another or desire to lose their separateness. But what each appreciates in the other is the virtue that they have in common, that is to say, a likeness to himself, and not the distinctiveness of another personality.
6. For discussions of Christian love from this standpoint, see: J. Burnaby, *Amor Dei* (London, 1938); A. T. S. Nygren, *Agape and Eros* (London, 1932–39) 3 vols.; R. Travers Herford, *The Pharisees* (London, 1924).
7. See J. Speirs, *Chaucer the Maker* (London, 1951); W. L. Purcell, *Love and Marriage in Three English Authors: Chaucer, Milton, Eliot* (Stanford Studies in Humanities, 1963); John Bayley, *The Characters of Love* (London, 1960).
8. Cf. *The Vicar of Bullhampton*, p. 162.
9. *The Duke's Children*, I, 265.
10. *He Knew He Was Right*, p. 910.
11. *An Old Man's Love*, p. 246.
12. *The Vicar of Bullhampton*, p. 16.
13. Ibid., pp. 139, 145.
14. *Ralph the Heir*, II, 240.
15. *An Autobiography*, pp. 123–4.
16. *Can You Forgive Her?* II, 281; I, 464.
17. C. S. Lewis, 'Four Letter Words', *Selected Literary Essays* (Cambridge, 1969) p. 174 n. Montaigne said: 'Celuy qui dit tout, il nous saoule, et nous desgouste; celuy qui craint à s'exprimer nous achemine à en penser plus qu'il n'en va. Il y a de la trahison en cette sorte de modestie, et notamment nous entr'ouvant comme font ceux cy, une si belle route à l'imagination.' (*Essais*, III, v.) Rebecca West wrote recently: 'The Victorians differ from us in the way they thought and they felt, and we are apt to think that we think and feel in a more gipsy way. . . . The Victorians often would not name the facts of life, but they would allude to them with candour. We understand perfectly what is the matter with Charles, the hero of Newman's first novel, when we read of his reaction to a meeting with an old friend, an Anglican clergyman, with his new wife. (*The Sunday Telegraph*, 17 July 1977).

18. D. H. Lawrence, *Letters*, 2 vols. (London, 1962), I, 282, 318, 324; II, 990.
19. *Framley Parsonage*, pp. 283; 284–5.
20. *Can You Forgive Her?*, I, 64.
21. Ibid., pp. 38; 473.
22. Ibid., pp. 127; 31; 137.
23. Ibid., I, 473.
24. Ibid., I, 54.
25. Ibid., II, 438.
26. *Phineas Finn*, I, 127; 116; II, 35.
27. Ibid., I, 308; 114.
28. Ibid., II, 79.
29. Ibid., II, 87–8; 51.
30. Ibid., II, 156; 377–9.
31. Ibid., I, 25.
32. Ibid., I, 37.
33. Ibid., I, 6; 9–10.
34. Ibid., I, 47–8.
35. Ibid., I, 57; 47; 153; 165.
36. Ibid., I, 167.
37. Ibid., I, 172, 174.
38. Ibid., II, 322; 328; 395.
39. Ibid., II, 323; 339.
40. Ibid., II, 381.
41. *The Vicar of Bullhampton*, p. 153.
42. *The Way We Live Now*, II, 471.
43. *Harry Hotspur*, p. 243.
44. *The Prime Minister*, II, 400.
45. *The Vicar of Bullhampton*, p. 264.
46. *The Small House at Allington*, II, 423.
47. *The Last Chronicle of Barset*, I, 6.
48. *Can You Forgive Her?* II, 295.
49. *He Knew He Was Right*, p. 12.
50. *An Autobiography*, p. 123–4.
51. *The Vicar of Bullhampton*, p. 263.
52. Ibid., p. 263.
53. *He Knew He Was Right*, pp. 719–20.
54. *The Vicar of Bullhampton*, pp. 61–63.
55. *He Knew He Was Right*, p. 915.
56. *The Way We Live Now*, II, 423.
57. *The American Senator*, pp. 80, 378.
58. *The Way We Live Now*, II, 383.
59. *He Knew He Was Right*, pp. 204, 205.
60. Ibid., p. 70.
61. Ibid., pp. 866, 868.
62. Ibid., pp. 30, 867.
63. Ibid., p. 898.
64. Ibid., p. 562.
65. Ibid., p. 658.
66. Ibid., pp. 314–317.

CHAPTER 10

1. *An Autobiography*, p. 94.
2. Ibid., pp. 90–1.
3. Ibid., pp. 92–93.
4. *The Way We Live Now*, II, 119–20.
5. Ibid., II, 106.
6. Ibid., II, 113.
7. Ibid., II, 295.
8. Ibid., II, 449; 106.
9. *The Fixed Period*, I, 22–4.
10. W. L. Collins, 'Autobiography of Anthony Trollope', *Blackwood's Magazine*, CXXXIV, Nov. 1883, 577–90.
11. *The Fixed Period*, I, 181–6.
12. Ibid., I, 41; 38–9; 52; 21.
13. Ibid., I, 83; 39; 175–8.
14. Ibid., I, 176; 177; 185–6.
15. Ibid., II, 110.
16. Ibid., I, 109; 70; 17; 180.
17. *Ralph The Heir*, III, 28; II, 120–1.
18. Ibid., III, 36.
19. Ibid., III, 38; I, 13.
20. Ibid., III, 35; 237.
21. Ibid., III, 33–4.
22. Ibid., III, 31–2.
23. Ibid., III, 250; 249.
24. Ibid., I, 134; 289; 290–1.
25. Ibid., I, 288, 297.
26. Ibid., I, 287; II, 33.
27. *Phineas Redux*, I, 49.
28. Ibid., I, 85.
29. Ibid., I, 135.
30. Ibid., I, 84.
31. *Phineas Finn*, I, 103–4.
32. *The Prime Minister*, I, 59; 229.
33. *Phineas Finn*, I, 411.
34. *Four Lectures*, pp. 41; 55.
35. *The Prime Minister*, II, 381; 372; 469; I, 305; II, 372; I, 124.
36. *Phineas Redux*, I, 352.
37. Ibid., I, 216; 285; I, 285: II, 334.
38. Ibid., I, 81; 83; 56; 137; 82–3.
39. Ibid., I, 53–4.
40. Ibid., I, 139; 54.
41. Ibid., I, 45.
42. *The Prime Minister*, I, 135–6.
43. *Phineas Redux*, II, 42–44.
44. *Phineas Finn*, I, 404.
45. Ibid., I, 100.
46. *Phineas Redux*, I, 358–9.

47. Ibid., I, 426; 428.
48. *An Autobiography*, p. 223.
49. *The Prime Minister*, II, 377.
50. *The Duke's Children*, II, 339–41.
51. *Phineas Finn*, II, 95.
52. *Phineas Redux*, I, 428.
53. *The Prime Minister*, II, 280.
54. Ibid., I, 360–2.
55. *Can You Forgive Her?*, II, 236–7.
56. *The Prime Minister*, II, 114.
57. Ibid., I, 67.
58. *Phineas Finn*, I, 17; 18.
59. Ibid., II, 96–7.
60. *Phineas Redux*, I, 396.
61. *The Duke's Children*, II, 260; 258; 259.
62. *Phineas Finn*, I, 408.
63. *The Prime Minister*, II, 186–7.
64. *Phineas Finn*, I, 17; 6.
65. *The Prime Minister*, I, 222–3.
66. *Phineas Redux*, I, 395–6.
67. *The Prime Minister*, II, 313.
68. *Phineas Finn*, I, 157.
69. Ibid., I, 158–9.
70. Ibid., I, 302.
71. *The Prime Minister*, II, 367–8.
72. *Phineas Redux*, I, 429.
73. *The Prime Minister*, II, 180; I, 79.
74. *Phineas Redux*, I, 47.
75. *The Prime Minister*, I, 198.
76. *Phineas Finn*, I, 405.
77. *The Prime Minister*, II, 325–6.
78. *The Duke's Children*, I, 69; II, 339.
79. *The Prime Minister*, I, 136–7.
80. Ibid., I, 64; 74, 80. Cf. II, 4–5, on 'ideal' Prime Minister.
81. Ibid., II, 291; 269; 363; 387.
82. Ibid., II, 469.
83. Ibid., II, 201–2.
84. *Can You Forgive Her?*, II, 53–4.
85. *The Prime Minister*, I, 125.
86. *Can You Forgive Her?*, II, 59; 61; 153.

CHAPTER 11

1. *Life of Cicero*, II, 393.
2. *Rachel Ray*, p. 47.
3. Ibid., p. 13.
4. *John Caldigate*, p. 434; 284; 431–2.
5. *Rachel Ray*, p. 66.

6. *John Caldigate*, p. 283; 318.
7. Ibid., p. 423.
8. *Rachel Ray*, p. 8.
9. *The Vicar of Bullhampton*, pp. 45–6.
10. Ibid., p. 134.
11. Ibid., pp. 172; 282.
12. Ibid., p. 124.
13. Ibid., pp. 90; 288.
14. Ibid., pp. 34; 449; 474.
15. Ibid., p. 175.
16. Ibid., p. 368.
17. Dr Wortle's School, p. 27.
18. Ibid., pp. 42–3.
19. Ibid., pp. 78; 50; 49.
20. Ibid., pp. 63; 49; 64.
21. Ibid., pp. 25–6.
22. Ibid., p. 88.
23. Ibid.
24. Ibid., pp. 96; 97.
25. Ibid., pp. 213; 4–5; 96.
26. Ibid., pp. 84; 92.
27. Ibid., p. 91.
28. Ibid., pp. 99; 100; 101; 131.
29. Ibid., pp. 210–11.
30. Ibid., pp. 257–8.
31. *Barchester Towers*, p. 34.
32. *The Last Chronicle of Barset*, I, 225.
33. Ibid., I, 107.
34. *Barchester Towers*, pp. 505–6.
35. *The Vicar of Bullhampton*, pp. 116–7; 245; 117; 243.
36. Ibid., p. 306.
37. *Phineas Redux*, I, 29–30.
38. *The Way We Live Now*, I, 151.
39. *Phineas Redux*, I, 352–3.
40. *Framley Parsonage*, p. 166.
41. *Barchester Towers*, p. 171.
42. Ibid., pp. 177; 178. This passage explicitly refutes the view that Trollope's gentleman is a Stoic ideal.
43. Ibid., p. 172.
44. Ibid., p. 170.
45. Ibid., pp. 185–7.
46. Ibid., pp. 172; 48.
47. Ibid., p. 46.
48. *The Last Chronicle of Barset*, p. 225.
49. *Barchester Towers*, p. 45.
50. Ibid., p. 186.
51. *The Last Chronicle of Barset*, II, 439; I, 107; II, 233–4.
52. Ibid., II, 421–2; 292.
53. Ibid., II, 421.

54. *Barchester Towers*, pp. 63–4.
55. *The Last Chronicle of Barset*, I, 184; 180.
56. Ibid., I, 331; 197.
57. Ibid., II, 333–4.
58. Ibid., I, 74; II, 220.
59. Ibid., II, 220.
60. Ibid., I, 115–17.
61. Ibid., II, 222.
62. *Ralph The Heir*, I, 258.
63. Michael Oakeshott, *On Human Conduct* (Oxford, 1975) p. 81.

CHAPTER 12

1. *National Review*, April 1886, p. 221.
2. H. Laski, *The Danger of Being a Gentleman* (London, 1932).
3. *The Prime Minister*, I, 2–7; 49–50.
4. Ibid., I, 30–31.
5. Ibid., I, 31–3.
6. Ibid., I, 41, 170.
7. *Life of Cicero*, I, 16.
8. Ibid., II, 204; 213.
9. Ibid., I, 19.
10. *Is He Popenjoy?*, I, 135; 13–4; II, 297–8.
11. Ibid., I, 232.
12. Ibid., I, 235.
13. Ibid., II, 118.
14. Ibid., II, pp. 87–93.
15. Ibid., II, 117; 97; 117.
16. Ibid., I, 95–6.
17. Ibid., II, 111; 296.
18. *The Last Chronicle of Barset*, vol. I, p. 196.
19. Ibid., I, 132; 192.
20. *The Way We Live Now*, I, 17; 132.
21. Ibid., I, 99.
22. Ibid., I, 209.
23. Ibid., I, 267; 230–31.
24. Ibid., II, 429.
25. Ibid., I, 275.
26. Ibid., I, 36; 428.
27. Ibid., II, 46; 49; 58.
28. Ibid., II, 44; I, 138; II, 44; 467.
29. Ibid., I, 116–17; 422.
30. Ibid., II, 70.
31. Ibid., I, 296; II, 273; 271.
32. Ibid., II, 270–1.
33. Ibid., II, 362.
34. *The Prime Minister*, I, 283; 5–6.

Name Index

Subject Index

About the Author

SHIRLEY ROBIN LETWIN (1924-1993) was born in Chicago and received her Ph.D. from the University of Chicago. She taught political theory and history at Harvard and other universities in the United States before moving to England, where she taught at the London School of Economics and Cambridge University. Her other books include *The Anatomy of Thatcherism.*